Human Communication across Cultures

HUMAN COMMUNICATION ACROSS

CULTURES

A Cross-Cultural Introduction to
Pragmatics and Sociolinguistics

Vincent Remillard and Karen Williams

SHEFFIELD UK   BRISTOL CT

Published by Equinox Publishing Ltd.

UK: Office 415, The Workstation, 15 Paternoster Row, Sheffield S1 2BX
USA: ISD, 70 Enterprise Drive, Bristol, CT 06010

www.equinoxpub.com

First published 2016

ISBN   9 781 78179 354 1   (hardback)
       9 781 78179 355 8   (paperback)
       9 781 78179 458 6   (e-PDF)

British Library Cataloguing-in-Publication Data

A catalogue record for this book is available from the British Library.

Library of Congress Cataloging-in-Publication Data

Names: Remillard, Vincent Leonard, 1942- author. | Williams, Karen
    (Linguistic) author.
Title: Human communication across cultures : cross-cultural introduction to
    pragmatics and sociolinguistics / Vincent Remillard and Karen Williams.
Description: Sheffield, UK ; Bristol, CT : Equinox Publishing Ltd, [2016] |
    Includes bibliographical references and index.
Identifiers: LCCN 2016007857 (print) | LCCN 2016018501 (ebook) | ISBN
    9781781793541 (hb) | ISBN 9781781793558 (pb) | ISBN 9781781794586 (e-PDF)
    | ISBN 9781781794593 (e-epub)
Subjects: LCSH: Language and culture--Study and teaching. |
    Communication--Study and teaching. | Pragmatics--Study and teaching. |
    Sociolinguistics--Study and teaching.
Classification: LCC P40.3 .R345 2016 (print) | LCC P40.3 (ebook) | DDC
    306.44--dc23
LC record available at https://lccn.loc.gov/2016007857

Typeset by CA Typesetting Ltd, Sheffield, UK

Printed and bound in the UK by Lightning Source UK Ltd, Milton Keynes and Lightning Source Inc, La Vergne, TN

Contents

Preface for Instructors

Most undergraduate college students in the United States have taken years of English courses, and many have learned the basics of a second language. But what is taught and studied in these courses hardly reflects *how* language is acquired and used. To do so requires the study of pragmatics and sociolinguistics. The study of pragmatics reflects how we use language and attempt to understand one another in various contexts in which we are involved. Sociolinguistics, as opposed to pragmatics, focuses on the social rather than the situational use of language. Sociolinguistics explores how language is used within social constructs such as where we live, our age, our gender, our ethnicity, our religious background, our social class and our level of education.

The study of language through pragmatics and sociolinguistics can reveal who we are, personally, professionally, and socially. To "know thyself" and others has inspired a number of institutions of higher education in teaching, planning or considering a variety of courses in one or more of the categories listed below, or perhaps a category not described here:

a. An introductory sociolinguistics course that is part of **an existing program of study** in linguistics, foreign language, English, anthropology or another related field.

b. An introductory sociolinguistics course serving as **an option within a Humanities common core**, either open for all interested students or as a requirement. Such a course serves as an excellent companion for nearly any major or field of study, such as advertising, anthropology, business, communications, gender studies, law, psychology, and sociology.

c. A course offered as **an alternative to satisfying foreign language requirements for students who are unable or unwilling to study a second language**. Students in this category can include those with learning differences, adult or non-traditional students, or international students who already speak more than one language fluently.

d. A course that **replaces foreign language requirements** in institutions that are eliminating or downsizing their foreign language departments due to budget cuts.

e. A course created to **support the increased focus on globalization** seen at many higher education institutions.

f.   An **education course** that prepares future teachers to accommodate culturally and linguistically diverse students in the classroom. Such courses have recently been mandated for accreditation through NCATE (The National Council for the Accreditation of Teacher Education).

g.   An **online course** in the Humanities and Social Sciences that utilizes an audio, visual and social networking tool such as *Collaborate* or *Blackboard*.

With these potential markets in mind, we have written this highly interactive textbook/workbook on sociolinguistics and pragmatics, or more generally on how human communication takes place in various cultures. Each chapter of the book includes a brief introduction, a discussion of the topic, multiple activities designed for in-class use and/or homework assignments, a concise conclusion, and useful references such as relevant websites and suggested further reading. We include answers for some of the activities, but most are designed for instructors to pick and choose from according to their own level of linguistic expertise. While the text features numerous examples from a variety of current world cultures, it is designed to allow instructors and students to include their own updated examples as well.

Among the highlights and key features of this text are:

a.   **Adaptability**: As stated above, the text is useful for a wide variety of courses and formats. It is appropriate for not only students in the United States, but also in other countries where similar courses are being taught in English.

b.   **Flexibility**: Instructors can provide an overview of all topics included in the book, or go into more detail on particular topics. For example, if an instructor wishes to devote more class time to language and gender issues, he or she can use more of the additional activities and references from that chapter, while spending less time on another chapter, such as the one on the structural features of language. Based on the particular needs of the course, another instructor could focus more on structural features, while assigning the language and gender chapter for individual reading, or omitting it altogether.

A special note concerning **Chapter 2, The Structural Features of Language**: An instructor with limited knowledge of linguistics in the formal sense could use this chapter as a reference for other chapters rather than as an independent topic.

c.   **Customizability**: Instructors are able to substitute their own examples, activities, and assignments, keeping the material up to date and relevant for their particular audiences. As one example, an instructor in business communications could add his or her own videos to class lectures that

highlight differences in verbal behavior in given cultures (such as greetings, turn taking and effective and ineffective politeness strategies) and
non-verbal behavior (such as appropriate body language for international business settings). Another instructor might have many foreign
language majors in the class, and therefore choose to augment the bilingualism chapter with relevant videos or assignments requiring interaction with bilingual people at the school or in the community.

This text is the result of many years of teaching and researching pragmatics
and sociolinguistics. We believe it fills a gap in the existing market by being a
text that is (1) written in an informal and engaging manner, (2) includes cross-
cultural material, (3) is highly adaptable and customizable to a variety of courses,
and (4) has been tested not only in traditional classrooms, but also in online
courses. Without a doubt, we have both found this area of study to be one of the
most gratifying to teach, and student feedback regarding this text has been over-
whelmingly positive for us over the years. We hope you enjoy using and adapting
it to fit your particular needs.

Vince Remillard
Karen Williams

Preface for Students

Welcome to the study of how human communication operates across cultures! Most of you come to colleges and universities after having taken years of English and foreign language courses, which, in large part, focused on grammatical accuracy. But traditional grammar hardly reflects how language is acquired and used, or its complexity.

There are two areas of study that do address language in this sense: pragmatics and sociolinguistics. The study of pragmatics shows how we communicate and understand one another in each situation we encounter. In so doing, others are constantly judging us based on our use of language, just as we judge them. Examples abound in such utterances as: *You talk too much*, *You're exaggerating*, *You're bossy*, and *You're rude*, to mention only a few. The study of sociolinguistics, on the other hand, seeks to explore how language is used in social interactions. For example, there are differences in the way we speak due to where we live, our age, our gender, our ethnicity, our religious background, our social class or our level of education.

To facilitate the study of pragmatics and sociolinguistics, we have written a highly interactive textbook/workbook addressing how human communication takes place in various cultures. Each chapter of the book includes a brief introduction; a discussion of the topic, along with references recommended for further research (both written and online); and an extensive collection of activities designed for both in-class usage and homework assignments. While the text features numerous examples from a variety of current world cultures, it is designed to allow both instructors and students to include their own updated examples as well.

The curricular goals for this book are twofold. First, by illuminating how human communication operates across cultures, we hope that the text will demystify language for you and increase your interest and confidence in the study of English, as well as any other language you might be learning. Second, we believe that the study of how language and communication operate together will make you more sensitive to and understanding of the cultural models that operate in your life and those of others.

Moreover, the information learned through the study of language, communication and culture is relevant to any profession in which communication is involved. Even among speakers of American English, language conveys different

social and cultural values depending on a multitude of factors. When one inter-
acts with speakers of English in other countries (such as the United Kingdom or
Australia, for example) and with speakers of other languages, the cultural models
conveyed can be even more challenging.

We hope that you will enjoy this area of study as you discover how language
is used in communication and how it reflects cultural values. Prepare yourself
to embark on a journey in learning what you didn't even know you didn't know
about human communication across cultures.

Vince Remillard
Karen Williams

Acknowledgements

The materials contained herein have been used and tested in several courses with hundreds of our undergraduate students at Saint Francis University, and Mercyhurst University in the United States. We thank our students for their patient and helpful participation and feedback.

We thank in particular the following colleagues at our respective educational institutions for their academic advice and encouragement:

Dr. Wayne Powel: Provost, Saint Francis University
Theresa Wilson: Director of the Center for Excellence in Teaching and Learning, Saint Francis University
Robert Griffin: former Assistant Director of Distance Learning, Saint Francis University
Louise Wilson: Adjunct Instructor, Saint Francis University
Dr. Alice Edwards: former Chair of the Department of World Languages and Cultures, Mercyhurst University

Finally, we wish to extend our sincere gratitude to Dr. Deborah Tannen for cooperation in granting us permission to use excerpts from her books on conversational style, discourse, and gender.

Any inaccuracies or shortcomings in this text are borne by the authors alone and are not due to any of the above. We extend our gratitude to our spouses and families for their patient and continued support.

Author Biographies

Dr. Vincent Remillard is Professor Emeritus of French at Saint Francis University in Loretto, PA, where he served as Chair of the Department of Foreign Languages, Dean of General Education, and Director of International Education. During his tenure there, he taught numerous courses in French language, literature, and culture, as well as in various fields of linguistics. He also developed a cross-cultural pragmatics and sociolinguistics course as an option to the traditional language requirement for the General Education Program. He received a BA in French from the University of Massachusetts, Amherst, a MAT in French from Assumption College in Worcester, MA, and a PhD in French Literature from the Pennsylvania State University. He has made several presentations statewide, regionally and locally on Standards, oral proficiency and the relationship of these to the teaching of literature, linguistics and culture. He has served as an Executive Council member of the Pennsylvania State Modern Language Association where he co-authored manuals on oral proficiency and standards for foreign language learners. As Past President of the Pennsylvania State Modern Language Association he testified in legislative hearings on the linguistic legitimacy of including American Sign Language among the languages that would satisfy the language requirement in Pennsylvania secondary schools.

Dr. Karen Williams is Professor of Spanish at Mercyhurst University in Erie, PA. She teaches numerous courses in Spanish, linguistics, and sociolinguistics. She received a BM in Music Performance from Iowa State University in 1992, an MA in Spanish Linguistics from the University of Georgia in 1995, and a PhD in Linguistics from the University of Georgia in 1999, with specializations in Hispanic Linguistics, Phonetics, Second Language Acquisition, and Sociolinguistics. She has served as a member of the Executive Council of the Pennsylvania State Modern Language Association (PSMLA) and as webmaster for the PSMLA website. She has published articles on various aspects of language and pedagogy and has given numerous presentations at local, state, national, and international conferences on foreign language teaching, translation, interdisciplinary language studies, sociolinguistics, and general education.

Chapter 1

Language, Communication and Culture

> We will consider the interrelationship between language, communication and culture, and define the aims and parameters of this text.

A year having passed, [Prajapati] wanted to speak. He said *bhur* and the earth was created. He said *bhuvar* and the space of the air was created. He said *suvar* and the sky was created (Hindu myth)

Language as Creation

Mythical accounts, such as in the Hindu one cited above, were often used to explain how the physical universe arose. In the book of Genesis of the Judaic tradition, God creates the universe by stating a series of *Let there be...* utterances. In the Christian Gospel of John, we read how the Word became incarnate so that God was revealed in the flesh: "In the Beginning was the Word and the Word was with God, and the Word was God...and the Word was made flesh." The Hindu, Jewish and Christian narratives, as do many other mythical accounts and world religions, conceive language as a creative force.

Beyond accounts of language's role as a force of physical creation, secular writers since the ancient Greeks have long recognized the role of language as a creative social force. One has only to read works like *The Social Contract* to see that Rousseau is creating a new paradigm by which nations can be governed. In the history of the United States, President Abraham Lincoln, in his *Gettysburg Address*, created a national vision by transferring (somewhat arbitrarily) the principle of equality for all within *The Declaration of Independence* to the Constitution, where equality is not explicitly affirmed. New realities continue to be created by the use of language in our everyday lives, such as when duly appointed authorities certify others as doctors, teachers and spouses.

Even in daily usage, we use language to create amicability, emotions, beliefs, cooperation, violence, propositions, and personal and social goals, to name only a few usages. As we use language in these ways it reflects who we are.

How does language operate to accomplish all this? To answer this requires an understanding of the nature and function of language.

Language and You

Let us begin by surveying your current views about language, communication and its relationship to a society's culture, so you can compare them to what your perspective will be after working with the materials in this text. This will serve to make you aware to what extent the knowledge gained herein has changed and challenged your current way of thinking about this topic.

With which of the following statements about language would you feel inclined to agree or disagree? Naturally, you will have mixed feelings about some of the propositions, but for the purpose of the exercise try to react simply and honestly, answering the question without looking for hidden or devious meaning, purpose or "trick." Mark your answers in the following manner:

1 = strongly agree   2 = agree   3 = little to no opinion   4 = disagree   5 = strongly disagree

_____   The languages of primitive peoples are simpler than those of more advanced cultures.

_____   Children learn to talk from role models and caregivers.

_____   People who have an advanced level of skill (ability, competency) in a language are pretty much able to "say what they mean and mean what they say."

_____   The cultivated speech of the educated person is more logical than that of the ignorant or illiterate one. The former would never say, "Nobody ain't done nothin."

_____   If someone uses words like *yinz* for *you* and pronounces the word *wash* as *worsh*, these are just instances of poor English.

_____   It's possible to speak without a dialect.

_____   Slang is used whenever someone is too lazy to use careful speech.

_____   People from the Boston area should not pronounce an "r" at the end of the word *idea* because it isn't written that way.

_____   African American English is a low-grade form of speech.

_____   The language you speak is the limit of your thinking.

_____   Women speak more than men do.

_____   The best way to find the meaning of a word is to consult a dictionary.

1. Take a few moments to jot down notes as to why you made these choices, even if it means indicating that you had no opinion.
2. Get together with one or more members of the class and discuss with them how they answered and the reasons they gave for their responses. How do they differ from yours? What do you think of the validity of their perspective? Would you now want to modify any of your responses? If so, how?

Basic Principles

We will begin our exploration of language, communication and culture by stating some of the principles underlying the various topics treated in this text.

1. "Human language is a more complex system than all the directions contained in the thickest style manual of the most state of the art computer" – Stephen Pinker, *The Language Instinct*

   The production of everyday human language is a creative force that arises from an infinite generative power we all possess as language users. We produce language with such ease that we are unaware of the complex operations taking place. This principle can be illustrated by combining 1,000 nouns with 1,000 verbs (and you have many more thousands of these in your vocabulary). This alone would yield one million possible two-word sentence combinations ($1,000 \times 1,000 = 1,000,000$)!

   Going beyond two-word combinations, if one were to consider all the possible combinations for a 20-word sentence (a sentence even shorter than this one), the best estimates are that it would take 10 trillion years to utter them all (Farb 1977: 4)! Of course not all of the word combinations would be meaningful, but even the number of grammatically appropriate ones would be enormous. This is what accounts for why most sentences we hear and produce daily have never been uttered before.

   Nor is language limited to possible word combinations. One must know how sound, grammar and meaning operate together. These are the sub-fields contained within the academic discipline known as **linguistics**. The complexity involved in how all these sub-fields interact as we produce language was evident from the beginning of linguistic studies in America by Leonard Bloomfield in his 1933 seminal work, *Language*, when he stated that: "the mechanism which governs speech must be very complex and delicate" (Bloomfield 1933: 32).

   Research since then has confirmed Bloomfield's insight even more convincingly. Indeed, the common everyday maneuvering of language forms far exceeds in complexity any other human learning endeavor. The studies of quantum theory, organic chemistry or literary deconstruction, any of which takes many years of schooling to even begin to master, pale in comparative complexity to our routine manipulation of language forms.

2.   "Just as birds have wings, man has language" – George Henry Lewes, *Problems of Life and Mind*

The notion that language is an incredibly complex system, however, is difficult to recognize at first, given that at six years of age and even younger, we are able to communicate our needs, tell stories, make descriptions and even do some hypothetical and abstract thinking with ease. How do we accomplish this? Current research would suggest that much like birds that innately perform through their hard wiring the intricate physical principles required for flight, human wiring permits intricate linguistic operations. And we perform such operations before any "school" learning about language takes place. Thus, we are left with hardly any remembrance of such an accomplishment. A quip that musician John Lennon included in some lyrics referring to life in general also applies to language in particular: "[it] is what happens when you're busy making other plans."

3.   "No matter how eloquently a dog may bark, he cannot tell you that his parents were poor but honest" – Bertrand Russell, *Human Knowledge: Its Scope and Limits*

The complexity and innateness of human language can be more appreciated when compared to animal languages. We are often impressed, even astonished, with how well dogs, cats and dolphins may understand our commands and make known their own needs. But can these animals request rather than suggest you scratch their back? Do they have verbal strategies to politely tell you, *Please move* or more directly, *Bug off*? Can they express how they wish to be treated in future interactions?

These and many other functions are routinely performed by us because, as Lisa Mundy has stated, we "constantly use language to position ourselves, create ourselves, and present ourselves" (Mundy 1996: 10). This is expressed in arguing, convincing, lying, interrupting, and gossiping, as well as in relating our conditions and stories, such as our medical ailments, our origins, our attempts to get along with others, etc., to mention only a few of our uses of language. It is in so doing that we cast the personality we want others to believe we have and don't have, or who we want to be associated with and who we wish to reject. These functions, as we will see in later chapters, are part of the study of **pragmatics**.

4. "People tend to look through language and not see language as a phenomenon in itself that's affecting what's going on" – Deborah Tannen, "What They Talk About When They Talk About Talk," *Washington Post*, February 1996.

In addition to the functional part of human language as we interact with one another, language is also a reflection of the society in which it operates. This is what the study of **sociolinguistics** addresses. It reveals the society and culture in which we participate. It is a reflection of our ethnic origins, the geographical area we live in, the generation we grow up with, the social stratum we belong to and which gender we identify with, just to mention a few social features. Language, in short, functions to reinforce, and to even generate, social and cultural values.

> Based on the four principles above, which of your responses in the questionnaire would you be inclined to reexamine? Explain.

Verbal Behavior

The study of language, both its forms and functions, has as one of its main purposes to make you more aware of your verbal behavior and its relationship to your identity. And it is only in comparing your verbal behavior to others that you come to define your cultural identity and that of others. You should suspect that those aspects of your verbal behavior that you consider natural, normal and logical are only cultural conventions. Only in uncovering these assumed notions can you benefit from a deeper insight and a keener awareness of how you use language on others and how others use language on you in your personal, social and professional relationships.

Text Aims and Parameters

The aim of this text is to bring together findings from academic research relating to language, communication and culture, and to illustrate how it affects us in our daily lives. Many of the research findings will challenge you to change the ordinary way you think about these three subject matters.

Our intent in this text is not to repeat notions about language study you may have acquired in previous formal schooling, either in language arts or foreign language courses. What you learned there was largely **prescriptive**, that is, how you "should" use language. Instead, we will view language **descriptively**, that is, how you and others actually use language. With this in mind, the goals of the succeeding chapters are as follows:

Chapter 2: The Structural Features of Language, outlines the formal components of human languages, independent of their use in context. The discipline that treats language from this perspective is **linguistics**. In this chapter we will cover the linguistic sub-fields of **phonetics, phonology, morphology, syntax** and **semantics**.

Chapter 3: Pragmatics, explores pragmatic or speaker meaning in verbal events and its relationship to context.

Chapters 4–8: will treat the following pragmatic forms we use to convey speaker meaning in communication, both in American culture and cross-culturally:

Chapter 4: examines the use of **Speech Acts** followed by an introduction to speech act theory and its relationship to felicity conditions.

Chapter 5: surveys speech act **Routines**, such as openings and closings, greetings, terms of address and honorifics, apologies and thanks, and complimenting, as well as their role in communication.

Chapter 6: illustrates the **Cooperative Principle and Implicature** underlying exchanges through which speakers are able to infer meaning.

Chapter 7: demonstrates **Politeness Strategies** and how they are used and viewed in social relationships.

Chapter 8: takes up **Conversational Organization** and examines the structure of conversation that underlies pragmatic/speaker meaning.

In **Chapters 9–12:** we will focus on language in its use in society, including the various areas of study within the sociolinguistic field.

Chapter 9: Social Factors, highlights the influence that various social factors such as gender, ethnicity, age, social class, and geographical location have on the way we use language. It also stresses the crucial role that language plays in constructing identity.

Chapter 10: Dialects, delves into the socio-historical and linguistic variables that affect communication across the United States, followed by an introduction to the complicated nature of our notions of "standard" language vs. "nonstandard" language. The chapter concludes with a discussion of dialects in other languages.

Chapter 11: Ethnicity, considers the relationship between language and ethnic variables, including both the linguistic and socio-political aspects involved with African American English.

Chapter 12: Gender, investigates the role that gender plays in language usage, both in American culture and in other cultures. It will be stressed that generalizations in this area are difficult to make, and that social norms and expectations differ greatly between cultures.

Chapter 13: Bilingualism, explores both individual and societal bilingualism. It will also address linguistic and sociolinguistic phenomena that occur when more than one language comes into contact, including code-switching.

Within each chapter you will find activities that will exemplify and assist you in understanding the principles presented. At the end of each chapter there are additional activities or assignments, websites and selected materials for further reading and viewing that complement the concepts presented in this text. These activities are intended to help you understand, apply and expand on what you learn.

Conclusion

- Human language is a creative force. It underlies our personal and social perspectives, indeed every aspect of our daily life.
- Human language is such an incredibly intricate system that it can only be acquired by virtue of our biological makeup. It far exceeds in complexity any learned activity or system.
- Human language is a profound tool for accomplishing all sorts of interpersonal activities. It consists of communicative functions that we use to establish our identity, and in so doing, defines us culturally.
- Human language is the sign of who we are and who we want to be. It is the reflection of our physical, social and cultural being.

We will now move on to define further the creative and complex system of human language by describing the structural features of language prior to studying pragmatics and pragmatic forms that describe a speaker's communicative purpose.

Additional Activities

We invite you to examine five of the statements contained within the orientation questionnaire. These statements were chosen because they usually receive "strongly agree" or "agree" ratings by students. This can be completed as an individual activity solely for reflection, or be completed and shared with the class.

1. **There are only a few gifted individuals who are creative users of the English language.**

   a. Take any picture, drawing, cartoon, etc. and ask as many people as you can find to give a one-sentence description of it. Compare the sentences. Are any of the sentences identical to others?

   b. Go to the library and access the titles of all the books that have three words in their title. Are any identical to others?

If you agreed or strongly agreed to this statement initially, why do you think you did so? What does this indicate about how you initially perceived creativity in language?

2. **Children learn to talk from role models and caregivers.**
While role models and caregivers are required for a child to speak a language (there are no documented instances of a child speaking a language otherwise), why don't children also learn the many errors these speakers make (usually inadvertently) as they produce language? Indeed, spontaneous speech is lined with errors of all sorts such as mispronunciations, grammatical anomalies, deviant word order, incorrect word usages, etc. But children do not repeat such errors after they hear them. Indeed, they will produce them in accurate grammatical forms.

   Consider the following activity. Regardless of the written rule we all learned in English class that indicates that you add an "s" to a noun to make it plural, the fact of the matter is that there are three different sounds we use to form plural nouns when we speak:

[s] as in the plural of the word cap – cap**s**
[z] as in the plural of the word toy – toy**s**
[Iz] as in the plural of the word dish – dish**es**

Can pre-school children subconsciously apply this rule to words they have never heard or produced before? Try the following:

a.   Take two or three 4-6 year old children and ask them for the plural of the following made-up words: *scrug, prag, clush, clat, frim, grod, jik, stush,* and *tresh*. For example, say to the child: "I have one *scrug* now but will have two _____ later."
b.   If the child cooperated, did s/he ever produce an incorrect plural for the words given above or for any other nonsense words you provided?
c.   How are children able to consistently produce the correct plural forms if they have never heard these words before?
d.   It is common for a child to produce *fishes* as a plural form for *fish*. Did they learn this though errors on the part of role models and caregivers? Or would they produce *fishes* regardless? Why?

3.   **People who have an advanced level of skill (ability, competency) in a language are pretty much able to "say what they mean and mean what they say."**

In a poem entitled *The Code*, Robert Frost narrates the story of an outsider turned farmer in Vermont, who, while pitching hay with his two helpers, notices an approaching storm and tells them they need to cock the hay before it rains. A half hour later one of the helpers, in disgust, throws his pitchfork to the ground and goes home. The outsider-farmer is totally puzzled by this behavior and asks the remaining helper, "What did I say?" The helper responds that the seemingly innocent statement of cocking the hay before the storm arrives was interpreted by the helper who left as finding fault with his work. The outsider-farmer, however, had never intended to insult the offended helper. He thought he had only stated a fact; that is, they needed to make sure they got the hay in the barn before it began to rain.

This incident illustrates what we have all experienced many times, regardless of our degree of competence in a language. Saying what we mean and meaning what we say goes far beyond the semantic (dictionary) value of words. Utterances are subjected to the contextual situation and the social norms of the culture in which they are used. More precisely, communication is a question not only of the words you use, but also of *how, when* and *why* you say *what,* and *to whom.*

a.   Think of an incident in your life where you made a very ordinary statement for which you received a totally different reaction than you expected.
b.   Using the contextual description given above (how, when and why you say what to whom) analyze where your message went awry. In the Frost poem cited above, for example, rural helpers in Northern New England (to whom) would take offense if they were told to do something (what) that they were competent of doing, even knowing the moment it must be done (when), and for what reason(s) (why).

The helper may also have been offended by the way the directive was given (how). In short, in the rural culture of Vermont (as in any culture), there are unwritten verbal codes. In this case, Frost succinctly states this through the words of the helper who stayed on:

Don't let it bother you. You've found out something.
The hand that knows its business won't be told
To do work better or faster

4. **It's possible to speak without a dialect.**

   a. Ask several people to locate the place in the English-speaking world that they consider as having the least dialectical speech. Plot the location of their response to the proximity of where they have lived and to what social class they belong. Is there any relationship between these variables and how they define standard and dialectical English?

   b. Find 5-10 speakers of English and have each person pronounce the words below in a sentence without you using the word itself, and record their responses:

      Ex. (syrup) Vermont is especially known for its maple _____

tomato	marry	cot
roof	sorry	almond
apricot	garage	either

      Did everyone pronounce these words identically?

   c. Now have one or two other individuals listen to the recording. Did they agree with your findings?

5. **Women speak more than men do.**
This statement is an example of the kind of unexamined claims that become so readily accepted that they become almost proverbial. And yet, responsible research in measuring the amount of talk by both sexes has never borne out this proposition. Instead, a host of contextual and cultural variables condition the amount of speech produced by anyone, male or female.

   a. Choose five pictures on varied topics (sports, relationships, nature scenes, etc.) and have one male and one female speak about them. Record their conversation and compare the length of their talk.

Picture number	Male spoke longer	Female spoke longer	Both spoke about the same amount of time
1			
2			
3			
4			
5			

Were there differences in the actual amount of time they spoke? If so, what would account for this? Was there anything in the pictures that would influence the amount of speech produced?

b.   To examine how others perceive the amount of talk, have five males and females listen to each recording and then have them complete the same form as the one above based on their impression of how much each person talked.

Was there a difference between their impressions? If so, what might account for these differences?

You may be surprised to learn that most linguists would disagree or strongly disagree with *all* of the statements in the orientation questionnaire on p. 2 due to the extensive research conducted on these topics. As you study the materials in this text you will want to refer back to the orientation questionnaire and modify your responses based on what you have learned.

Web Resources

Note: Many of the topics introduced in this chapter will be discussed in further detail in subsequent chapters. The two websites below offer a good place to start your exploration of the many facets of language:

- For virtually all topics covered in this text, you will find relevant information on this companion website to the PBS special "Do You Speak American?" http://www.pbs.org/speak/. The site is very well-organized, but the amount of information is so extensive that you might wish to begin by browsing the site map: http://www.pbs.org/speak/sitemap/
- For another version of a basic description of the field, check this link from the Linguistic Society of America: http://www.linguisticsociety.org/what-linguistics

Chapter 2

The Structural Features of Language

> We will introduce you to the discipline of structural linguistics, outline its history and provide a brief overview of its subfields.

Good heavens! For more than forty years I have been speaking prose without knowing it (Molière, *Le Bourgeois Gentilhomme*)

Language is the most massive and inclusive art we know, a mountainous and anonymous work of unconscious generations (Edward Sapir, *Language: an Introduction to the Study of Speech*)

Introduction

There are several popular meanings that people associate with the terms **linguist** and **linguistics** but these have little or no relevance to the content of this chapter or text. So that we may better understand what will be understood in this text by the use of these terms, we will begin by eliminating some of the popular ways they are interpreted.

First, we will not be studying the origin of languages and how any given language has changed over time. This area of linguistic study is known as historical linguistics, which is not the subject of our text. Second, the term *linguist* will not be used to refer to commentators who claim expertise in evaluating current language uses and practices based on selected canonical sources, such as grammars and dictionaries. These individuals are sometimes labeled as linguists, but in a strict sense, they are not. Their interest is focused on the perceived social norms of language use. Finally, the term *linguist* will not be used to refer to polyglots, who are people who claim to speak several languages. These individuals are deservedly praised for their linguistic ability, but this text is not focused on language acquisition.

So then, what are we talking about in using the terms *linguist* and *linguistics*? In this chapter, linguistics will be used to refer to the scientific study of language forms, independent of context. The language forms to be presented are those relating to sounds (**phonology**), grammar (**morphology** and **syntax**), and meaning (**semantics**). Linguists carry out structural studies of these language forms.

MOD 2

A basic knowledge of these language forms is relevant to understanding how language is used in different contexts and cultures, as we will see in the following chapters.

A Brief History of Linguistics

Since most students in the United States have never been exposed to linguistics as described above, an understanding of the historical perspective of this discipline is useful in order to provide a framework for understanding this area of study. The current discipline of linguistics began as recently as the last century with Ferdinand de Saussure (1857–1913). Saussure, who lectured on general linguistics at the University of Geneva in Switzerland from 1907–1911, is often recognized as the first modern linguist. Ironically, he never wrote a text on the materials he presented in his lectures. Expressing his thoughts in writing often frustrated him, as many of you who have struggled in composition courses and writing term papers may well understand. Rather, it was through his students, who assembled the notes from his lectures and published in 1913 a text entitled *Cours de linguistique générale* (*Course in General Linguistics*) that we have come to know Saussure's ideas on language.

A key precept of Saussure's view of language was the arbitrariness of the MOD 2 symbol (*signifiant*) in relation to the meaning it conveys (*signifié*). Words, he said, have no innate meaning, regardless of what they sound like or may have meant in the past. As a personal example, Dr. Remillard's mother, a native speaker of French, for example, was extremely intolerant of any use of profanity in her presence. And yet, she would never hesitate to use the word *phoque*, the French word for *seal*, when talking about a seal, regardless of the fact that she was aware of its almost identical pronunciation in English to the much used "taboo" word, *f*ck*. The relationship of the sounds of the word to its meaning in English never entered her mind when speaking French.

The relationship of the symbol to its meaning is also arbitrary not only from one language to another, but also in relation to past meanings. Speakers of English today, for instance, use the subject pronoun *you* for referring to both the singular and the plural second person pronouns without knowing that it was only used as a plural pronoun before the seventeenth century. Such prior uses of this word, however, have little to no relationship to its use in the English language today.

In these and other principles he presented, Saussure was providing a perspective of language wherein language forms (sounds, grammar, and meaning) relate to one another, not aesthetically, morally, or historically, but rather structurally. He conceived the study of language as one wherein the constituent forms are in relationship to one another. For him, the linguist was much like a biologist who studies a life form such as a tree in relationship to all other life forms, and how each of these life forms is constituted.

Structural Linguistics

In the United States, the study of linguistics arose at about the same time as Saussure was lecturing at the University of Geneva. The need for understanding how languages operate was fueled in this country by the desire to preserve the many Native American languages that were becoming extinct as their number of speakers rapidly diminished. Methods and techniques for analyzing and classifying sounds, words and how the words combined to form sentences, were first addressed.

As opposed to the more theoretical perspective championed by Saussure and his disciples, the study of linguistics in the United States thus developed from studying languages from a field perspective, that is, gathering, collecting and analyzing actual language use by native speakers. These field studies led to a codification of Native American languages in the early part of the twentieth century. Following this, two leading figures in American linguistics, Edward Sapir and Leonard Bloomfield, would each write a text entitled *Language*. Sapir, in his 1921 publication, described Native American languages and focused on the relationship of these languages to culture. Bloomfield, in his 1933 publication, presented a **behaviorist** approach to the study of language, wherein the linguist acts like a **descriptive** scientist who observes, classifies and measures physical phenomena. For Bloomfield, language studies that did not meet this concept of science were to be discarded.

Bloomfield's approach to the study of language would dominate the thinking in the field of linguistics for another generation. The focus on studying languages from a behaviorist perspective was common in university courses in this country from the decade of the 1930s through the 1960s. When Dr. Remillard took his first course in linguistics in 1969, every student in the class had as a final project to do a phonological, morphological and syntactical description of a language s/he had never heard or seen before, using the behaviorist methodology Bloomfield presented. In his case, the language was Swahili. Dr. Williams did an abbreviated form of this when she analyzed certain aspects of spoken Hungarian in 1994.

It was not until the 1960s that linguists began to conceive of their discipline from a different scientific perspective. The breakthrough occurred after Noam Chomsky published *Syntactic Structures* in 1957 which he later followed up with the *Aspects of the Theory of Syntax* (1965). Until then, the discipline of linguistics had focused on the finite nature of language forms, that is, the sounds, word formation and the grammar of a particular language as prescribed by Bloomfield and his followers. But Chomsky recognized that syntax, which is the possible order of words and phrases in a sentence, was infinite (as we demonstrated in Chapter 1). Instead of analyzing the syntax of individual utterances, what Chomsky proposed was a **cognitive** approach to syntax that consisted of phrase structure rules that could be formulated to generate the deep structure of all (and only) the possible phrases and sentences of any given language, not just those used by any given speaker. Transformations could then be applied on the components of the deep structure generated by the phrase structure rules until the surface structure or actual speech resulted.

The cognitive approach in linguistics used to explain syntax would then spur the study of semantics, which made behavioral linguists somewhat uncomfortable since meaning did not lend itself to the finiteness of sounds and grammar. The cognitive approach to linguistics even went beyond syntax and semantics. In the last three decades or so, we have since witnessed an increasing focus on the relationship between the language forms, context and communicative functions (pragmatics) as well as on language's relationship with sociological factors such as ethnicity and gender (sociolinguistics).

Language Forms

The historical development of structural linguistics presented above serves as a backdrop for discussing the linguistic forms (sounds, grammar, and meaning) that constitute a language. Our purpose in presenting the language forms herein is not only to have you appreciate the features that constitute a language but especially to provide you with adequate knowledge of language forms so that you can understand how they operate in interpersonal relationships and social groups, topics dealt with in succeeding chapters. Since this is not a structural linguistics text, much of our treatment is brief. We realize you may want or need (especially if you are conducting research) to pursue further information on language forms. For this purpose, we have included several websites within and at the end of this chapter that will direct you to more in-depth treatments of these forms.

Phonetics: The Study of Speech Sounds

We will begin our overview of language forms by defining and explaining the basic terms associated with the study of **phonetics**. Phonetics, the study of speech sounds, has many practical applications, such as in language education (including English as a Second Language and English Education), human/computer interfacing or interfacing between computers, audiology and speech therapy. It is also used to accurately describe pronunciation differences between dialects, a sociolinguistic topic to be treated later in this text.

The area of phonetics that describes how speech sounds are produced is called **articulatory phonetics**. The sound inventory of any given language includes both vowels and consonants.

Vowels

Different vowel sounds are produced by changing the position of the tongue and the lips. In pronouncing vowel sounds, the air passage is not obstructed but is modified by the shape of the tongue and the lips. Vowels are categorized according to three features:

MOD 4

1. tongue height (high, mid, low)
2. tongue position (front, central, back)
3. lip position (spread/round)

While we have learned that in writing there are five or six vowels in English, in the spoken language we function with at least 11 vowels, and depending on the dialect, even more.

Consonants

Consonant sounds are produced by **articulation** and the lack of or use of **voicing**. Articulation involves the place in the vocal tract (lips, teeth, hard palate, etc.) you use to produce the consonant. For example, the sound [p] is **bilabial** (*labia* < *Latin = lips*), because you use both of your lips to articulate it. The lips, then, are the **point of articulation**. Articulation also involves the process of how you expel the air from your vocal tract, called the **manner of articulation**. For example, the [p] mentioned above is additionally labeled as a **stop** because the air flow must be completely stopped during its production.

MOD 4

    Voicing refers to whether or not the vocal cords vibrate for the production of the consonant. For an unvoiced consonant, such as [p], the vocal cords do not vibrate. But with a voiced consonant, the vocal cords do vibrate. Indeed, if you voice the [p] you will end up producing a [b]. Voicing, then, is the only difference between these two consonants. This can be demonstrated by placing your fingertips on your throat and alternating between the sounds. (In producing the [p] and [b] consonants, do not produce the vowel that follows [i], as you do when you recite letters alphabetically).

    There are several other unvoiced consonants in English in which voicing changes the consonant. One example is [s] (like the sound of a slithering snake) and [z] (like the sound of a buzzing bee). For the former, there is no vibration, but for the latter, there is.

The International Phonetic Alphabet

The International Phonetic Alphabet (IPA) was created as a tool to describe sounds. In theory, the IPA uses a separate symbol for every sound used in every human language, although in practice, it is not so simple.

We will be using IPA symbols in this text (you've already seen a few examples above), and your instructor may choose to expand this section and teach you more details about the system. For quick reference, we are including a simplified chart of English consonant symbols below. Many of the symbols are visually identical to the letter of the alphabet that corresponds with that sound, but some are not. In case your instructor chooses not to focus on IPA symbols, we also provide pronunciation descriptions that do not use these symbols, so it is not necessary to memorize them in order to understand the basic phonetic concepts presented in this book.

> Optional Expansion: To view the full IPA table online and for more information on its uses visit this website: http://www. internationalphoneticalphabet.org/

You may wonder why phoneticians don't just use the English alphabet to represent a given sound, but this poses problems. For one, a given letter can be represented by more than one sound. Think of the letter "c" in English. Does it sound the same in the pronunciation of the word *cat* as it does in *cement*? The correct IPA symbol for the sound it makes in the word *cat* is [k], but in the word *cement*, it is [s]. Conversely, a given sound can be represented by more than one letter. The [k] sound mentioned above is represented by the letter "c" in the word *cat*, but by "q" in the word *quick*. A particularly troublesome case of the lack of direct correlation between a sound and a letter can be seen in the English letter combination of *ough*. Pronounce the following words, and you'll see just how many sounds can be represented: *trough*, *though*, *tough*, *through*, and *bough*. In this text, we use quotation marks to indicate a letter of the alphabet, and either brackets or slashes to represent sounds.

With languages having a written form, there are none that have a perfect correlation between sound and the written symbol, but some are closer than others. Spanish is considered to have a higher correlation between sound and symbol than English, for example. One of the reasons that learning to spell in English is so challenging is that when we borrow words from other languages, we change the pronunciation, but not the spelling. An example from French is *ballet*, and one from Japanese is *karaoke*. In essence, a child learning English spelling must learn the spelling rules of many different languages!

In addition to the study of vowel and consonant segments, phonetics also includes the study of **suprasegments**, such as **stress**, **tone** and **intonation**. This area of phonetic study, however, extends beyond the scope of this text.

	Bilabial	Labio-dental	Inter-dental	Alveolar	Post-alveolar	Retro-flex	Palatal	Velar	Glottal
Stop	p b pay bay			t d tie die				k g cot got	ʔ
Fricative	w (wʰ) white	f v fever fever	θ ð thigh thy	s z sip zip	ʃ ʒ shoe pleasure		j yes		h hello
Affricate							tʃ dʒ church judge		
Nasal	m man			n nip			ñ onion	ŋ sing	
Tap						l ɹ lip leer			

Should you desire it, further information on the role of supra-segments can be obtained online at: http://www.britannica.com/science/phonetics

Phonology: The Study of the Sound System of Language

Phonetics is often considered part of the study of **phonology**. In its larger sense, however, phonology deals with the whole area of sound in language, including not only how sounds are produced but also how they are structured and patterned within a given language. In this text, we will limit our discussion of phonology to defining and explaining the concept of the **phoneme**, and include some activities and websites that illustrate phonemes more fully.

Phonemes are the sounds of a language that a native speaker of a language recognizes as different or distinctive. It is essential to realize before going any further that sounds an English speaker interprets as different can be interpreted as the same sound to speakers of another language. And conversely, sounds an English speaker interprets as the same can be interpreted as different to speakers of another language.

One way we determine which sounds are considered the same and those which are considered to be different in any language is by using **minimal pairs**. A minimal pair is a pair of words whose pronunciation differs by only one sound. (Remember again here that letters and sounds are not the same thing). Take, for example the English sounds [l] and [r]. In minimal word pairs, such as *lip-rip* and *clack-crack*, only the [l] and [r] are in contrast while the other sounds are identical. But a change in meaning has occurred solely by one sound being substituted for another in these pairs. When this occurs in a language, as it does here in English, the sounds ([l] and [r] in this case) are said to be distinctive or phonemic.

In Korean, however, these two same sounds are not distinctive. This can be illustrated by the distribution of [r] and [l] in the following Korean words with their translation in English:

rupi/ ruby	*mul/water*
kiri/road	*pal/big*
saram/person	*ilkop/seven*
ratio/radio	*ipalsa/barbe*

The [r] occurs only in word initial or syllable initial position and the [l] only at word final or syllable final position (marked in bold). For Korean speakers, even though both of these sounds exist in their language, they are not phonemic. If you were to pronounce *rupi* as *lupi* it would still be understood as meaning *ruby*. Likewise if you were to pronounce *mul* as *mur* it would still be understood as meaning *water*.

Non-distinctive sounds in a language, such as the [l] and [r] in Korean, are called **allophones**. A feature of allophones is that they never occur in the same MOD † place and are thus said to be in complementary distribution as can be seen in the Korean example above. Think of complementary distribution as you would

Batman and Bruce Wayne. Whenever Batman is present Bruce Wayne is absent and vice versa.

An amusing yet relevant error that illustrates the non-distinctiveness of [l] and [r] in Korean was alleged to have occurred when a Korean diplomat stated (in English) how pleased he was to hear of President Clinton's winning *erection* in 1996 rather than his *election*. What is happening in Korean with the [l] and [r] is analogous to what occurs in English with aspirated consonants, which are consonants that require the release of a puff of air. The degree of aspiration of the consonants, [p, t, k] in English depends on their location in a word.

Take the consonant sound [p] as an example: English speakers pronounce a very aspirated [p] in word-initial (or syllable-initial) position, as in the words *pot* or *depend*; a less aspirated [p] in the word-medial position, as in *spot*; and a barely aspirated or unaspirated [p] in the word-final position as in *tap*. (You can feel this difference yourself by putting the palm of your hand in front of your mouth while pronouncing each of these words). The degree of aspiration of [p] in English is not phonemic/distinctive because, regardless of how much or little aspiration you use for pronouncing the [p] in any position of a word, it will not change the word's meaning. Consequently, when a foreign speaker pronounces an English word, such as *tap*, with a strong aspiration on the [p], it will retain its meaning for you, regardless of the degree of aspiration used. If you have an acute ear you will likely only sense that it is not a native pronunciation.

You may be thinking that of course the aspiration of consonants does not change the meaning of the word! But indeed it does in other languages. In Hindi, for example, the aspirated and unaspirated initial [p] is a phonemic/distinctive sound of their language. The word pronounced as [pʰbl], for example, means *fruit*, if the initial [p] is strongly aspirated, which is represented here by the superscript "h" in [pʰ]. But if the initial [p] is not strongly aspirated, [pbl] means *moment*. This minimal pair reveals a completely different meaning to the Hindi speaker. For the speaker of Hindi, the aspiration and non-aspiration of [p] would be distinctive, or phonemic, in that it changes the meaning of the word. As speakers of English, we would, at best, not hear much difference between these two words so that in learning Hindi we would have to train ourselves to hear and say it.

In sum, phonemes are sounds that native speakers of a language perceive as distinctive and allophones are sounds perceived as essentially the same. The distinction you make between the [l] and an [r] sounds as speakers of English is no more "natural" than the non-distinctiveness of these sounds for speakers of Korean. Similarly, speakers of English not making any phonemic distinction between the degrees of aspiration with [p] is no more "natural" than the distinctiveness of these sounds made by speakers of Hindi.

We have only provided you with a cursory introduction to phonetics and phonology. The following website includes a series of useful and engaging videos describing phonetics and phonology in more detail: http://www.thelingspace.com/phonology-episodes (You can explore the entire site to view other linguistic and sociolinguistic topics as well).

Morphology: The Study of Word Parts MOD 4

When sounds are combined, words are created. As literate individuals we generally view words as a whole. But words are actually made up of parts called morphemes. A **morpheme** is the minimal sequence of sounds that carries lexical meaning or gram-   MOD 4
matical function. Here are some examples that illustrate how morphemes work:

> *boys*: This word contains two morphemes: *boy*, a content morpheme since it has lexical meaning in itself; and *–s* (pronounced as a [z]), which has the grammatical function in English of creating the plural.

> *scarecrow*: this word constitutes only one morpheme (not two) as it refers only to a crude figure of a person rather than anything to do with a kind of bird.

> *unbelievable*: this word consists of two grammatical morphemes, the prefix *un-* and the suffix *-able,* and one content morpheme, *believ*(e).

> *ungrateful*: this word consists of one grammatical morpheme, *un* and one content morpheme, *grateful.*

Based on the definition of a morpheme and using the examples above, divide the following words into their morphemes and explain if the morpheme is lexical or grammatical:

1.   dishes
2.   unholy
3.   holiday
4.   biology
5.   Massachusetts
6.   saneness
7.   blackboard
8.   blackball
9.   immoral
10. repeat
11. rewrite
12. indivisibility
13. psychosomatic
14. constitution
15. phlebitis

It is interesting to note that pre-school children conceive words as morphemes, and not as we (who have learned to read) have come to think of them in their written form. This can be illustrated when a six year old child creates grammatical forms accurately such as pluralizing words she has never heard before. Suppose the child heard the noun *bead* [bid] for the first time. She would pluralize it to *beads* [bidz] with a plural ending in the [z] sound. She would also know that other words she had not heard before, like *cat*, are made plural by pronouncing an [s] rather than a [z]. And with a word like *dish*, a third plural sound, she would form the plural as [Iz], so as to produce *dishes*.

Create nonsense words such as *prag, drush, blin, seck, flous, glup,* etc. and ask a pre-school child to give you the plural form of each. Since the child will likely not understand what *plural* means, you can do this by saying, "I have one *prag* in this hand but in my other hand I have two _____."

Did the child accurately produce one of the three English plural forms, with the proper suffix creating the sound [s], [z] or [IZ]?

Is the grammar rule that states that words are made plural in English by adding an "s" an accurate one for speaking? Why not?

Why do children pronounce the plural of *fish* as *fishes*? Is this really a mistake? Can you think of other plural forms that are irregular such as *data* from *datum*? Where do such forms come from? Do you think there are many of them in English?

Speakers of other languages create grammatical plural morphemes in various ways. Spanish makes plurals through various versions of "s". If the Spanish word ends in a vowel, then the "s" [s] alone is added to the spelling for the plural; for instance, the word for *brother*, which is *hermano*, becomes *hermanos*. On the other hand, if the Spanish word ends in a consonant, then "es" [es] would be added to the plural form. Thus *ciudad* (city) becomes *ciudades*.

MOD4

In spoken French, the plural is marked by the preceding article *les* [le] as opposed to *le/la* (masculine and feminine singular markers). Even though the "s" is added to most of the following nouns in the written convention, it is usually not heard.

When it comes to other grammatical morphemes, such as verb endings, languages differ significantly. In English, there is a grammatical morpheme verb ending in the present tense only with the third person singular (he walk*s*, she see*s*, it hurt*s*) while in Spanish the present tense has a different ending for each subject. In spoken French, only the first and second person plural endings of the present tense (*ons, ez*), are pronounced. Japanese can omit the subject pronoun (*I, you, he, she, we,* and *they*) from a sentence if the verb and context make it clear. German and Latin assign different endings to nouns depending on how the noun relates (subject, object, etc.) to other words in the sentence.

Unlike grammatical morphemes, we have much greater flexibility in English with content morphemes. Indeed, we use content morphemes to create new words. This is done by compounding words as with the following: *mailman*, *greenhouse* and *blackboard*. Other examples of content morpheme creativity is in   MOD 4 forming acronyms (*Scuba, UNESCO, PC*); abbreviations (*ads, bikes, math, labs, apps*); eponyms, which are words created from someone's name (*Gatling gun, Franklin stove, Sandwich*); and blends (*motel* from *motor+ hotel, guesstimate* from *guess+estimate, emoticon* from *emotion+icon*, and *fremeny* from *friend+enemy*).

Provide two or more additional examples for each of the following:
compounds
acronyms
abbreviations
eponyms
blends

Syntax: the Study of How Words are Combined   MOD 4

The next sub-field of linguistics, **syntax**, deals with how words relate to one another in terms of how they combine to construct phrases and sentences. A linguistic axiom of syntax is that native speakers of a language operate with a set of innate and consistent rules by which they recognize and produce what linguists call well-formed or grammatical phrases and sentences.

This does not mean that a phrase or sentence has to be meaningful or truthful. As an example, consider this sentence from Anthony Burgess's novel, *A Clockwork Orange*:

> The Korova Milkbar was a milkplus mesto...

Semantically, this sentence conveys little or no meaning and the Korova Milkbar is not really a place. And yet, we recognize this sentence as grammatical because it conforms to the way speakers of English perceive how a sentence is formed. One would only have to substitute different lexical items to produce the following meaningful sentence:

> The pepperoni pizza was a great treat.

Moreover, grammaticality does not refer to prescriptive rules of writing, such as using the predicate nominative after the verb *to be* rather than the object pronoun (*It is I* rather than *It is me*); or not using a preposition at the end of a sentence (*We will put in our time* rather than *We will put our time in*); or not splitting an infinitive verb (*To go boldly where none have gone before* rather than Star Trek's *To boldly go where none have gone before*); or never using the term *however* at the beginning of a sentence. These rules may apply to the sense of grammaticality of other languages, or to someone's arbitrary aesthetic taste, but they are not innate constructs of English syntax.

In short, a grammatical sentence is what you intuitively sense in your native language as sounding right or normal, and an ungrammatical sentence is one that sounds strange or unusual.

MOD 4

The following activity will illustrate the above: For each of the sentences below label them as grammatical (G) or ungrammatical (U). After you have finished, compare your responses to those of others in your class.

1. _____ I drink my juice in the morning.

2. _____ I breakfast my juice in the morning.

3. _____ The work seems tiring.

4. _____ The work seems dining.

5. _____ I wait the results.

6. _____ I await the results.

7. _____ The book me is pleasing to.

8. _____ The book is pleasing to me.

9. _____ The fish with a grin pulled the fisherman in.

10. _____ The fish with a grin pulled in the fisherman.

11. _____ The fish pulled the fisherman in with a grin.

12. _____ The fish lulled the fisherman in with a grin.

13. _____ He came in by the side door.

14. _____ He came by the side door in.

15. _____ I don't mind it.

16. _____ I don't bind it.

17. _____ I don't find it.

18. _____ I don't blind it.

19. _____ He snores the bed.

20. _____ He leaves the bed.

Did you find that your answers were largely the same? Why do you think this was so? Also, for each ungrammatical sentence, try to explain why it is not a well-formed sentence in the English language.

A grammatical theory should account for why you and native speakers of your language can identify grammatical from ungrammatical sentences. But while a sentence or a phrase may sound natural or commonsensical to you, that does not mean it is so for speakers of another language. The equivalent translation of a sentence like: *The book me is pleasing to* is a perfectly well-formed sentence in French (*Ce livre me plaît*), and the same is true for Spanish (*El libro me gusta*), but not for English.

While the word order in French and Spanish phrases occasionally differs from what you would expect as an English speaker, the normal word order in both these languages is overall the same as it is in English: Subject – Verb – Object (SVO). Japanese speakers, however, combine words differently. The word order in their language is Subject – Object – Verb (SOV). In case you think this is a deviant way of combining words, you will be surprised to know that if we list the word order of all languages, Japanese word order is indeed more common than ours. Other languages, such as Irish and Arabic, use a (VSO) word order and a very small percentage use (VOS). If we rank word order preferences for all languages we find the following:

SOV = 44%
SVO = 35%
VSO = 19%
VOS = 2%

The point to be made here (especially as we approach the discussion of semantics and later, pragmatics and sociolinguistics) is that you need to suspend judgment as to what is commonly accepted as natural or common sense in respect to language forms and their function in communication.

> The following website offers a brief definition of syntax, followed by some observations about how syntax works in real life: http://grammar.about.com/od/rs/g/syntax.htm
>
> This next website is designed for ESL teachers. It includes a number of interactive online quizzes covering various aspects of language, including sentence structure: http://a4esl.org/a/g.html
>
> This final website offers some very good basic information about descriptivist syntax, although you must scroll through numerous ads to read the entire entry: http://www.wisegeek.com/what-is-syntax.htm

Semantics: The Study of Meaning

The final sub-field of linguistics, **semantics**, deals with the systematic ways words relate to one another and create meaning in phrases up to the level of the sentence. The study of meaning beyond the sentence falls into the realm of pragmatics, which will be treated in the following chapter.

The popular notion of meaning is that a word means what a dictionary says it means. But dictionaries, while helpful to varying degrees, have serious limitations when it comes to understanding grammatical meaning, as seen with the words below.

Look up the definitions of the following words in a dictionary and write a description of their meaning to a person learning English:

a

to

this

phosphatase

bring (as opposed to take)

Concrete words, on the other hand, are not as challenging to define, but most have quite diverse meanings. Take, for example, the word *chair*. The first meaning that came to your mind is most likely an object used for sitting. And how is that different from a *seat*? *Chair* can also mean the head of a particular group, organization, or committee. In this latter sense, *chair* also functions as a verb, as in to *chair* a committee. And then there are meanings of *chair* for the cage that hauls up coal from a mine shaft or the metal piece that supports a railroad track. Even the most exhaustive dictionary entries are unable to account for all the emerging dialectical and idiolectical meanings by which a concrete word could be understood by speakers in a linguistic community.

In addition to the various definitions, words relate to other words in several ways, like with **synonyms** (words that sound different but have the same or nearly the same meaning); **antonyms** (words of opposite meanings); **homonyms** (words having the same sound but with different meanings such as *pair* and *pear*; and **metonyms** (words used in place of others that have the same meaning, such as *brass* for *officer*), to mention only a few ways individual words are tied to other words.

MODH

Beyond dictionary definitions and word relationships, the meaning of a word must be considered in its reference to the real world. But what do words like *or*, *bye, assuming, seeming,* etc. refer to in the real world? Much of language consists of phenomena that have no real world referent. While Barack Obama is Barack Obama, a dog is a dog, and a rose is a rose, who is the Easter Bunny or Harry Potter?

Could we not just then extend the meaning of a word to include a mental image or concept? This allows one to imagine the Easter Bunny and Harry Potter as well as other figures such as Santa Claus and leprechauns, none of whom exist in the real world. But mental images can't be conjured up for words like *and, to, merely, will, for, no,* or *how.* And even when we have mental concepts of ordinary objects, these concepts represent, at best, an idealization. Your concept of a *radio,* for example, may not include radios of all possible kinds (car radios, satellite radios, stand-alone radios, and counter radios, to name a few). Mental concepts also differ from person to person as well. When you read the word *dog,* what image comes to mind? Perhaps you think of your childhood dog, or the type of cute Labrador puppy that is often featured on calendars?

Meaning is also not limited to the level of the word. Words combine to form phrases and sentences which involve knowing the truth value and conditions. When one says *George W. Bush was President of the USA from 2001–2009,* one recognizes the truth value of this sentence and the conditions (he was elected twice and did not die or resign during that period). On the other hand if one says *George W. Bush is golfing,* can you really know if this is true? For you to know, you would have to know the conditions in which this would be true, e.g., he has golf balls, tees and clubs, and he is not a paraplegic. But if you were golfing with him, you would know the truth value by witnessing it yourself. Meaning, here, consists of knowing more than the sum of the words in a sentence.

Consider the following sentence:

> The Easter Bunny left Easter baskets in our home.

Has a truth condition been met? Explain. Does the sentence have truth value? Explain.

Now consider the truth value and condition of the following sentence and compare it to the sentence above:

> The Easter Bunny is playing golf.

Meaning also involves going beyond literal declarative sentences, such as those given in the examples above. In language we use commands, counterfactual sentences, questions and exclamations not only to convey factual information but also for such purposes as irony, sarcasm and metaphors of all types. For example, the phrase *That's fantastic!* could be used to convey sincere approval, or to express intense sarcasm. And telling a non-native speaker of English that *It's raining cats and dogs* might bring a rather apocalyptic image to his/her mind!

Meaning at the level of the sentence also intersects with syntax. In English, and many other languages, word order changes the meaning of a sentence. *The boy ate the bear* is quite different from *The bear ate the boy.* We can also create ambiguous sentences such as *I found my dog eating a candy bar.* Two interpretations are possible here: Is your dog eating a candy bar, or were you eating a candy bar when you found him? Both could be considered correct depending upon the context. It is not the word order (syntax) that is in question in this sentence, but rather the intended meaning.

Conclusion

Linguistics, as it has developed as an academic discipline over the last century or so, has focused on the linguistic forms that make up a language. These forms have been categorized within the following sub-fields:

- **Phonetics** and **phonology** are the study of speech sounds and the system in which these sounds operate.
- **Morphology** and **syntax** are the study of the grammatical aspects of a language with the former focusing on word parts and the latter on how these words combine with one another to form phrases and sentences.
- **Semantics** is the study of word, phrase and sentence meaning.

Communication, however, requires a level of language usage far beyond these linguistic forms. In any living language, users combine linguistic forms within the physical and social world in which the language is used. In so doing, meaning functions not only at the linguistic or literal level produced by the forms of the language, but also within a given context. When the context is considered along with the linguistic forms, we are dealing with **pragmatic** or **speaker** meaning. Meaning in this larger sense first requires an awareness of the components of context, a topic we will treat in the following chapter.

Additional Activities

1. Put your hand on your throat and pronounce the following minimal pairs. What is the difference that you notice?

pit	bit
tap	tab
ten	den
bit	bid
fan	van
grief	grieve
sap	zap
hiss	his

2. Hold a sheet of paper in front of your face with your thumb and index finger at the top of the paper. Say the following minimal pairs out loud. Describe what happens to the sheet of paper with each word. Why is this case?

pit	spit
pin	spin
tone	stone
ton	stun
kin	skin

3. Decide whether or not these words are examples of minimal pairs by writing *yes* or *no* in the third column. Then, in the fourth column, explain in a short answer why the words *are* or *are not* minimal pairs. (Note: This exercise requires some familiarity with the IPA symbols. To refresh your memory, you may refer back to the chart earlier in the chapter).

Words	Phonetic Spellings	Minimal Pairs? (Yes/No)	Explanation (Why? or Why Not?)
hung hut	/hʌŋ/ /hʌt/		
fraught frat	/frat/ /fræt/		.
string ring	/strIŋ/ /rIŋ/		
cat chat	/kæt/ /čæt/		
rhymes crime	/raymz/ /kraym/		
space splice	/speys/ /splays/		

4.   Consider how the following minimal pairs could change the meaning of the sentences in which they are located. If the recipient hears the second rather than the first, how would this affect his/her behavior during the course of the conversation? What might be his/her reaction or next statement? (Note: The languages in parentheses indicate speakers who may make such an error.)

   a.   I am going to use my *razor/racer* to shave. (Spanish)
   b.   I *bit/hit* my lip.
   c.   I want to *sit/shit* on this chair.
   d.   My *head/Ed* is *hot/ought*. (Italian)
   e.   I want to introduce you to my friend *Ellen/Hellen*. (French)

5.   Pronounce the following phrase aloud: *Mele Kalikimaka*

   This Hawaiian word was taken from English pronunciation. However, since there are only eight consonants in Hawaiian, and vowels must separate consonants (i.e., no blends like /sp/ or /str/ or /bl/ are permissible in Hawaiian), extra vowels have been added. What were the two original English words?

6.   A Finnish speaker may create the following sentences in English.

   a.   She buys gifts me.
   b.   I sing song you.
   c.   We bought home Loretto.
   d.   He goes store me.

   Consider what the Finnish speaker is trying to say in each sentence. How would you say each of these sentences? What might these phrases tell you about Finnish syntax?

7.   Language usage is infinite. All individuals are highly creative speakers, as they can combine the finite parts (words) in an infinite number of combinations to create phrases and sentences. Because we are faced with this constant creativity, we have to interpret the meaning of each message received anew. We will hardly ever hear the same thing said in exactly the same way, and certainly never in an identical setting. Once you are aware of that fact, you'll begin to notice never-before-uttered sentences all around you.

   Following is a brief sampling of original sentences that Dr. Williams has observed just by watching an evening of FOX Network animation shows:

1. Roger on *American Dad*: "I'm becoming uncomfortably lucid."
2. A desperate 37-year old woman on a blind date on *Family Guy*: "Me and my three eggs are having the best time!"
3. Marge Simpson (on The Simpsons), after having drank a large quantity of water, tells a salesperson that she's feeling over-hydrated. The salesperson replies, "That just means that your bladder is full of science!"

Try to explain each of these sentences to a non-native speaker of English. In so doing you will need to resort to linguistic meaning and the context in which they were uttered. As an optional extension of this activity, find your own examples of unique phrases from print materials or spoken examples.

8. What sub-field of linguistics is involved in each of the following examples/descriptions?

Sub/field	Word(s)	Examples
	fan/**v**an	Voiced and unvoiced sounds are examples.
	bit/**p**it	Units of sound whose distinction causes these words to have different meanings.
	unsatisfied	This word has four parts, which is an example of this.
	shoulder	This word has more than one definition. One is a part of the body (a noun). Another is to bear a burden (a verb).
	John walks.	This sentence is composed of a noun phrase followed by a verb phrase.
	reformat slight**ly**	Prefixes and suffixes are examples.
	cantaré	In Spanish this includes a part that means *sing* (*cant-*) and a part that means future tense plus the first person singular (*-aré*).
	sisters	One day two blondes walked into a tanning salon. One blonde said, "A tan for two please!" The cashier agreed, filled out a form for them, and asked, "Are you two sisters?" They chuckled and replied, "No, we aren't even Catholic."
	ten/**d**en	Apicoalveolar sounds like /t/ and /d/ are examples.
	tom[a]to tom[eI]to	Allophones, which do not cause minimal pairs, are a part of this type of analysis.
	N/A	A root word or a stem is an example.
	N/A	The vocal apparatus is important to this study. This includes the lungs, pharynx, larynx, glottis, vocal cords, nose, mouth, tongue, teeth, and lips.
	N/A	Fricative sounds include labiodental fricatives (/f/ and /v/), apicodental fricatives (/θ/ and /ð/), apicoalveolar fricatives (/s/ and /z/), and alveopalatal fricatives (/ʃ/ and /ʒ/).

Web Resources

- For a good basic overview of linguistics and its subfields, visit this website: http://grammar.about.com/od/grammarfaq/a/What-Is-Linguistics.htm
- Because students in colleges and universities are not often aware of linguistics as an academic discipline, they often think it must be very esoteric and not related to the real world. This is unfortunate in that it limits student potential and perspectives. In the website given below, an extensive list is given of various professions and jobs in the areas of business, education, and government, for which linguists are sought.
- http://ling.bu.edu/about/linguistics
- ESL teachers must often try to recognize and correct pronunciation errors which are due to interference from a student's first language. While this is certainly not from an academic original source, the following site includes a useful list of common pronunciation errors made by ESL learners divided by language:
- http://en.wikipedia.org/wiki/Non-native_pronunciations_of_English

Further Reading

Akmajian, A. (2010). *Linguistics: An Introduction to Language and Communication, 6th ed.* Cambridge, MA: The MIT Press.

Fromkin, V., Rodman, R., and Hyams, N. (2013). *An Introduction to Language.* Belmont, CA: Wadsworth.

Chapter 3

Pragmatics

> We will consider what is meaning and more specifically the difference between linguistic/literal meaning and pragmatic/speaker meaning.

The language of friendship is not words but meanings (Henry David Thoreau, *A Week on the Concord and Merrimack Rivers*)

Introduction

It was not unusual in a previous era for first semester college students in an English composition class to be assigned a 250-word essay on the meaning of meaning. The topic always stunned students. Most had never even thought to think about meaning! Totally befuddled, students took several days to even try to grasp what the instructor may have wanted them to address. Most students made an honest effort to meet this challenge but fell far short of what they could have written if they had been introduced to how languages operate, and specifically to the linguistic study of **semantics**.

But unless you had been a student in the decades of the 1960s and thereafter, research in semantic meaning was not extensive. Until then, of the four linguistic sub-fields, semantics was the most neglected. This was due to the fact that semantic analysis did not lend itself to the same rigorous methods that had been developed for the study of phonology, morphology and syntax. It was only after these three subfields had been developed that semantic studies really began to develop, focusing initially on linguistic relationships in lexical and sentence meaning, as you learned in Chapter 2.

It quickly became evident to researchers in semantics, however, that meaning is not limited to linguistic relationships. Indeed, a person may have native fluency in a language (**linguistic competence**) without being aware of how to use the language appropriately in various contexts within a culture (**communicative competence**). In other words, what we mean as speakers of a language is not only found in the meanings of words, but also in our knowledge of the physical and social world in which we are participating, along with our intended communicative purpose. It is this knowledge that native speakers of a language often assume is normal, common sense, legitimate, necessary, etc., which makes even the most common everyday utterances have several possible meanings.

Dr. Remillard offers an example with this exchange that took place after church services between a three year-old boy and the pastor who had previously recognized this toddler as a very active boy. The pastor said, "You must keep your parents on their toes." The toddler looked down at his toes and at those of his parents. His non-verbal reaction reflected that he only understood the pastor's linguistic or literal meaning. But this was not likely to be the pastor's speaker meaning, that is, his intended meaning. In this case, the pastor had previous social knowledge of the toddler's physical activities. The pastor may have been thinking of how tired such an active boy could make his parents feel. In so doing, he could also have meant to imply that he understood why his parents were expressing frustration with him. He may even have been alluding to how the parents' frustrations with the boy were being felt in church activities by other members in the parish. He could have also felt empathy for the parents in their never-ending task of having to be very watchful. Or he may have extended his knowledge of active boys to this three year-old and never had any thought other than that this child was exasperating his parents. Regardless, the point is that in most verbal utterances a multitude of possible speaker meanings usually arise.

As for the three year-old in this example, he had not yet arrived at understanding all the possible contextual factors in which the pastor was functioning, even though he was already reaching fluency in the language. But as adults our contextual experiences in life make us aware of the varying degrees of meaning beyond literal interpretation. If there are so many varied interpretations for any given verbal event, most of what speakers mean is conveyed to us quite obliquely. How, then, can we come to know what someone truly means?

There is, in fact, no magical formula. Our best recourse to understanding what others mean lies in the use of intelligent guesswork. Intelligent guesswork goes beyond just having a hunch, however. It consists of combining the meaning conveyed in the linguistic message within the context of the utterance. This level of meaning goes far beyond just semantics in the linguistic senses discussed in the previous chapter. It involves, in particular, how linguistic forms are used, which is the subject area of **pragmatics** (from the Greek *pragma*, meaning *deed* or *affair*).

Pragmatic/speaker meaning has been defined in several ways. Explain the following definitions of pragmatics:

1. How language is used to perform different functions Mihaliček & Wilson (2001: 19)
2. The study of how more gets communicated than what is said (Yule 1996: 3).
3. A listener's intelligent guesswork in conversation (Pecei 1999: 5).

Entailments and Presuppositions

We have chosen to only briefly address two areas of pragmatic studies, **entailments** and **presuppositions**, in this text, as they both focus more on linguistic/ literal meaning rather than on pragmatic/speaker meaning derived from knowledge of the context. If you were to say, *I saw a robin*, it entails that you saw a bird. We can infer this meaning based solely on the semantic relationship between a robin and a bird, independent of the setting where the robin was seen.

As for presuppositions, knowledge of the physical and social world is minimally required, if needed at all. When we ask questions such as *Who is in the room?*, we presuppose that someone is in the room. When we give a command such as *Don't touch the painting*, we presuppose this warning was needed. In these instances, we infer what is meant based on the words and grammatical structures (question, negation, command, etc.).

The study of pragmatics which we will focus on in this chapter and throughout the rest of the text deals with speaker meaning as inferred from the **context,** or the knowledge of the physical and social world between interlocutors (speakers and listeners).

Context

But what are all the components that make up context? Following the outline proposed by Dell Hymes (1974), context consists not only of **setting** (where/ when something is said), but also of **participants** (who says it), **topic** (what is said) and **goals** (why it is said). Hymes also includes contextual concepts such as **key, instrumentalities, norms of interaction** and **interpretation**, and **genre**, all of which address how something is said. Let us look at each of these contextual components more closely in terms of speech events:

Setting: This refers to the time and place (*where/when*) of the speech event. The setting includes concrete places (stadium, mosque, school, home, etc.) that affect the linguistic utterance. The speaker's meaning in an utterance needs to be measured by the location and the moment it is used. If a fan says *I hope God is with us* at half-time during the Super Bowl, it may be meant very differently than when that fan uses it while taking communion during a church service.

Participants: This refers to all the individuals (*who*) involved in the speech event. It is not necessary, however, for all the participants to be involved directly in the conversation, as in the case of a lecture where the speaker addresses the people in attendance but the audience remains silent.

Topic: This refers to the subject matter *(what)* of the speech event as well as its relationship to the language form used (dialectical/formal/casual speech). You probably discuss different topics around the dinner table with your family than you do with friends at a bar. Even if you do discuss the same topics in both settings, the language forms, especially the vocabulary, will likely be altered.

Goal: This refers to all the outcomes and personal goals or purposes *(why)* of the speech event. A baccalaureate commencement, for example, has as its goal the outcome of awarding degrees to those participants who have completed a course of study. Each of the degree recipients also has unique goals, as do the members of the audience such as parents and friends.

As for the additional contextual components Hymes treats (**key, instrumentalities, norms of interaction** and **interpretation**, and **genre**), these all refer to how something is said. The **key** is the manner, tone or the attitude the speaker uses; **instrumentalities** are the means of communication (oral, written, the use of Twitter as opposed to e-mail, etc.); **norms of interaction** are the rules of speaking such as when it is proper to be loud or silent, or when to speak or not speak; **norms of interpretation** address such factors as how we greet one another in various cultures or when it is appropriate to criticize or be friendly; and **genre** refers to the form of the speech event such as a poem, joke, lecture, etc.

Knowing how to use a language involves knowledge of these contextual components, put simply as *how, when, where,* and *why* we say *what to whom.*

How context influences what is said can be illustrated by the very simple language forms used for naming people. A person named John Smith could be addressed using the following forms:

Mr. Smith
John Smith
Johnny
Smitty
Dude
Douchebag
Sweetheart
Dad
Handsome
Sir
Boy
Mr. Chairman
Uncle
You
Son
JS

> Which names would you associate with specific social relationships?
> Which names would you associate with emotions?
> Which names would you associate with the social status of the speakers?
> Which names would you associate with intimacy?
>
> How would the setting influence the use of one form over another?
>
> Take any of the names above and describe to whom, how, when, where, and why you would use that name.
>
> In learning another language the various linguistic forms for naming can be as numerous and frequently used as in English. What would this indicate to you as a foreign language learner in regard to literal and speaker meaning?
>
> Is naming just simply saying something about the relationship or does it involve doing something, too? Explain.

Conclusion

Knowing how to use language involves knowing both linguistic/literal meaning and pragmatic/speaker meaning.

- Linguistic meaning is associated with the surface forms of a language, that is, its sound system, grammar and semantic meanings and associations.
- Pragmatic meaning links the surface forms of a language with knowledge of the context underlying the speech event taking place.

In the following five chapters (4-8), we will examine various pragmatic forms. Along with context, these forms serve to reveal speaker meaning in terms of the various performative functions. For example, in giving a command is a speaker insisting or suggesting? In expressing an emotion, is the speaker being sarcastic, condescending or sincere? Is the compliment itself sincere or a means by which the speaker is "buttering someone up" so as to influence that person to do something? These are communicative functions that when combined with the contextual factors in which they are uttered allow us to apply intelligent guesswork for decoding speaker meaning.

As we examine these pragmatic functions we will focus on their use in several cultures.

This field is known as **intercultural pragmatics**. It includes not only what we identify as foreign cultures but also the different English-speaking cultures around the world.

Additional Activities

1. When someone utters a sentence such as *It's hot in here*, the semantic meaning is that the temperature is too high. Can you think of three other possible speaker meanings? What contextual factors would influence your choice for each of these meanings? Even being aware of the context, is it possible that your choice of meaning could be inaccurate? Explain.

2. What is the semantic meaning and possible pragmatic meanings of the sentence *I'm hungry* in the following three contexts?

   a. You are with friends on a trip.
   b. You are at home with your parents.
   c. You see your favorite dish on the menu of a restaurant.

3. In each of the following conversational extracts, is the meaning related to semantics or pragmatics? Explain.

   a. Wow! That is a really interesting story!
   b. Are you ever any better?
   c. What did the Polish-American writer Isaac Singer mean when he said: "Of course I believe in free will, I don't have any choice."
   d. *Antidisestablishmentarianism* can be understood by breaking up the word into its constituents: *anti*, *dis*, *establishmentarian*, and *ism*.
   e. The constitution of the USA states only that the President must be 35 years-old. It does not state any other conditions such as race, gender or religion.

4. It is possible for different utterances to have similar pragmatic meanings. What is the similar pragmatic meaning of these three utterances?

   a. Don't you like the meal I prepared for you?
   b. Would you want to have seconds?
   c. You look so slim!

5. A radiator shop had the following sign at its entrance: "The best place in town to take a leak." Give three different semantic meanings for this phrase, and the context for each one.

6. You are at an exercise recreation center working out on a machine. Someone comes up to the adjacent machine and says *These machines are too close to each other*. What are some possible pragmatic meanings for this utterance?

7. Give your own example of something that was addressed directly or indirectly to you. Provide the semantic and pragmatic meanings of what was said based on the context. Create another context for this statement. Will the pragmatic meanings be the same? Explain.

8. Look at the citation by Thoreau at the beginning of this chapter and explain it in terms of what you learned about meaning from this chapter.

Website Resources

- The Linguistic Society of America provides a good overview of semantics and pragmatics: http://www.linguisticsociety.org/resource/meaning-semantics-and-pragmatics
- This website offers a more detailed analysis of pragmatics as a study: http://www.gxnu.edu.cn/Personal/szliu/definition.html
- This comprehensive website provides a wealth of information and numerous links dealing with pragmatics, as well as information on various pragmatic subcategories that will be addressed in the next few chapters: http://www.universalteacher.org.uk/lang/pragmatics.htm

Further Reading

Birner, B. (2012). *Introduction to Pragmatics*, 1st ed. Hoboken, NJ: Wiley-Blackwell.
Huang, Y. (2015). *Pragmatics*. Cary, NC: Oxford University Press.
Yule, G. (1996). *Pragmatics* (Oxford Introduction to Language Study Series). Oxford: Oxford University Press.

Chapter 4

Speech Acts

We will continue to discuss speaker meaning through the pragmatic form of speech acts, followed by an introduction to speech act theory and its relationship to felicity/appropriateness conditions.

When I say before the...altar, "I do", I am not reporting on a marriage: I am *indulging* (italics are mine) in it (J. L. Austin, *How to do Things with Words*)

It's a war [reforming the Church] that you don't fight with weapons, but with your tongue (Pope Francis, as reported in *La Repubblica*, Oct. 1, 2013)

Introduction

When the word *acts* is used, our first thoughts usually turn to physical acts, such as running in a marathon, throwing a football, walking a dog, driving a car, etc. If we then think of ourselves as undertaking these physical acts we have performed a mental act. But it was when British philosopher J. L. Austin gave notice to another kind of act, namely, **speech acts**, that speaking became more widely associated with the performing of an act. In a series of lectures given at Harvard University in 1955, Austin demonstrated how speaking involves actually doing something with language. It was here that Austin provided the example cited above of what happens when one says *I do* at a wedding ceremony. The use of such an utterance does much more than describe what happens. It draws on language to do something, in this case, to create a reality that did not exist before.

It is when we are doing something with language that we are performing speech acts. Pope Francis, in the quote given above, recognizes that the vehicle for getting something done in reforming the church is language. On the other hand, if we describe an event or happening, such as *John was at the picnic* or *The Pirates beat the Cardinals*, or when we utter an ethical principle such as *Do unto others as you would have them do unto you*, we are speaking, but not acting.

While we may not normally think of language use in terms of speech acts, we may still sense that someone is trying to get us to do something when we draw out the inferences from that person's utterances. Consider the following speaker utterances (U) and the inference (I) that the listener drew from each of them:

U	That presidential candidate will ruin this country.
I	Someone wants me to vote against a candidate.
U	Has the garbage been emptied?
I	Mom wants me to take out the garbage.
U	You owe five bucks on Penn State's victory over Ohio State.
I	I am now expected to pay on my bet.
U	Is that outfit you are wearing intended for the wake?
I	My best friend is humiliating me for my choice in clothes.
U	I am naming you as the executor of my will.
I	I have been charged with all matters relating to your belongings upon your death.

In other contexts, different inferences could have been drawn with the utterances listed above. What other inferences could have been drawn and what would be the context (setting, participants, etc.) in which they arose?

What possible inferences could you draw from the following utterances? Provide the context which justifies such an inference on your part.

The election of a black President in 2008 was inspiring.
I was sorry to hear about the demise of your brother.
I promise to do better the next time.
I pronounce you man and wife.
You need to do more work on this report.

Taxonomy of Speech Acts

Austin went beyond simply providing examples of how language is used to get things done. He proposed a framework to illustrate how a speech act is understood, not only for its semantic meaning, but especially for its force (what someone is trying to accomplish) and its effect (the reaction to what is said). The framework for speech acts Austin devised consisted of:

Locutionary Acts: These acts are the sounds, words, phrases and sentences which when combined convey semantic (literal/direct) meaning, as when a speaker says *Stand up* and wants you to rise from your sitting position.

Illocutionary Acts: These acts refer to the force of the action, or what the speaker is trying to do. In a directive, for example, the force can vary depending on the semantic value of the verb and the context in which it is being used. For example, a person can be urged to stand up, *I order you to stand up* or s/he can be coaxed into doing so, *I suggest you stand up*. You'll find a more extensive explanation of the force of directives and other illocutionary acts in the next section.

Perlocutionary Acts: These are the intended or unintended effects that the illocutionary utterance had on the hearer, such as the speaker succeeding in getting the hearer to stand up.

A further example of perlocutionary acts can be seen in a situation where your teacher said to you that your report needed more work to receive a good grade (an illocutionary directive with the force of a command) after you had worked on it for several hours. The perlocutionary effect of this statement on you could be one of annoyance if you thought it was good, and would be expressed by you in an utterance like *I worked for hours on that report*. Another possible perlocutionary effect on you could be one of embarrassment, expressed in an utterance like *I was worried that the report did not come up to your standards*. On the other hand, the effect on you could be one of inspiration if you thought that with more work you could express better what you wanted to say, as evident in an utterance like *Wow, I can now see some very relevant things to include and change in the report*.

Classifying Illocutions

The taxonomy of illocutions created by Austin was somewhat incomplete and flawed. Since then Searle (1979) and others have formulated a fuller classification with more accurate definitions for each illocution:

Directives are attempts to get someone to perform a physical act. This illocution can range from a strong force, as in a command, an order, a dire warning or a more modest force, as in a request, a suggestion or an invitation.

> Get the shovel.
> Be careful of snakes.

Rogatives are a more recent addition to Searle's taxonomy. They are also directives, but of a different sort. They occur when the hearer is asked to perform the verbal action of supplying information rather than a physical act, as in a directive.

> Are you done?
> Tell me what's going on.

Representatives are attempts to get someone to believe something and can vary in force, ranging from claims and conclusions to opinions and hedges.

> The class is over in two hours.
> Unlike humans, dogs are probably governed by instinct alone.

Expressives are reflections of the psychological state of the speaker and can have the force of an apology, a congratulatory statement, an expression of sympathy, or even a negative evaluation.

> My sincere regrets for your loss.
> Your wine leaves much to be desired.

Commissives are attempts to commit the speaker in varying degrees to some future course of action and can have the force of an intention, a threat, a promise, a pledge, etc.

> You're going to fail this course if you don't hit the books.
> My money is on Ohio State to beat Alabama.

Declarations are propositions that result in a change in the world. Declarations come in various forms, such when a judge sentences someone to prison, a minister pronounces a couple as married, or a university president appoints a provost.

> University President: *"By the power vested in me by the Board of Trustees I award you the degree of Bachelor of Science."*

> Ordained Minister: *"I pronounce you husband and wife."*

Note: Do not limit the definition of the term *declaration* to the grammatical structure of a declarative sentence. Many or most illocutions are in the form of a grammatical declarative. When you say *I think the weather's going to be nice today*, this can be a representative (an opinion, belief, etc.) or even a commissive, if conveyed with the intention of a pledge, but not as a declaration (unless, of course, you have the force of creating good weather).

Illocutionary Performative Verbs

The illocutionary type of an utterance can sometimes be identified by use of a performative verb. For example, in the sentence *I order you to take charge of the platoon*, the verb performs as a directive with the force of a strong demand. But in the sentence *I think the course in solid geometry is very difficult*, the verb acts as representative of an opinion. In the sentence *I congratulate you on your new job*, the verb is an expressive of an emotion. A commissive is implied in the sentence *I promise you my support in your application for that job position*. If an owner of a firm says *I appoint you as my Chief Executive,* she is making a declaration of a change in organizational structure. Each of these verbs performs or describes the illocutionary type.

Additional Considerations

Two other considerations must be taken into account in considering performative illocutionary acts. First, like a physical act, it is generally necessary for the subject of the action (at least implicitly), to be performing it. Grammatically, this is reflected in the first person singular *I* or plural *we*. But in the case of a directive, this would not be the case because it can be addressed to someone else. For example:

> You (2nd person singular or plural) *are entrusted with carrying the torch to the site of the Olympics.*

> Pedestrians (3rd person plural) *are warned not to walk on the grass.*

Second, with performatives, even if the subject is in the first person, as in *I invited my friends to the party*, the action must be in the present tense for it to be a performative. Otherwise, it is simply a description of what occurred, not what someone is doing.

Explain why the verb in each of the following sentences fails as a performative:

I inspire you to do better.
I congratulated the winners.
I order my dog to stop.
In my capacity as the garbage collector I pronounce you husband and wife.
He entertains the troops.
I convince you of my intentions.

Speech Acts: Direct vs. Indirect

The force of the illocutionary act is said to be direct whenever the locution (sounds, words, phrases and sentences) is directly performing its function. The meaning in such utterances is directly related to the linguistic structure, as when your mother uses the following directive:

> Take out the garbage.

In sentences that have performative verbs, direct speech acts can be identified if the verb is being used performatively, as in the following utterance:

> I promise to be home by midnight.

But if the performative verb does not describe the illocutionary type, the speech act is an indirect one as in:

> I promise to go to the police if you do that.

In this latter utterance, a threat (such as *The police will question you* or *You will have to go to court*) is underlying the promise.

When the utterance does not contain a performative, you can determine whether or not it is a direct speech act by seeing if the sentence type corresponds to the meaning. For example, if a contractor calls a client and says *I can't start the job until I first get 50% of the cost of the materials up front*, this was really a command (directive) for the client to forward the money and not a statement of fact (representative).

To distinguish between direct and indirect speech acts, Austin (1975) proposed a set of what he called felicity conditions, summarized below:

1. **Preparatory Conditions**

   a. There must be a conventional procedure having a conventional effect.

      With a surface directive, such as *Shut the door*, there must be a door to get to, or a way to get to the door. Otherwise, the speaker has another intended meaning.

   b. The circumstances and persons must be appropriate, as specified in the procedure.

      Again, with the surface directive, *Shut the door*, it would only count at a time when it could be done (not when the person has already passed out from the cold entering the door) or by someone who is capable of doing it (not a paraplegic, for example).

2. **Content Conditions**

   The procedure must be executed (a) correctly and (b) completely.

   The command, for example, must be in a language you understand (English, for most readers of this text), and you must agree to do it, what Austin calls a satisfactory uptake. Violations of the preparatory conditions (a), and the content conditions (b), are what Austin labeled as misfires.

3. Sincerity Conditions

> Often (a) the persons must have the requisite thoughts, feelings and intentions, as specified in the procedure, and (b) if consequent conduct is specified, the relevant parties must then do so.

Another way to view these conditions may be to recognize them as appropriateness conditions, since they all speak to the appropriateness of the speech act.

As an illustration of these conditions, consider the convention of assigning a grade for your performance in this course. You can insist (a directive) that your instructor give you an A for the course but you do not have a conventional procedure or circumstances to carry this out (preparatory conditions). The registrar will not accept your claim. Therefore, the procedure can't be executed (content conditions). Your insistence on getting an A may not even be what you intend (sincerity condition) especially if you know you can't mandate the grade. It may indeed be just your way of expressing your displeasure with the instructor and his/her grading procedures.

> Show how the professor meets all the felicity/appropriateness conditions when s/he declares that the student above has earned a grade of B for the course.

Another way to distinguish direct from indirect speech acts is to see what the listener's response would normally be in the context in which a statement is uttered. In the sentence *I think the course in solid geometry is very difficult*, the work of the linguistic structure is to convey a representative, in this case, an opinion. But the performative verb of thinking in certain contexts could indirectly be interpreted as a directive, conveying something like *Don't take the course*, or even a commissive, in the sense of *If you take the course I would wager that you would not succeed in it*. Here, the sincerity condition on the part of the speaker has been violated. In this instance, the speaker's intention may not have been to render his or her opinion but rather to perform indirectly a directive or a commissive.

> What is the role of April Fool's Day jokes in regard to indirect speech acts? What kinds of illocutions are used to play a joke on someone on this occasion? What is the real illocutionary attempt?

> Before Dr. Remillards' son left to go on a week-long trip with his friends, his mother said, "*Your room is a mess.*" What kind of illocution did she use? Was it a direct or indirect speech act? Explain. His son became very angry at his mother's utterance. What felicity conditions could have justified his behavior? Explain.

Cross-cultural Speech Acts

In foreign cultures, direct and indirect speech acts may differ from those in our own society due to differences in how the felicity conditions operate. For example, in our country, one cannot divorce his/her spouse by simply stating *I divorce you*. We may use it as a threat (commissive) but it does not work as a direct speech act since there is no conventional procedure for doing so in our society (preparatory condition 1a). But in some Muslim societies, if a man utters this sentence three times consecutively, it does indeed work and consequently the wife is effectively divorced. In such societies this would be an illocution of a declaration type since it works as a proposition that results in a change in the world.

In regard to Searle's taxonomy of illocutionary acts, it has been assumed that it applies to all languages. Michelle Rosaldo (1982), however, has challenged this notion in the research she conducted while living among the Ilongots in the Philippines. It became evident to her in the verbal interactions she had with them over almost three years that the Ilongot social system operated with a different underlying philosophy than our own. In brief, in Ilongot speech acts it is relations rather than intentions that count. Ilongots don't see language as the expression of internal states as we do in our use of representatives, commissives and expressives. In their society the emphasis is rather on cooperative bonds, which is the foundation of their social system.

As a result, Rosaldo characterized the taxonomy of the Ilongot speech acts as consisting only of directives and declarations. Among the Ilongots, the various intents involved in trying to make someone believe something (representatives), committing oneself to do something (commissives), or expressing one's psychological state (expressives), function only as directives or declarations.

On the other hand, directives are used predominantly in daily life, such as by husbands to their wives so that they know what to do, and wives to the children, so that they gain knowledge. Directives are not interpreted as rude or too forward in their community but rather serve as cooperative bonds in their society. Indeed, commands are so prevalent among the Ilongots that they are even heard where they would not be expected in Western societies, such as at the beginning of stories and in uttering magic spells.

Conclusion

Speech acts, like physical and mental acts, consist of using language to do things. There are three related acts involved in a speech act:

- **Locutions**, which are the linguistic form of the utterance (sounds, grammar and meaning).

- **Illocutions**, which consist of the various forces (representatives, directives, commissives, expressives and declarations) underlying the locution.
- **Perlocutions**, which are the intended or unintended effects that the illocutionary utterance has on the hearer.

Speech acts are **direct** whenever the locution and its function are the same and **indirect** whenever they are not. In the latter, the surface meaning of the speech act is being performed by another speech act.

This introduction to speech acts has not included the kinds of speech acts that underlie a great deal of daily living, namely verbal routines or rituals. These widely used verbal acts will be the topic of the following chapter.

Additional Activities

1. Analyze the following verbal interaction in terms of locution, illocution, and perlocution:
    Student: I think the French test was hard.
    Professor: For you maybe, but not for the rest of the class.

2. Give three possible perlocutions for the following locution:
    I love hip-hop music.

3. How many different illocutions can you create for the following locutions? Provide the contextual basis for each possible illocution.
    I'm out of gas.
    I hate your guts.
    I believe he's neurotic.
    I'll do better next time.

4. Create locutions that would have the following illocutionary force, with and without performative verbs.

Illocutionary Force	Locutions
Reporting	
Asking	
Threatening	
Proposing	
Suggesting	
Promising	
Scaring	
Inspiring	
Confusing	
Pleasing	
Infuriating	

5. Create a locution that could have the illocutionary force of intimidating someone and another locution that has the force of deceiving someone.

6. Consider the following statement: *You're standing in my light.* On the surface it appears to be a claim, that is, a representative illocution. But in what context could it be a directive?

Website Resources

- If you like visual aids, this website offers a graphic visualization of speech act theory: http://www.mindmeister.com/6473296/speech-acts
- Further exercises that will assist you in learning and identifying speech acts can be found at the following website: http://disciplinas.stoa.usp.br/enrol/index.php?id=7389

Further Reading

Martínez-Flor, A. and Usó-Juan, E. (2010). *Speech Act Performance: Theoretical, Empirical and Methodological Issues*. Amsterdam, Netherlands: John Benjamins.

Chapter 5

Routines

> We will discuss the role of routine verbal formulas in interpersonal conversation.

Men do not after all meet on the ground of their real acquaintances and actual understanding of one another but degrade themselves into the puppets of convention (Henry David Thoreau, *The Journal of Henry David Thoreau, 1837–1861*)

Introduction

When Thoreau stated the above, he was probably frustrated by individuals who were unable to use, or refused to use, language beyond routine conventions. And yet, routine verbal formulas are essential on various occasions for purposes of social solidarity. They occur in **openings** (*Hello, Hi, Yo, What's up*, etc.) and when **closing** conversations (*Bye, See you later, Have a good one*, etc.); in expressing **thanks** for what someone said or did (*Thanks, How nice of you*, etc.); in **apologizing** for intended and unintended offenses (*I'm sorry, Forgive me, How stupid of me*, etc.); and in **complimenting** (*Nicely done, What a great idea!* etc.).

One has only to spend a day not greeting others or taking leave of them with no expression of closure; or not expressing appreciation for services rendered; or not apologizing for gaffes; or not thanking those who assist us, to realize how connected these routines are to accepted social customs. Indeed, not to use them is considered rude to the point that further communication between interlocutors may not take place.

Verbal routines function as a lubricant in linguistic communities so that further conversation can often then take place. The cultural sensitivity associated with these routines, when coupled with the linguistic knowledge required to use them with the appropriate terms of address, or of kinship (as well as with honorific terms in some languages), make them highly sensitive verbal features among speakers. In this sense, they can be considered speech acts since they involve getting something done with language, such as expressing gratitude, demonstrating concern, smoothing relationships, etc., regardless of their ritualistic nature. But unlike speech acts discussed in the previous chapter they are finite in number.

Thoreau was perhaps accurate to say that people are not interested in actually getting to know one another and prefer to "degrade themselves into the puppets of convention," but when routines are not used, or used inappropriately, they can degrade and even devastate social relationships. On the other hand, the absence of verbal routine may signal a special closeness in the relationship, as when two individuals know each other so well that a routine is not required, or the social bonding between them may be so strong that seemingly inappropriate routine responses are used as a marker of a special relationship.

Openings

Greetings

Conversational openings in our society often begin with greetings that may also include terms of address (first name (FN), last name (LN) and title and last name (TLN)), and **phatics**, commonly known as small talk, such as commenting on weather or health. Greetings are communicative openings that are used to acknowledge someone's presence and may also signal one's desire to move on to further conversation. They can take on various verbal forms depending on contextual factors, such as when, where, why and to whom the greeting is addressed. In some contexts greetings are not used, such as in the case of an emergency (*Help! Fire!* etc.), or when the purpose is to get someone's attention (*Excuse me, but do you know your car lights are on?*). Linguistic variations in greetings are also modified or not used at all depending on the communicative channel (telephone, e-mail, instant messaging, etc.).

Cross-Cultural Greetings

The forms and practices of greetings vary widely from one culture to another. Greetings (as well as other routines) become so ingrained in us that their usage becomes in our minds a "common sense" act. But even within the same speech community, their use varies. Dr. Remillard cites a personal example:

> I was born and raised in the USA as part of a French Canadian ethnic group, speaking only French until I was six years-old. I still remain fluent in that language but within an American context. When in France, however, I must always remind myself that, no matter how inconvenient I think my imposition is on someone else (which usually leads in America to skipping the greeting and getting right to the topic), greeting formulas are expected.

> This was made clear to me when I needed immediate information on a bus route in Paris. A bus arrived at the stop and I only had enough time to enter

and ask quickly the conductor's bus route. Observing the best of American cultural practices in this context, I did not want to delay the conductor any more than necessary. Upon entering the bus, then, I went straight to asking for information on his bus route. My direct entrance into the topic due to my concern for the conductor's schedule was met by the latter's unmistakable facial frustration. The driver responded to my request by a verbal salutation (*"Bonjour Monsieur!"*) before he would even say anything about the bus route. The unintended breach of the conventional usage of the greeting routine on my part (especially since I am a native speaker of French, thus conveying that I should know better) was interpreted by the bus driver as rude, or even boorish.

Dr. Remillard's experience bears testimony to the fact that simply knowing linguistic formulas is insufficient for communicative effectiveness in greetings. There are a host of contextual factors that must be considered. In American English, for example, the use of a simple greeting, such as *Good morning*, requires one to know the physical setting in which it is or is not used (where); the times and occasions of its use (when); the people to whom it needs, or needs not, to be addressed (who); and its various uses other than for greetings, such as sarcastic usage (how), like when one says *Good morning* as a wake-up to someone who has not paid attention to what was said, regardless of the time of day.

Greeting practices differ from culture to culture. According to Charles Ferguson, for example, the good morning formula in Syrian Arabic can be used for someone who has just had a haircut, a bath or a shave. In the Bengali and Wolof languages there are no different greetings (*Good morning, Good afternoon*, or *Good evening*) based upon the time of day. In the Wolof society, greetings are used much more frequently than what we would be accustomed to since their use is required upon two persons becoming visible to one another, even as much as 100 feet or more away. Walking down a plaza, for example, the Wolof expectation is to greet everyone along both sides of you. Even if there is an empty space along your path, you would be expected to greet people farther away from the empty space, even as far as the limits of your visibility.

On the other hand, the French will not greet one another within the distance we would expect someone to do so in American culture, especially if they are occupied with doing something else at the time. Philippe Labro in his novel, *L'étudiant étranger* (*The Foreign Student*), writes that, as an exchange student at Washington and Lee University in Virginia he was called to task before a student international committee because of reports that he often did not greet other students when they expected him to, such as when they were in the hall as he was entering the classroom. The impression he conveyed was one of arrogance, even though he was doing nothing more than focusing on where he had to go, as he would have done in his own culture.

Polly Platt, author of the book *French or Foe: Getting the Most Out of Visiting, Living and Working in France*, describes an incident where an American found Parisians to be extremely rude in many instances, even when he spoke French. This was particularly evident when he had requested the *New York Herald Tribune* in the establishments where it is sold. Instead of asking directly if they had the *Tribune*, as was his custom in the USA, Platt proposed that after greeting the clerk he use the following verbal opening in French: *"Excusez-moi de vous déranger mais j'ai un problème"* (Excuse me for disturbing you but I have a problem). The man followed Platt's advice and was overwhelmed at how helpfully and kindly the clerk responded. Indeed, the clerk went out of his way to find him his newspaper!

What cultural values do you see operating in these formulas that made for such a successful experience?

Even the symmetry in greeting exchanges we practice within the American speech community is not practiced in some other societies. Unlike American greetings, which are largely symmetrical in their sequential exchange (both greet each other and try to ask the same number of questions), thus conveying a cultural model of equality and/or shared aims, the Wolof greetings are based upon a cultural model of inequality. The person of lower status, as determined by age, caste, gender and wealth, is required to greet the person of higher status. In Wolof society one is expected, then, to "greet up."

In telephone conversations it is common in the United States to skip greetings and enter immediately into the topic if we recognize the person on the other end. In Japan, the caller is always expected to identify himself or herself first. This is also the practice in France, followed immediately by the often-used practice of excusing oneself for bothering the person taking the call.

> Using the cultural criteria in your speech community for saying *Good morning*, describe to a non-native English speaker everything s/he needs to know in order to use it correctly. Assume that this person does not even have this as a greeting formula in his/her own language.

Terms of Address

Terms of address often accompany greetings in conversational openings, and their use, like greetings, are conditioned by contextual and cultural factors. Reciprocal first name (FN-FN), (title) last name ((T)LN-(T)LN), and non-reciprocal forms of address ((T)LN-FN), are social relationship markers we use with one another in interpersonal conversations. These terms of address convey a range of personal associations, from extreme intimacy (as with parents, significant others, spouses, etc.) to formal relationships (as with doctors, teachers, bosses, elders, etc.).

People	Your term with them	Their term with you	Reciprocal or Non-reciprocal?
Teachers			
Relatives			
Parents			
Peers			
Police person			
Clergy person (or equivalent)			

What terms of address do you use with the following people, and what terms do they use with you? Label each relationship as either reciprocal or non-reciprocal.

Explain briefly in terms of social status (distance, deference, formality, politeness, etc.) and personal relationships (intimacy, casualness, condescension, etc.) what governs the usage of these terms of address in your experiences.

Other terms of address are those relating to kinship, such as *aunt, uncle, brother*, or *sister*. Other than family members, we can use them with individuals who are not relatives but to whom we want to signal intimacy or respect. For this reason, we can address them with terms such as *auntie* or *uncle* in our greetings and in other routine verbal statements.

Cross-Cultural Terms of Address

Kinship Forms

In China, kinship terms are even more commonly used among individuals who are not kin than in the United States. Beverly Hong (1973) notes that the term *bobo* in Chinese, for example, literally means *father's older brother*, but is used by younger people in addressing seniors. It conveys not only extreme respect to the addressee but also the humbling of the speaker. This kinship term of address has lost favor since the Communist Revolution, and the subsequent move toward social solidarity that ensued. It is more common now, according to Hong, to hear the term *shushu* used to address seniors, literally meaning *father's younger brother*, as it implies respect between equals. Less respect is reflected in the term *ayi*, meaning *mother's younger sister*, which can be used with females who are non-relatives.

Pronominal Forms

In various societies, the transition from the greeting to the topic will require one to know the use of the appropriate pronominal (pronoun) markers, especially whom to address with the second person *you*. Romance languages (French, Spanish, Italian, etc.) use *T* or *V* (from the French *Tu* or *Vous*, which take on slightly different verbal forms in other Romance languages, such as *Tú* and *Usted* in Spanish). In German, the T-V relationship exists as *du* and *Sie*, and in Chinese as *ni* and *nin*. While all of these forms convey the informal and formal *you* respectively, their use as pronouns in terms of address reflects the personal relationship and the social distance existing between individuals. The T form is associated with relationships involving intimacy and solidarity and the V form with distance and respect.

The T-V usage in these societies, moreover, is not static. Various studies and individual reports have shown that evolving social conditions such as egalitarianism and solidarity make their usage unstable. In the case of English, the T-V pronominal system began to disappear beginning about the sixteenth century but is occasionally heard today in archaic forms such as *Hear ye,* used in courts of law, or in the traditional wedding vows *With this ring I thee wed.* The disappearance of these second-person pronoun forms, especially in American English, was linked to the growing sense of egalitarianism that developed from the sixteenth century on.

Honorifics

In Japanese, a complex and extensive set of linguistic politeness/respect markers called **honorifics** must be used in terms of address in all contexts. In addressing others, according to Sachiko Ide *et al.,* (1986), the speaker must decide to use the most appropriate honorific based on cultural standing. Someone with the last name *Sato*, for example, could be called:

> *Sato – san* (honored)
> *Sato – sama* (exalted respect)
> *Sato – senpai* (exalted colleague)
> *Sato – sensei* (high professional status)

Ide notes that there also exist honorifics for humbling oneself, such as when one wants to lower oneself in relation to the person being exalted, even to the entities and activities associated with that person. Someone may show exalted respect to Sato by adding the honorific *-sama* to his name while referring to him-/herself with a humbling honorific such as *-to*. The humbled person can also use humbling honorifics for the entities or activities s/he is involved with. For example, with the word *bun*, which refers to the sentences one used in a composition, the honorific *-setu* can be added to mean *my (bad) sentences.*

Phatics

As mentioned earlier in the chapter, openings often include phatics, or small-talk expressions. Phatics in our society can consist of formulas of a neutral type, such as in a reference to the weather (*Nice day, eh?*), self-oriented types (*I'm getting too old to put up with this!*), or other-oriented expressions (*How's the family, the business, the new job, retirement*, etc.). Phatics serve to avoid the awkward silence which can occur after greetings and can also be used as a cooperative and exploratory device, such as in a transition to the topic to be considered, or to a new topic.

> While most languages make use of phatics in openings, the topic and the forms of the phatic used differ. In France, the transition from greetings to the neutral type of phatic dealing with weather is not nearly as frequent as it is in American society. In Arabic, the phatic form in openings contains reference to God. For instance, when a colleague of Dr. Remillard in Egypt had his servant hospitalized to undergo an operation, he would ask him upon his hospital visits how he was doing. The servant would not respond directly to his question, but rather with phatic linguistic forms evoking God, using such expressions as: *Let the glory be to God* or *Let God be praised*. (Note: We are using the term *God* here, not to make any distinction between *God* and *Allah*, but simply because *God* is the English translation of the Arabic word *Allah*, and these sentences were spoken in English. As a cultural note, you might be interested to know that Arabic-speaking Christians were using the word *Allah* before the dawn of the Islamic faith.)
>
> Conversational openings in other languages and cultures where we would use greetings are often quite different from what we would expect. Listed below are sample greetings in other linguistic communities.
>
> | Language | Phrase Translation |
> |----------|--------------------|
> | Chinese | Have you eaten rice yet? |
> | Arabic | Peace be on you. |
> | Irish | God be with you. |
> | Irish | God and Mary (many saints may be added here) be with you. |
> | Samoan | Where are you going to? |
>
> What cultural perspective may have influenced the use of each of these verbal formulas in the societies listed above?
>
> | Language | Influence |
> |----------|-----------|
> | Chinese | |
> | Arabic | |
> | Irish | |
> | Samoan | |

> Even in our own society, new greetings have developed as a result of emailing and text messaging. Make a list of all the greetings you use in different communicative channels. What cultural values are operating in the use of these formulas?

Closings

As with openings, closings in American society make use of a variety of verbal formulas (*Goodbye, Bye, See you later, Till we meet again*, etc.) depending upon the contextual conditions.

Terms of address used in greetings are often repeated when solidarity is desired in closings. Sometimes there is a shift from formal to informal terms of address that occurs from greetings to closings, either for purposes of casualness or solidarity. For example, after being greeted as *Dr. Remillard* (TLN), Dr. Remillard has often asked colleagues who may be a new acquaintance to address him as Vince (FN). Similarly, Dr. Williams often invites students to call her Karen after they graduate.

Phatics can also be part of closings. Some are mitigating, as when you are required to end a conversation (*Sorry, I have to leave*), or performed in deference to the listener (*I see you're busy now, so I will leave you to finish up*). Sometimes a consolidation address can be used (*What a pleasure it was to see you again!*) or an admonition (*Be careful now*). Additional possibilities include an expression regarding the welfare of the listener (*Hope you feel better*), a promise to continue the relationship (*I'll call you soon*), or an expression relating to a wider network (*Say hi to the wife for me*).

Feelings of discomfort often accompany closings in American society. In social gatherings, speakers often experience awkwardness when they close a conversation, due to a fear of offending someone or of appearing to be dismissive. One practice often used in American social gatherings to close a conversation and avoid awkwardness is to tell a joke just before using a final closure statement.

> Context, and particularly the communicative channel, influences the choice of a closing formula. What are some of the formulas you use in e-mail messages and text messaging?

Cross-Cultural Closings

The feelings of discomfort that Americans often experience in closings are not as acute in other societies. It is very common among the French to close conversations more suddenly than we are accustomed to. The use of the Italian word *Ciao* is often heard in such instances or simply the word *allez* (go).

In regard to terms of address used in closings in French, one interlocutor may suggest that both parties *tutoie* (use the T form) one another in subsequent conversations if the conversation up to that point was with the V form. There is not as much fluidity, in this respect, in the use of honorifics among Japanese speakers. Appropriated honorifics, used in Japanese terms of address, must also be respected in closings.

In the Cree culture of NW Canada, conversational closings (and openings) are not even used. Formal greetings and leave takings are avoided so as not to give the impression that the relationship is limited to that event. Among the Cree, the cultural value of the continuity of social relations is, according to Regna Darnell (1985), "the key to effective action in all areas of native life."

Apologies and Thanks

Routine expressions of apologies and thanks, like openings and closings, serve to characterize polite behavior in society. Apologies are used for indebtedness to others and, as such, are attempts to repair real or imagined regrets, ranging from mortal accidents to simple social inconveniences or missteps.

With the thanks routine, on the other hand, we express gratitude. With both thanks and apologies, the objects of gratitude and indebtedness can be real or potential, related to a tangible product or a social service, as well as something requested or not.

As with openings and closings, apologies and thanks are used to establish and maintain relationships. As language forms, they consist of routine statements expressed sequentially by the interlocutors, as seen in the following examples:

Thanks for the help.	Sorry to have interrupted you.
No problem.	That's quite alright.

Note in the above examples that the responses can be applied to either utterance:

Sorry to have interrupted you.	Thanks for the help.
No problem.	That's quite alright.

The interchangeability of responses occurs whenever **indebtedness** is involved. But whenever remorse is required, interchangeability of responses would not normally be appropriate. Here, the first pair works, but the second does not.

Thanks for the help.	Sorry to have bumped you.
You're welcome.	You're welcome.

Cross-Cultural Apologies and Thanks

In foreign cultures one must also recognize that there are routine formulas that could be easily misinterpreted by someone from the American speech community. Even the simplest words have to be interpreted in context. Take for example, the word for *thanks* in French, *merci*. In France, at a dinner table, if you were asked if you would like another serving, the appropriate expression for accepting the serving would be *Thanks* in English. But in France, the response *Merci* would convey *No, thanks*.

In terms of apologies, the Japanese formulaic expression, *sumimasen*, roughly translated as *This is not the end*, may sound like a threat to an American. In Japan, however, it is used as an apology or to show thanks, as when you are leaving the home of the person who invited you.

In learning Japanese, where indebtedness and self-esteem are so much more highly considered than in American society, one must be particularly aware of how apology routines are used in different contexts. Coulmas (1981) notes that Japanese speakers have as their goal to avoid embarrassment and not to encroach on the rights or needs of others. Consequently, they apologize much more frequently than we would anticipate them to do so. Even routines such as greetings and closings can be followed with apologies. Compliments are often accompanied by downgraders. For the utterance *You prepared a great meal*, the response may be: *Not really...*

Describe from the above how the Japanese social practices relating to indebtedness and self-esteem can be understood in contextual terms, that is, *how, when* and *why* you say *what* to *whom*.

An example answer would be: *They apologize in many more settings = when.*

M. L. Apte (1974) found that in South Asian languages, gratitude and indebtedness are very closely connected. In expressing gratitude in the exchange of goods, a *thank you* is avoided so as not to be indebted to the other speaker. Even services for family members are not accompanied by expressions of gratitude since it is considered a duty to perform them in the context of the family structure.

In foreign societies, the linguistic forms for expressing apologies and thanks (as well as in the use of openings and closings) are not only different but can be more complex than in our own. Javanese speakers in Indonesia and Nahuatl speakers in Mexico, for example, must also decide between high, middle and low speech styles, based on status and familiarity that befits the social relationship.

In addition to speech styles, in some languages, such as Javanese and in Japanese, there is a set of **honorifics** that refer to various matters such as a person's social status, what that person owns, and even the parts of that person's body.

Honorifics are attached to different parts of speech (nouns, verbs and adjectives). Wardhaugh (1986) points out that in the utterance *Eat now*, the lexical choices a Javanese speaker makes depend on the style and honorifics required by the context. While this is not a ritual expression of gratitude, it does provide an example of all that a speaker must consider in uttering routine as well as all other utterances.

Speech Level	*Eat*	*Now*
High style, high honorifics	*dahar*	*samenika*
High style, no honorifics	*neda*	*samenika*
Middle style, no honorifics	*neda*	*saniki*
Low style, high honorifics	*dahar*	*saiki*
Low style, low honorifics	*neda*	*saiki*
Low style, no honorifics	*mangan*	*saiki*

Complimenting

Verbal formulas used for compliments in American English have been shown to be more restrictive than those used for greetings, closings, thanks and apologies. Manes and Wolfson (1981) collected 686 compliments used among a varied population in regard to age, sex and occupation. They found that two adjectives (*nice* and *good*) were used 42% of the time. Two other adjectives (*beautiful* and *great*) were used more than 24% of the time. Combined, these four adjectives occurred in two-thirds of all the compliments. As for verbs, these researchers found that just two (*like* and *love*), were used in 86% of the compliments.

Not only were these few adjectives used most frequently, compliments were also limited to a few syntactical structures. More than half of the time, the following structure was used. (The abbreviations used here are NP for noun phrase, ADJ for adjective, and PRO for pronoun.)

> NP   (is/looks)   (really) ADJ
> The book (is/looks)   (really) good.

Two other structures constituted more than 31% of the syntactical structures:

> I (really) (like/love)   NP
> I (really) (like/love) the book.

> PRO is (really) (a) ADJ NP
> He   is (really) (a) nice person.

In the end, these three structures made up 85% of all those used in complimenting.

While the verbal formulas used for compliments are much more restricted than with other routines, they have greater flexibility in their occurrence. They can substitute for openings (*I like your house!* and closings (*That was a nice party*), and be included in thanks (*What a generous gift!* and apologies (*I'm sorry that I could not have prepared a meal like you do.* They can also be used as independent speech events to repair confusion and ambiguity (*I can never get this together like you can*).

Their wide range of usage tends to make compliments appear more creative than other routines. This perception may be due to a certain wish fulfillment that makes us believe in the sincerity of compliments addressed to us. One needs only to recall the Aesop fable of how the fox outwits the crow to realize how vulnerable one can be to compliments. There is also the fact that the verbal formulas for compliments are not usually taught as are the other routines. We are taught the formulaic versions of gratitude as children (*Thank you* and *I'm sorry*), as well as what to say in greetings and closings. But compliments, such as *Tell him you really like his new tie*, are usually not taught. Instead it is expected to be generated by the desires and goals of the speaker.

Compliments, like other routines, serve to establish and maintain social solidarity in a speech community. This may account for the restricted number of compliment formulas, as it requires speakers to avoid any suggestion that would convey social distance, such as in the use of condescension or insincere affectation.

Cross-Cultural Complimenting

Like all routines, compliments are reflective of the context in which they are used and of the cultural values in a society. In America, we often compliment for newness and bigness while in France, oldness and smallness are more highly valued. As another example, there are very few situations in American culture where it would be acceptable to compliment a woman on gaining weight; in Zimbabwe, however, it is seen as a positive thing, as a heavier weight reflects prosperity and health.

There are also differences in how people are expected to respond to compliments. In China, Korea and Japan, where humility is paramount, people tend to downgrade personal compliments from social acquaintances, especially those that refer to personal attributes. In general, Americans are more likely to accept compliments. Research done by Miriam Raveto (2012) shows that Italians and Germans are also likely to accept compliments, but in slightly different ways.

Conclusion

Routines serve the essential function of encouraging social solidarity among interlocutors. While they are highly formulaic, their use is particularly sensitive to context and cultural values.

Routine speech acts are verbal utterances used in:

- **opening** and **closing** conversations
- expressing **thanks**
- **apologizing**
- **complimenting**

We will now move on to examining the Cooperative Principle and how it functions in communication as well as how it relates to context and speech acts.

Additional Activities

1. Charles Ferguson (1976) relates that he decided to do nothing more than not say "*Good morning,*" to his secretary but only give a friendly smile. He had to abandon this practice after the second day to prevent what he called an explosion that could have had serious consequences.

    Try to do something similar with one of the routines discussed above. What were the consequences? What does this tell you in regard to the value of verbal routines or what some consider as nothing more than ritual snippets?

2. Select an episode from a soap opera and record the forms and uses of the five routines covered in this chapter. Are they different from what you experience in everyday life? If so, how?

3. Select one of the languages mentioned in this chapter (or any other language) and research how their pronominal forms function as terms of address. You need to consider several social aspects relating to participants in your description, such as occupational hierarchy, age, class, and gender. Other contextual factors such as setting, topic and goal also need to be included in considering their usage. Finally, what are some of the consequences that arise from the violation in the use of these pronouns?

Website Resources

*   The website listed below addresses Japanese apologies, thanks and compliments. The website takes into account the various contextual factors that govern the use of these routines, proving that it is more than just a matter of memorizing formulas and using them as you would in your own culture. http://www.carla.umn.edu/speechacts/ japanese/Compliments/Compliments.htm
*   This website offers extensive lecture materials and lesson plans for teachers who are addressing linguistic routines in their classrooms: http:// americanenglish.state.gov/resources/teaching-pragmatics
*   This website is geared towards international business. For each country listed, there is a variety of cultural information, including communication norms: http://www.cyborlink.com/

Further Reading

Aijmer, K. (1996). *Conversational Routines in English: Convention and Creativity* (Studies in Language and Linguistics). New York: Routledge.

Chapter 6

Cooperative Principle and Implicature

> We will consider the cooperative principle and implicature under-lying verbal exchanges through which speakers are able to infer meaning.

Don't believe anything you hear and only half of what you see (Anonymous)

Introduction

The quote cited above has probably been used as words of advice by parents and elders with children as they faced hardships, deceptions and disillusionments. For many, these words may have served as consolation as well as practical and sound advice during moments of despair. And yet, beyond that, the advice really isn't functional. Why? Simply put, if we all consistently avoided believing what others say, conversation would cease and with that, society would end as we know it.

In fact, we don't abandon communication with others, regardless of all the possible problems associated with it, whether they be deceptions, misinterpretations, or banalities and trivialities, to name only a few communicative problems. H. P. Grice, in the William James lectures at Harvard University in 1967, maintained then that there must be an **internalized operational understanding** (postulate/assumption) that we and others will not lie, cheat, mislead, etc., even though this is surely not always the case. This understanding also applies not only to the production of utterances (telling a lie, speaking incoherently, talking too much or too little, etc.) but also to every facet of verbal interaction. For example, when we are asked a question we expect that we will be given time to answer the question, or that the question even has a possible answer, and if so, we will be listened to.

Grice called this understanding among interlocutors the **cooperative principle**. He stated that in spite of all the problems involved in interpreting the motives underlying what another person says, an agreement or pact is formed which impinges on four areas of communication: *quantity*, *quality* (for which the more precise term **accuracy** will be used in this text), *manner* and **relevance**. Grice called these areas of communication **maxims** (general principles). In the next section, we will look more closely at each of these maxims.

Maxims

Quantity: Make your contribution as informative as required and no more so than is required.

If you show someone how to cook a potato in the microwave but neglect to say beforehand that you should puncture the potato three times so that it does not explode, you did not provide enough information. Or when you complain to your neighbor that his kids damaged your shed and he then withholds further cooperation by shrugging you off with a flippant expression such as: "*You know how kids are today*," or with the proverbial expression "*Boys will be boys*," he is discouraging any further discussion by using a cliché that does not provide you with information to resolve the problem.

On the other hand, we have all been victims of people who provide us with more information than necessary. Simple requests which require a yes/no response are sometimes answered with a barrage of excuses and conditions. A common example in higher education is the professor who lectures beyond the class time. Student perception that the maxim of quantity is about to be violated is reflected when they close their books, shuffle their feet, and pack their bags, etc., five minutes before the class time is over.

The following was an e-mail response from a professor to a colleague following a routine question as to how he was doing:

> Unfortunately, we have not been in the best of health this week. My wife caught a nasty intestinal virus after she took my daughter to NY to attend the funeral of her 30 year-old cousin. He died of congestive heart failure. He left behind a 25 year-old wife and a one year-old daughter, whom they had just adopted from Africa the previous year. His wife has no family here. Her parents are Belgian and live north of Brussels. We were close to my cousin. He was an usher at our wedding.

What part of the quantity maxim was violated in this instance? Can you cite an instance from your own personal experience of when the maxim of quantity was violated? What resulted?

Accuracy: Do not say what you believe to be false or for which you lack adequate evidence.

We have all experienced and indulged in conveying information we knew to be false. In discussing matters of politics, adequate evidence is often violated and thus becomes the tripwire of an argument. Many heated disagreements arise while discussing political and social topics as a result of interlocutors not accepting someone's information as accurate.

> Can you cite an instance from a personal experience when the maxim of accuracy was violated that then led to arguing? What was said that triggered the misunderstanding and how was it interpreted by the offended party?

Manner: Avoid obscurity of expression and ambiguity. Be brief and orderly.

Many examples from the world of advertising are violations of this maxim. Indeed, the field of advertising is often intended to be ambiguous, which is achieved by use of obscure expressions. When there were tobacco commercials on TV, a famous one stated *[Brand name] tastes good like a cigarette should.* This is, at best, an obscure claim at face value.

> Select advertisements that you have heard or seen recently and analyze them for their obscurity of expression and ambiguity.

Examples of ambiguity can be found in just a sentence or a word. If you say in a sentence *I saw the man with the telescope,* this could mean you saw a man through the telescope or you saw a man in possession of a telescope. Ambiguity can also arise from word usage, such as when driving you ask someone as you arrive at an intersection if this is the right turn. Are you referring to a right turn as opposed to a left turn, or a correct turn?

> Can you cite an instance from personal experience or from the experience of someone else of when the maxim of manner was violated? What was said? What was the result of this verbal interaction?

Relevance: Be relevant to the subject you are discussing.

If someone asked how you liked a movie and you responded that it rained all day, this response would not connect easily to the question. Such blatantly irrelevant responses, however, often lead listeners to apply the cooperative principle. In the context of someone who indulges in irrelevant responses, for example, this could be interpreted as a joke or an attempt by the speaker to avoid an unpleasant subject, or maybe even an instance of schizophrenia.

> Can you cite an instance from personal experience or from the experience of another person of when the maxim of manner was violated? What was said? What was the result of this verbal interaction?

Implicature

It is when a maxim is deliberately or flagrantly violated that conversational implicatures arise. To use an example that Grice provides, consider this answer to the question of how a new employee is doing at the bank: "Quite well, he gets along with his colleagues and he hasn't gone to prison yet." The clear implication here is that the employee is dishonest. Grice says that the speaker in this example is flouting the maxim of relevance (which, incidentally, is the basis of irony and sarcasm).

Unlike simple maxim violations, such as when an inadequate amount of information is given (quantity), or when the information is inaccurate (accuracy), or ambiguous (manner), any of which can lead to communicative mishaps, the flouting of a maxim is clearly evident to both the speaker and the hearer. With simple violations it is not apparent that the speaker has provided inadequate information, lied, or was unclear.

Cross-Cultural Examples of the Cooperative Principle and Implicature

Implicatures occur, such as in the example above, when we fill in the blanks between what is said (semantic meaning) and unsaid (speaker meaning). The unsaid often requires knowledge of the context and culture. Dr. Remillard offers a personal example of implicature during one of his trips in France:

> I once needed to get a load of clothes washed before I left one town. When I entered the laundry with three full bags of dirty clothes at 3:00 in the afternoon (two hours before they closed) and asked the proprietor if she could have my clothes washed by 9:00 the following morning, her immediate answer in French was '*Non, impossible!*' If I had taken her response for its semantic value only, I would have just left the store (and probably accused her of not liking Americans). But I knew she was flouting the maxim of accuracy as my prior experiences in France had led me to understand that a request for quick service requires the speaker to justify the reasons for the request. I then pleaded tactfully that I had no clean clothes left and that I needed them to continue my trip the following day. She then asked me to wait while she consulted her helpers after which I was able to negotiate an 11:00 o'clock pick up time the next morning. In fact, my clothes were ready at just about the time of my initial request.

Another example of flouting of a maxim in a foreign culture is reported by Elinor Ochs Keenan (1976) who lived among the Malagasy in Madagascar, an island off the SE coast of Africa. She found in a study of village life there that because people live very close to one another there are hardly any secrets. As a result, information others do not have is very valuable since it provides one with power and prestige.

A further reason for withholding information is that they believe they are responsible for the consequences that may arise from giving too much information. In that event, they would bear the cultural taboo they call *tsiny* (*guilt*). They see this taboo as having dire consequences for the person giving the information, as well as for his or her family. The Malagasy, then, will deliberately withhold information, thus flouting the maxim of quantity.

In interpreting a maxim, one must account not only for the semantic value of what is being said, but also for the context and the cultural environment surrounding the utterances. It is especially when context and culture are not considered that incorrect interpretations and misunderstandings arise.

Describe a context where the expressions listed below would deliberately violate a maxim. What could be implied by their use? Think of when you may have used them or similar expressions:

1. I am so awed by that dress.
2. What a great friend you are!
3. You're the best!
4. All good students give 110%.
5. Boys will be boys.

Some Further Considerations

The reasons for violating a maxim are numerous in everyday life and may be done for admirable reasons. For example, you may deliberately lie or not provide enough information, thus violating the maxim of accuracy, so as to protect yourself from stating something for which someone may take advantage of you. Or you may decide to violate this same maxim by withholding relevant information, so as to imply that you want to protect someone's reputation, feelings, or good name. In applying for a job, you may decide to deliberately violate the maxim of quantity by providing more material than requested, so as to enhance your prospects for your potential employer.

The cooperative principle may even be overtly banned, such as when soldiers are instructed by UN conventions that in the event they are captured they are only required to give their name, rank and serial number. Likewise, CIA and military agents are sometimes sworn to never in their life provide any information on matters of national security for which they were assigned.

One can also violate the maxims but still be in compliance with the cooperative principle. This is done by deliberately stating that a given maxim is about to be violated, such as when using a word like *but* or an explanatory clause. For example, you can announce a violation of the maxim of quantity by saying *I know you have heard this several times but...* A violation of the maxim of accuracy can be announced when you state that Type-2 diabetes can be prevented by use of cin-namon capsules, but then insert a clause such as *Of course you realize that evidence is still to be gathered on this matter.*

> Following the example given above on violating the maxims of quantity and accuracy while remaining in compliance with the cooperative principle, can you give similar examples of apparent violations of the maxims of relevance and manner?

There are several instances when the maxims can be violated at the semantic level, but when the context is then considered, the cooperative principle remains in effect. For example, when a parent asks a child if she had any questions relat-ing to the assigned homework, the reply from the child could be that she had already done it. This could be a violation of the maxim of relevance, but within the parent-child context it is commonly understood to mean that she had no more questions since she already finished it. Grice calls these kinds of verbal interchanges *conventional implicatures* (as opposed to flouting *conversational implicatures*), since they occur customarily in conversation and thus are not bla-tant violations of the cooperative principle.

It is our knowledge of the context and culture as well as our linguistic knowl-edge that leads us to distinguish between these two kinds of implicatures. Indeed, knowing the difference in any culture between conventional (apparent viola-tions of the cooperative principle) and conversational (deliberate implicatures of the cooperative principle) implicatures is an essential indicator of one's cultural competence.

The cooperative principle functions as an all-encompassing appropriateness condition in indirect speech acts (See Chapter 4). This has been made particu-larly evident among the present generation of computer users. Whenever we try to communicate an indirect request to our computer we are usually told that we have made an invalid request, thus indicating that we have violated the maxim of relevance. And yet, the actual problem is that computers are largely unable to interpret our request as indirect speech acts.

Other examples of the relationship between the cooperative principle and indirect speech acts occur when we overgeneralize, such as when we flout the maxim of accuracy in making statements like *He's never without his wife around him.* We know that this almost certainly can't be true in the literal sense, so we make an appropriate adjustment to interpret what has been stated. In this instance, we may interpret that his wife does not trust him when he is out of her sight.

The flouting of one or more of the maxims in indirect speech acts underlies the use of irony and sarcasm. When someone chooses a tie whose color does not match anything else s/he is wearing and someone says *That's an interesting combination*, s/he is using irony by violating the maxim of accuracy and is actually telling the wearer that the choice of ties is terrible, or even to take it off and pick another one.

Humor often results from a violation of one or more of the maxims. Consider the following proverb:

> Behind every successful man is a woman

What maxim is being violated here that makes the following clause (attributed to Groucho Marx) humorous?

> And behind her is his wife

Explain how the addition of this last clause converts this proverb from a direct to an indirect speech act.

Conclusion

- The **Cooperative Principle** is the underlying assumption in conversation that speakers and hearers will cooperate in effective and purposeful communication.
- The cooperative principle is recognized by how well speakers adhere to four maxims: **quantity**, **accuracy**, **relevance** and **manner**.
- Violations of these maxims occur for a wide variety of reasons, not the least of which is misunderstanding the context and culture in which they are used.
- **Implicatures**, on the other hand, arise when speakers and hearers understand that one or more of the maxims are being flouted, that is, purposefully and deliberately violated.

As we move on to the next area of pragmatic functions, politeness strategies, we will see again that it is connected to speech acts and the Cooperative Principle. While we need to divide these pragmatic functions for purposes of understanding how they operate in communication, the fact is that pragmatic communication is a seamless phenomenon.

Additional Activities

1. What maxim may be violated if you discovered that a private conversation you had with a friend had been recorded?
2. In the following two examples, Grice claims that no maxim is violated. In what context is this accurate? In what context is it not accurate?

    a. I am out of petrol.
    b. There is a garage around the corner.
    c. Smith doesn't seem to have a girlfriend these days.
    d. He has been paying a lot of visits to New York lately.

3. In the following two examples Grice claims that a maxim is violated. Which? Justify your response.

    a. Miss X sang "Home Sweet Home."
    b. Miss X produced a series of sounds which corresponded closely with the score of "Home Sweet Home."
    c. Where does C live?
    d. Somewhere in the South of France.

4. The cross-cultural examples of flouting among the Malagasy and the French are instances where an indirect speech act has occurred. In terms of their respective cultures, explain why this is usually so in their cultures but not in ours.

Website Resources

*   This website provides video examples of the cooperative principle in action, as well as video examples of Grice's maxims being violated: https:// sites.google.com/a/sheffield.ac.uk/all-about-linguistics/branches/ pragmatics/example-research-conversational-implicature-and-maxims
*   Scroll down to the exercises and try to determine the maxim(s) violated. Following the exercises you will find the author's interpretation of the maxim(s) violated.
*   This video is a compilation of scenes from the popular television series, "The Big Bang Theory." The scenes are specifically organized to show violations of Grice's maxims: https://www.youtube.com/ watch?v=vEM8gZCWQ2w

Chapter 7

Politeness Strategies

> We will examine how politeness strategies function in social relationships.

All the world's a stage,
And all the men and women merely players:
They have their exits and their entrances;
And one man in his time plays many parts,
His acts being seven ages.

(William Shakespeare, *As You Like It*)

Introduction

Shakespeare's insight as to the diverse roles we play in life can be connected to the various strategies (usually implicit) of politeness we use in verbal interactions. Politeness, however, is often portrayed to us not in terms of strategies, but rather as explicit formulaic utterances. Parents, caretakers and media sources usually present politeness to children in terms of learning and using routine verbal formulas (*thank you, please*, etc.) with the appropriate demeanor. But such verbal routines in themselves reflect shallow expressions of politeness when uttered with a lack of sincerity, and may even be interpreted as sarcastic, as when one hears *Thanks a lot*, accompanied by an infantile tone.

Politeness first involves knowledge and sensitivity to cultural and contextual factors, without which routine politeness formulas will sound superficial and insincere, or even worse, offensive, bad-mannered, foul, vulgar, boorish, or simply rude. For example, you would not usually barge into a professor's office and then immediately direct her to drop everything she is doing to assist you with a problem. If you did, the professor might very well feel threatened by your imperious strategy and demand that you leave. On the other hand, your probability of success would be greatly enhanced if you first greeted her with an appropriate professional term of address, apologized for the disturbance and then requested a convenient time to meet.

Face

What is operating in the example above, relates to the degree of impact on the professor's **face**. Brown and Levinson, whose research has led to an increasing awareness in how politeness operates in various societies, used the term *face* to mean one's self-esteem (personal) or public self-image (social). You may have heard it used in the phrase *saving face*.

Face Wants

In the context of everyday social interactions, sensitivity to face (self-esteem or public self-image) can be understood in terms of **face wants**. We expect others to recognize our face wants, and we are expected to recognize theirs. In the case of a distant social relationship, deference or respect is normally expected; with close relationships, solidarity or intimacy is the norm. **Face threatening acts (FTA)** occur when something is said that does not respect these face wants, as with the student demanding the professor's immediate attention. On the other hand, **face saving acts (FSA)** occur when something is said that lessens the threat, as with the student who apologizes to the professor for interrupting and then negotiates a meeting time.

As another example, consider the statement below, sent by an employer following the submission of the employee's first job report dealing with problems in the corporation:

> I wanted your report to reflect innovative approaches to the problems in the corporation.

For the employee, this could be a FTA. If, on the other hand, the administrator had said:

> We will need to reconsider your report so as to tease out and expand on some of its ideas as they relate to the corporation's problems.

This statement could lend itself to being a FSA. One must be careful not to limit the FTA or the FSA to the appropriate verbal formulas. Routine verbal formulas, in themselves, do not account for face threatening or saving. Close friends, for example, often belittle one another in jest by name-calling and using various insults, without any sense of a FTA. In such contexts where participants are in close solidarity, a more formal or socially appropriate politeness formula might be considered a FTA rather than a FSA.

What insulting formulas do you use with intimates that are meant in the opposite sense of their lexical value? Other than the participant you address it to, what other contextual factors are required for you to use them? Explain.

Positive and Negative Face Wants

Face saving acts occur when paying attention to *positive and negative face wants*. **Positive face wants** are expressed by the desire to be connected with others. This can take the form of sharing wants, being approved of or accepted, helping, or as in the job report example dealing with problems in the corporation, expressing a desire to assist rather than threaten the employee. Positive face wants will be verbalized in terms relating to common ground (*Let me help you, Thanks buddy, How about a drink*, etc.) and cooperation (*Let's go together, In the past we've been successful as a team*, etc.).

On the other hand, sensitivity to *face wants* is also evident when respecting someone's desire to be free or not be interfered with, that is, to be independent. This is the case in the earlier example of the student addressing the professor. In this case, **negative face wants** needed to be addressed. *Negative face wants* are verbalized in terms of not imposing on another person, such as in apologies for interrupting (*I'm sorry to bother you, but...*), or being indirect (*Children are asked to be quiet during the presentation*), non-presumptuous (*I didn't mean you had to make a donation*), or non-coercive (*We could use a helping hand.*)

A caution must be given here: do not interpret *negative* as meaning *bad*, but rather in terms of a polar opposite, such as a negative electrical current.

Politeness Strategies

Say Nothing

Face wants can be addressed non-verbally, that is, by saying nothing. In this strategy, the topic of concern is not directly addressed to someone. For example, imagine you are in the library and need to plug in your computer but can't find an electrical terminal. You look in front, to the side and to the back of the cubicle. Someone in the adjoining cubicle notices this and then tells you that there is an electrical outlet available on the floor next to the cubicle.

Off-Record

If you had not received the needed information as to the location of the electrical outlet by saying nothing, you could have uttered the following statement aloud:

Now what do I do?

In this case you have made a verbal request that was not addressed to anyone in particular. Your utterance then consists of an **off-record** strategy.

> Provide an instance from your own experiences of using an off-record verbal politeness strategy. To what extent was it a FSA or FTA? Explain.

On Record – Bald

If your request is directly addressed to someone, you then are **on record**. The first of the on-record politeness strategies that we will examine is the **bald** utterance, which is an utterance that gets straight to the point. In the example above of the person looking for an electrical terminal used above, this could take on the form of a directive addressed to someone, such as in an utterance like, *Help me find the terminal.* In the context of addressing this to someone you are not familiar with, there would be a lack of concern for face, a disregard of the FSA. It may even constitute a serious FTA.

One must be careful, however, not to interpret bald utterances as all having a high risk of face loss. In many professional situations, for example, among colleagues who are often required to be in constant communication to assist one another, directive statement words such as *bring, take, look at*, etc., are required in everyday interactions and as such would not constitute a FTA. Moreover, it is not uncommon to hear bald on-record statements used by participants in unequal power relationships, such as when a professor says to a student who wants to speak to him in his office *Pull up a chair and sit down.* In such contexts, bald statements have a low risk of face loss. In the instance of an emergency, such as when a gunman is shooting at will *Get down!* is all you would want to say to protect others. Bald on-record statements that provide maximum efficiency in contexts such as those just provided are uttered with little or no risk of face loss.

On Record – Positive and Negative Strategies

One way the risk of a FTA is attenuated is by the use of mitigating remarks, such as *Please, Can you...*, etc. But these may sound insincere or superfluous with bald statements. Instead, **positive** and **negative politeness on-record strategies** are usually more effective in lessening the degree of face risk.

Positive politeness strategies occur whenever the speaker addresses someone's positive face wants. In such cases, the speaker expresses a desire to be connected to the addressee in some way. More specifically, positive politeness occurs when one desires cooperation in the sense of solidarity, as in the following utterance:

> Got a minute to help me find the terminal?

When the participants are not in a solidarity relationship with the addressee, however, positive politeness strategies can convey dishonesty, intrusiveness or even deceitfulness, depending on the context. This is what makes us wary of sales-people who want to connect to us by stating that the product they are selling will make life easier or be of great benefit for you.

It is more common, especially in asynchronous social interactions (and much more common in societies where the hierarchy of social stratification is less fluid than in ours), to use a **negative politeness strategy** to meet our needs. In this case, the speaker takes note of someone's *negative face want* to be independent. Wherein positive strategies are based on the desire for solidarity, negative strategies reflect the concern for the hearer's desire not to be imposed upon. It is characterized verbally with utterances of deference, self-effacement, and formality. Consequently, a question form is often used with a softening modal verb, such as:

> Could you help me find the terminal?

In this case, the right to even ask a question may be included:

> Might I ask if you could help me find the terminal?

An apology can also be added:

> I hate to bother you, but would you be so kind as to help me find the terminal?

It is not uncommon in the use of negative politeness strategies to add hesitations, pauses and lengthier sentences than necessary.

> In what instances have you used negative and positive politeness strategies? Give specific verbal examples and explain contextually why you used one or the other. Include whether or not your strategy was successful and why. In the case of the negative strategy, were you trying to avoid a bald on-record response because you feared a denial of your request?

Cross-Cultural Politeness Strategies

Politeness strategy expectations will differ depending on the context and the speech community in which the utterance is used. Foreign cultures present the greatest challenge for non-native speakers in selecting a FSA and avoiding a FTA in verbal interactions. As with any of the pragmatic forms we have examined so far (cooperative principle, speech acts and routines), it does not necessarily follow that someone who is linguistically fluent in a foreign language has the communicative competence to know the most effective politeness strategies to use and which to avoid in any given context.

There are, however, politeness strategies that are more prevalent in some cultures than in others. Eva Orgiermann, in her study of politeness strategies identifies Russian and Polish as languages having a tendency toward the use of positive politeness strategies (2009: 282). Hollos and Beeman (1978) note that Hungarian children have a propensity to being direct in their communicative style, thus lending themselves to bald strategies.

While negative politeness is often favored in American cultures, it is emphasized even more so in France. On the other hand, positive politeness strategies are less commonly used in France than they are in the United States, and bald strategies are more frequently avoided with people you are not familiar with. In a setting such as Paris, an American speaking French asking a Frenchman baldly, *Montrez-moi où est la cathédrale Notre Dame (Show me where Notre Dame Cathedral is)* would most likely invite a snub, if not an outright rebuke, regardless of tone, even from an authorized official who is responsible for assisting tourists. This has, indeed, been the experience of many American tourists.

You would probably be just as unsuccessful in this instance if you resorted to a positive politeness strategy, such as, *Mon ami, où est la Cathédrale Notre Dame? (Hey buddy, where is the Notre Dame Cathedral?)* You may not even gain much more favor if you added a routine politeness expression to this strategy, such as *s'il vous plaît (please)*. Indeed, using too many grammatical politeness devices and formulas even in fluent French may evoke ridicule, or even mockery. Here is an example:

> *Auriez- vous la gentillesse de bien vouloir m'indiquer comment je pourrais me rendre à la cathédrale Notre Dame?*

> Would you be so obliging as to want to inform me as to how I should go to get to Notre Dame Cathedral?

Experiences in the use of politeness strategies such as these and in various settings (restaurants, museums, etc.) are often the basis for many Americans to claim that they encountered rudeness in trying to express themselves to the French in their language.

The most effective strategy in this setting would usually be to convey first, directly or indirectly, that you are aware that you are inconveniencing the addressee (a negative politeness strategy) and then to make your request:

Je m'excuse de vous déranger mais pourriez-vous m'indiquer le chemin pour me rendre à la cathédrale Notre Dame?

I'm sorry to bother you but would you tell me how to get to Notre Dame Cathedral?

In Japanese society, according to S. Ide (1986), politeness is governed by a set of explicit social rules. The prevailing rule is to be polite in a formal setting. Three other rules also function within this overriding rule:

1. Be polite to a person of higher social position.
2. Be polite to a person in power.
3. Be polite to an older person.

The context, especially those contextual components related to the participants involved, governs the order of importance of these three rules for the speaker. For example, social position and age are most important when talking to an elder. But if the elder is a woman, the degree of politeness is not nearly as great, since females hold lower status in the society. In another instance, power could prevail over social position, such as when a doctor addresses a patient or a teacher addresses a student.

Social rules are verbally reflected by the use of **honorifics** in Japanese. As described in Chapter 5, honorifics are linguistic markers that in themselves do not convey lexical meaning but rather reflect hierarchical social constructs. They are attached to the various parts of speech (nouns, verbs, adjectives and adverbs). Some honorifics, such as *to*, are markers of humility meant to lower the speaker's status in relation to the person being addressed, thus serving to emphasize negative politeness strategies. Honorifics such as *–san*, a noun suffix; *o-* a noun prefix; and *–are*, a verbal suffix, mark the high status of the addressee.

Taroo wrote a book with (speaker's) son.

Taroo	-san	ga	gusoku	to	o	hon	kak	-are	Ta
Taroo	HON	subject marker	Son	HUMIL	HON	object	write	HON	past tense marker

HON = honorific marker
HUMIL = humility marker

Note: Not only is Taroo honored but also the entity (book) and the activity (writing) associated with him are marked for respect.

There also exists a class of honorifics that are deferential markings at the end of the sentence to show respect to the addressee.

Satoo came.

Satoo	ga	ki	masi	Ta
Satoo	subject marker	come	HON	past tense marker

Using the honorifics given above, show honor to Akiko along with other entities and activities while humiliating the speaker:

Akiko is eating fish with the (speaker's) son.							
Akiko	Wa	ga	musuko	sakana	o	tabete	iru
Akiko	topic marker		son	fish		eating	present tense marker

Women in Japan generally use more deferential speech than men due to their lower social status. This is reflected in their overall higher frequency of honorific usage, lexical softening devices and sentence final particles, thus further accentuating negative politeness. This topic will be discussed further in Chapter 12.

To use these honorifics most effectively as part of politeness strategies requires both communicative and linguistic competence. As with the other pragmatic forms seen thus far (the cooperative principle, speech acts, routines, and politeness strategies), communication is interwoven in linguistic, contextual and cultural knowledge.

Conclusion

- Politeness is associated with **face wants**, defined in terms of self-esteem (personal) or public self-image (social).
- **Face threatening acts (FTA)** occur when something is said that does not respect face wants and **face saving acts (FSA)** are those that lessen the face want threats.
- Politeness strategies address face wants and range from **saying nothing**, to saying something by going **off-record** (stating indirectly one's face wants) or **on-record**. On-record politeness strategies (stating directly one's face wants) are **bald**, when one's verbal approach is direct; **positive**, when one's utterances reflect a desire to be in solidarity with or connected to someone; and **negative**, when one recognizes another person's need to be free or independent.
- The appropriate use of politeness strategies will differ in kind and complexity from one culture to another and reflect one's linguistic and cultural competence.

Politeness strategies, as well as the other pragmatic forms we have been studying thus far, usually take place within the framework of a conversation. In the following chapter we will address how the very structure of conversation both operates within and conveys speaker meaning.

Additional Activities

1. Imagine that you are in a restaurant with your date and with another couple. At the end of the meal the waiter leaves the bill on the table, and you suddenly discover that you left your money and your credit cards at home.

   a. How would you hint at this without saying anything?
   b. Let's assume you need or want to say something but don't want to go on record. What kind of hint could you use?
   c. If you went on record, provide a bald statement, a positive politeness strategy and a negative politeness strategy. Which of these utterances would be the most face threatening act and the most face saving one? Justify your choices. Your rationale will need to include additional information as to the context.

2. Of the following requests for information, which one would be the most effective if you were an American asking this question to the concierge in a Paris hotel? Justify your choice and briefly explain why the other three statements are less effective.

   a. *Auriez-vous l'obligeance et la gentillesse de me réveiller à 6 heures?*
      Would you be so willing and so kind as to wake me up at 6AM?
   b. *Réveillez-moi à 6 heures.*
      Wake me up at 6AM.
   c. *Excusez-moi, mais j'ai oublié mon réveille-matin et j'ai besoin de quelqu'un qui pourrait me réveiller à 6 heures?*
      Excuse me, but I forgot my alarm clock, and I need someone to wake me up at 6AM.
   d. *Vous avez l'air d'être très responsable, réveillez-moi à 6 heures.*
      You seem to be a very competent person; wake me up at 6AM.

3. With the provided context, identify the politeness strategy being used in each of the following sentences. The first four utterances are from Tamil, a language spoken in India; the final one is from Tzeltal, spoken by a group of indigenous people in Mexico. Justify your choice of strategy.

   a. Something that was too hot to eat or drink:
      koncam cu Taa irukku
      It's a little hot.
   b. Said to a very close friend:
      koncam uppu vaankalaam-nnu vanteen
      I've come to get a little salt.

    c.   A standard offer to a meal:
       caappiT Tu
       Eat!

    d.   Said of a picture on the wall:
       Ookoo! Puyu pooT Too pooT Tiinklaa?
       Oh! You've got a (nice) new photo on your wall, eh?

    e.   Needing money to purchase something:
       ya hk'an ala pesuk
       I want sort of a peso's worth.

4. Upon leaving the home of an American to whose home they were invited, a Japanese couple apologized for having disturbed the host couple. What politeness strategy is reflected here? Why would they have done so? What would be the reaction of the American couple not versed in Japanese politeness? Why?

5. Given what is described above concerning politeness strategies in France, explain why the following communication proved to be a particularly successful way of ordering food in French restaurants? (This is based on personal experiences that Dr. Williams, who does not speak French, had while visiting Paris. She had a colleague compose this statement for her to keep handy as an electronic note on her cell phone.)

Je suis un mangeur aventureux et je respecte le talent et la créativité du chef. Malheureusement, je suis très allergique à l'ail et aux oignons, y compris les poireaux, les échalotes, la ciboulette et les oignons verts. De plus, je suis allergique à l'oignon et l'ail en poudre. Pouvez-vous m'aider à commander?

I'm an adventurous eater and I value the talent and creativity of your chef. Unfortunately, I'm very allergic to garlic and onions, including leeks, shallots and green onions. Moreover, I am allergic to onion and garlic powder. Can you help me order?

Website Resources

- The following website offers general information and examples regarding politeness strategies: http://grammar.about.com/od/pq/g/Politeness-Strategies.htm
- This website provides further practice in identifying politeness strategies: http://media.humanities.manchester.ac.uk/humanities/flash/sociolinguistics/exercise04/exercise4.html
- This website gives some good examples of politeness strategies to be used by English as a Second Language (ESL) speakers: http://www.brighthub.com/education/languages/articles/64944.aspx

- If you scroll down this page, you'll see charts that may help you visualize Brown & Levinson's model of politeness strategy: http://cresenciafong. com/wiki/ref:brown1978universals

Further Reading

Brown, P., and Levinson, S. C. (1987). *Politeness: Some Universals in Language Usage* (Studies in Interactional Sociolinguistics). New York: Cambridge University Press.

Chapter 8

Conversational Organization

> We will analyze the structure of conversation that underlies speaker meaning.

If the rhythm of a sentence was right its sense could look after itself (Edgar Pelham in Frye, 1964).

Introduction

In our discussion of pragmatic forms (cooperative principle, speech acts, routines and politeness strategies), we have not treated the underlying structures operating in verbal interactions. And yet, without some structure, communication would disintegrate, as witnessed in those instances when individuals become overly inebriated and are not able to have meaningful conversations with one another. These individuals are usually at no loss for words, but their conversations are incoherent monologues or empty dialogues filled with overlaps and interruptions.

What, then, are these underlying structural properties of conversation that we use and take for granted and how do they affect speaker meaning? This is what will be addressed below as we look at the structural features that make conversation coherent and meaningful.

Turn-Taking

A basic structural requirement of conversation is the often intricate and delicate organizational framework of **turn-taking**. Much like the childhood game of "tag," turn-taking is the acknowledgment that, at different times in a conversation, you are "it;" that is, you have the floor to speak. While we may think of turn-taking in conversation as intuitive, we actually had to learn when it was our turn to speak. As children, in our haste to express ourselves, we were often admonished for speaking out of turn by a parent or caretaker who would say something like, *Wait until I am done talking to speak* or *It's rude to talk before our guest has finished speaking*. Later, when we went to school, we learned more formal turn-taking principles, such as raising our hand for permission to speak in class.

The point at which we take our turn to speak is called the **transition relevance place (TRP)**. Depending on the context of the conversation, the TRP can occur at the end of a phrase or sentence or even at the end of a longer conversational unit, such as at the end of an enumeration of items, after the punch line of a joke, or at the conclusion of a lecture or a story.

But how do we know where the TRP is in verbal interactions? One way you know is when the current speaker selects you to speak. The speaker can do this straightforwardly (e.g., *What's your answer? Tell me what you think, etc.*) or by use of various **adjacency pairs** (two utterances that follow one another) that in some manner or other, constrain the other person to speak. These adjacency pairs can consist of:

Question – Answer
    Where are you going tonight?
    To the movies.
Tag question – Answer
    You're going to class, aren't you?
    Not today.
Offer – Acceptance/Refusal
    Do you want to go the party tonight?
    Not really.
Judgment – Agreement/Disagreement
    I think it will rain today.
    Probably.
Assessment – Response
    The Indians are not yet good enough to play .500 ball.
    Yes, they are!
Directive – Response
    Get the shovel.
    Do it yourself.
Greeting – Greeting
    Hi John!
    Hello, Megan!
Compliment – Response
    What a beautiful shine on your car!
    I worked on it.
Apology – Response
    Sorry for the inconvenience; it won't happen again.
    It better not.

The examples of adjacency pairs listed above are prototypes, since in actual conversations insertions often occur. Sometimes one adjacency pair is embedded in another, as in the following example:

Greetings – Response
> Good morning (greeting). Nice day (judgment)!
> Yes, it sure is.

In addition to the various kinds of adjacency pairs, **prosodic signals** also permit us to identify the TRP, such as when the rhythm of speech slows down, or a longer pause than usual occurs, or a higher pitch is used at the end of a sentence. There are also non-verbal means used to identify the TRP, such as a gaze or the wave of a hand.

As for the time lapse between the speaker and the respondent, it will vary depending on context and culture. The TRP may consist of a slight gap or no gap, or of a longer period of silence than expected (lapse), or even no response at all (termed as significant silence since it can carry loaded meaning).

Overlapping and Interruptions

Instead of being selected to speak at a verbal or non-verbal TRP, interlocutors can also self-select. This occurs when there is no overt indication of speaker selection, when the interlocutor is oblivious or inconsiderate of someone else's turn, or when talking alone is meant to show enthusiasm. In such cases, a speaker enters the conversation straightforwardly or by use of a transitional entry device, such as an **utterance incompletor** (*well, but, and so*, etc.).

Self-selection can also involve **overlapping** another speaker's conversation. In many settings where two or more parties are in a conversation, the American normative practice is that one person speaks at a time with a transition between speakers consisting of a slight gap or no gap. Nevertheless, overlaps do indeed arise. For example, inadvertent entrances into the conversation occur due to a misinterpretation of the TRP. In other instances, the overlapping may be a supportive and cooperative verbal device. But whenever the overlap is intended to overpower another speaker deliberately, it ceases to be cooperative and is instead understood as an **interruption.**

To illustrate the difference between overlaps and interruptions among speakers in informal situations, consider the following conversation that Deborah Tannen recorded and analyzed in her book, *Conversational Style* (2005: 89–90). This conversation took place among three participants; David, an American Sign Language (ASL) interpreter, is talking about ASL to Deborah (the author) and Peter. (Note: This conversation can be more effectively understood by going online to the following link: http://faculty.georgetown.edu/tannend/CSmp3s/page89.mp3)

David: So: and this is the one that's Berkeley. This is the Berkeley...
            Sign for...Christmas
Deborah: Do you figure out those...
            those ... those um correspondences? or do –
                                        David: /?/
            when you learn the signs, /does/
            somebody tell you.
David: Oh you mean watching it? like
Deborah: Cause I can imagine
            knowing that sign, ... and not...
            figuring out that it had anything to do
            with the decorations
                ....
David: No. Y- You know that it has to do with
            the decorations.
Deborah: 'Cause somebody tells
            you? Or you figure it out.
David: No. Oh. ...
            You you talking about me, or a deaf
            person.
Deborah: Yeah
            You. You.
David: Me? Uh: Someone tells me, usually...
            But a lot of 'em I can tell. I mean
            they're obvious... The better I get
            the more I can tell. The longer I do
            it the more I can tell what they're
            talking about ...
Deborah: Huh.
            Without knowing what the sign is.
Deborah: That's interesting.
Peter: But
            how do you learn a new sign?
                ...
David: How do I learn a new sign?
Peter: Yeah. I
            mean supposing ...Victor's talking and
            all of a sudden he uses a sign for
            Thanksgiving, and you've never seen it before.

In this conversation, Tannen reports that Deborah and Peter were latching onto
one another's conversation rather than interrupting. Tannen goes on to say that

we have an example here of two participants engaged in verbal acts of solidarity arising from the enthusiasm of the moment. Deborah and Peter considered their overlapping as cooperative, in the sense that they were attempting to complete each other's turn. They are involved in synchronous verbal styles of the type called **high involvement** by Tannen. High involvement speakers tend to speak at a fast rhythm and are very animated in gestures and facial expressions.

Tannen goes on to say that David was uncomfortable in this same conversation as he tried to explain to them the sign for Christmas. His verbal style is asynchronous with theirs. He felt that Deborah and Peter's overlaps of his locutions were interruptions. This is reflected, according to Tannen, in David's inability to latch onto Deborah and Peter's conversation, as evidenced by the size of his gaps, his vacillating, repeating and using of circumlocutions. His verbal style is what Tannen calls **high considerateness**. It consists of not interrupting, of using a slight or larger gap between speakers and of not imposing.

It would not be surprising if David interpreted Deborah and Peter's high involvement verbal bantering as pushy, aggressive and domineering. On the other hand, Deborah and Peter might characterize high considerate speakers like David as indifferent, tedious, timid, or just dull.

Enact the following conversation, which was recorded by Alice Greenwood and analyzed by Deborah Tannen in her book, Gender and Discourse (61), consisting of three people involved in a humorous topic. Dara is 12 years-old, and her sister Stephanie is 11, while Max is 14. Max complains at the end of being interrupted. After the conversation Dara complained to her mother that she did not like Max even though it was Max who said he was inconvenienced. Based on this conversation, explain why Dara and Max came to these conclusions about each other.

Dara: Listen, listen, listen, listen.
Max: Say it in slow motion okay?
Steph: Betty bought a bit of bitter butter and
         she said this butter's bitter. If I
         put it in my batter, it will make my
         batter bitter. So Betty bought a bit
         of better butter to
Dara: You never heard
         that before?
Max: No. Never
Dara: Max, seriously?
Max: Seriously.
Dara: It's like the famous to
Steph: tongue twister.
Max: No. The famous tongue twister is
         Peterpiperpicked
Dara: Same thing. It's like
         that. It's like that one.
Max: You keep interrupting me.

Cohesive Communicative Devices

Repairs

Imagine what a conversation would sound like if all the parties did not observe turn-taking procedures and consequently spoke whenever they wanted to. Indeed, old comedy sketches, such as those done by the Marx brothers and the Three Stooges were created on this premise.

To remedy this sort of verbal anarchy there are structural devices used between and within turns called **repairs**. Consider what would happen in a conversation if someone used the wrong word to describe an object. Like a satellite shooting out of orbit, the conversation could head in an unintended direction. And then there are instances when someone is unable to think of the word to use. Does this mean that the conversation then ceases? Of course not! In all such instances, repairs allow speakers to correct their verbal gaffes. The repair can consist of an apology, such as the speaker excusing herself for violating the TRP, or a correction by the listener or speaker of the inaccurate information provided, or a request by the listener to repeat due to her inattentiveness.

Consider each of the following examples and identify the repair that is proposed:

Doug: Where is Jane supposed to be going for her internship?

Mary: Jane says she's going to England.

Bob: She says she is going to... Sorry, I did not realize you were responding to his question.

Speaker 1:   This wisteria plant flowers yearly.

Speaker 2:   Actually, it's a vine.

Speaker 1:   This doohickey is required for the light to go on in the trunk.

Speaker 2:   Oh, you mean the fuse.

Speaker 1:   I'm going to need to go to the store.

Speaker 2:   What?

Speaker 1:   I said that I need to go to the store.

Speaker: I thought...no, I'm sure he said he would arrive at 8:00 pm.

Backchannel Cues

In addition to repairs, conversations are rendered cohesive by some form of **active listenership**. Active listenership takes place by use of **backchannel cues** (*yeah, sure, cool, uh-huh,* etc.), or by use of non-verbal actions, such as a head nod, a raising of eyebrows, or other gestures and facial expressions. In many kinds of conversations, especially those in which confirmation of a point is required, speakers need to be assured that their interlocutor is actively listening. It is often unsettling whenever one realizes that no such feedback is forthcoming. It is at that point that the speaker says something like: *Can you hear me?* or *Is there a problem?* Verbal and non-verbal backchannel cues, then, are signs of attention which encourage the speaker to proceed with the topic. Without them, speakers are often ill at ease and will limit, shorten, or even shift the topic.

On the other hand, while backchannel cues support the speaker, too many such cues in succession may reflect the desire of the hearer to interrupt, and thus be used as a **pre-turn** such as *Oh yeah, we already know that, but my take on the question is...* The excessive use of backchannel cues may also reflect lack of interest (*Sure, but get to the point please*), pandering to someone's ego (*You're so perceptive*), or even disapproval when accompanied with a summary tone such as *Sure, sure, sure.*

The linguistic forms and practices in the use of backchannel cues will differ from one context to another. In the classroom setting, when participation is required, backchannel cues are encouraged. Timid students, those who do not want to appear to be seeking favor, or those who are not accustomed to being participatory in class, will hesitate to provide backchannel cues. On the other hand, students who are outgoing, not as influenced by peer pressure and have experience in being active participants in their education, will provide ample and varied backchannel cues.

Repetition

Another verbal device that renders conversations cohesive between and within turns is **repetition**. Repetition serves to connect conversational units to the experience described. Repetition may be used for various purposes, such as emphasizing a point, stalling, or mocking, to mention a few.

What are the purposes of repetition in the examples below?

During an argument:
    Go to hell.
    You go to hell.

Planning for the evening:
    Do you want to?
    Do I want to what?
    Do you want to stay in this evening?
    Sure.

Husband and wife in a restaurant as the server takes their order:
    I'll have a beer.
    He's driving, he'll have coffee.
    I'll have coffee.

Stylistic

Stylistic devices, often exemplified in literature, are also part of everyday speech and serve to render conversations cohesive. Among such devices are **puns**, **alliterations**, and other kinds of **word play**. Puns as a communicative device serve to put focus on the topic. When Dr. Remillard was hospitalized for a nasal condition, for example, he received a so-called get well message from his son focusing on his medical condition that included the following pun: *Nobody knows (nose) the troubles you've seen.*

Identify the pun in the following utterances:

1. My son and I have both earned doctorates.
   Oh, that means you're a paradox.

2. The fattest knight at King Arthur's round table was Sir Cumference. He acquired his size from too much *pi*.

3. I thought I saw an eye doctor on an Alaskan island, but it turned out to be an optical Aleutian.

4. She was only a whiskey maker, but he loved her still.

5. A rubber band pistol was confiscated from algebra class, because it was a weapon of math disruption.

6. A dog gave birth to puppies near the road and was cited for littering.

7. Two silk worms had a race. They ended up in a tie.

8. A hole has been found in the nudist camp wall. The police are looking into it.

9. A sign on the lawn at a drug rehab center said: "Keep off the Grass."

10. When cannibals ate a missionary, they got a taste of religion.

Alliterations, which are two or more words in a phrase or sentence that have the same initial sound, are also devices that serve to focus on a topic. The following alliteration could be used at the losing end of a situation or an event:

> Doomed by the dangling dong of destiny.

We bring this discussion of cohesive stylistic devices to a close with an example of the kind of word play that is often the source of joke telling:

> The Idaho potato met, fell in love with, and married the Maine potato and had one child, sweet potato. Sweet potato later in life met and fell in love with Paul Harvey, a famous news commentator. Idaho potato was furious that his daughter would marry a commentator (common tater).

Cross-Cultural Organizational Devices

The length, timing and allocation of turns may differ significantly from one context, or culture, to another. Also involved in turns, according to Deborah Tannen, is whether one is a **high involvement** or a **high considerateness speaker.**

The Cree people in the Western provinces of Canada, for instance, allow long gaps within turns so as to carefully consider what they will say next, and between turns so as to show respect to the other interlocutors (high considerateness). On the other hand, it is a normative practice in casual conversation in France for the listener to enter into the turn before the gap, usually on the last syllable of the speaker's utterance (high involvement). This creates simultaneity in conversation that often gives Americans the impression that the French are interruptive and difficult to converse with in a smooth manner.

Speaker allocation in some contexts and cultures is strictly followed. In Burundi, a language spoken in Africa by five million people, the order in which people speak in a group is strictly determined by seniority of rank. Everyone must speak before the first speaker can speak again.

Backchannel cueing in foreign cultures can be quite different from ours. With the Cree, for example, active listenership is indicated by saying *ehe* (*yes*) for a simple acknowledgement to what is said, but *tapwe* (*truly*) as an ending for a developed argumentation. The latter backchannel cue resembles the kind of assertive *Amen!* that one might hear in response to forceful preachers at religious revivals.

Other cohesive communicative devices (repetition, repairs and stylistic) are part of every language and culture but may differ in respect to kind and usage.

Conclusion

Structural properties underlie meaningful conversation and, like the pragmatic forms we have treated thus far, reflect the cultural models speakers operate with.

- Turn-taking practices are governed by verbal cues (adjacency pairs, prosodic signals) and non-verbal cues (gazing, raising of eyebrows, etc.).
- A slight gap or no gap is the American normative practice in turn taking, but for various reasons overlaps and interruptions commonly occur between turns.
- Within turns, speakers make use of cohesive devices (repairs, backchannel cues or stylistic devices), that serve to convey communicative intent, such as if an interlocutor is being supportive or disinterested while backchanneling; helpful or mind-numbing in the use of repetitions; and pedantic or focus oriented in the use of stylistic devices.

- Structural principles will vary from one context and culture to another, often challenging interlocutors in making judgments of other people's intentions.

We have now completed our study of pragmatics, the use of language in situational contexts. In the following chapters the focus will be on how language forms are used in social contexts such as in various dialectical and ethnic groups, as well as between genders. This area of study, known as **sociolinguistics**, is the topic of our next chapter.

Additional Activities

1. Record a political news show (FOX, CNN, PBS, BBC, Al Jazeera, etc.) and observe how conversations are controlled by use of the structural properties treated in this chapter.

    An extension to this activity could include a comparison between political news shows from networks within the United States and those outside of the United States.

2. Given the normative practice of the Cree people to allow long gaps within and between turns and the American practice of little to no pause between and within turns, what kind of misunderstandings could occur between speakers of these languages in this respect?

3. At this point you should be able to conduct a pragmatic analysis of an actual conversation which would encompass the use of the cooperative principle, speech acts, routines and politeness strategies. Be aware that if you decide to record a conversation on the spot for this purpose you must seek permission from the participants.

4. Another option would be to apply such a pragmatic analysis to a dialogue in a play or in a narrative, such as Dorothy Parker's short story "The Sexes." The dialogue contained therein lends itself particularly well to such analysis as it is essentially a conversation between a man and a woman, wherein the latter refuses to provide information to the man concerning what she interpreted as his attraction to another woman. This story could also serve for analysis of the role of language and communication in relation to gender which will be addressed in Chapter 12.

Website Resources

*   http://linguistics.usask.ca/Ling347/webp/turntaking/index.html is a very useful site offering information on turn-taking, including cross-cultural examples.
*   http://changingminds.org/techniques/conversation/interrupting/overlap_speech.htm provides brief entries regarding the role of gender and nationality on interruptions and overlaps.

Further Reading

Finegan, E., and Besnier, N. (1989. *Language: Its Structure and Use*. San Diego, CA: Harcourt Brace Jovanovich.

Chapter 9

Social Factors

We will consider the influence that various social factors such as gender, ethnicity, age, social class and geographical location have on the way we use language.

Language, never forget, is more fashion than science, and matters of usage, spelling and pronunciation tend to wander around like hemlines (Bill Bryson, *The Mother Tongue: English and How It Got That Way*).

Introduction

Do you think men and women speak differently? Do you sometimes use different words than your parents or grandparents do? Do you have a friend or family member from another part of the United States who speaks with an accent that sounds strange to your ears? Do you know anyone who speaks Ebonics?

You probably answered yes to at least some of these questions, and might even be able to produce several examples of language differences you have observed through your own experiences. The fact of the matter is that we all speak a unique form of language, an individual version called an **idiolect**. An idiolect, like a dialect, is affected by many factors, such as gender, age and ethnicity, but it also reflects language use that is unique to each of us. We change the way we speak in different situations, such as using less slang when talking to teachers than when talking with friends, or answering the telephone with a different greeting in a work situation than when answering a cell phone at a party. To continue the analogy made in the quote that opens this chapter, you wouldn't wear a business suit to a dorm party, nor would you wear a swimsuit to a job interview. Just like with fashion, we each have our own distinct linguistic "style."

If you have ever attempted to discuss different accents with friends or family, or debate the proper usage of a particular part of speech, you have already noticed that language is a lively topic for conversation. Most people are at least somewhat attuned to linguistic differences, whether or not they are able to classify or explain them. Individual language use is an intensely personal expression, and it is easy to trigger strong emotions and opinions when someone's language usage is analyzed.

As you have learned, **linguistics** and **pragmatics** aim to explore language in an objective manner. **Sociolinguistics**, however, goes beyond sounds and the ways words are formed and linked with other words. This branch of linguistics addresses the influence that various social factors – such as gender, ethnicity, age, social class and geographical location – have on the way we use language.

The Relationship between Language and Society

While it might be intriguing to pose the question of whether language shapes society, or society shapes language, the relationships could more accurately be described as bidirectional, with each aspect influencing the other. For example, do teenage girls in Western industrial societies tend to use more detailed terms for color because they are bombarded with ads for cosmetics and clothing from a young age, or does some inherent characteristic of female speech lead them to create and utilize a wider range of color terms? Stopping short of making a universal generalization, we could simply state that there is likely some connection between the color terms American teenage girls use and the world of advertising that surrounds them.

To further explore this question, the following activity was designed to elicit the use of color terms. It may or may not uphold the idea that women use a wider variety of color terms, but it would not be surprising if you see this pattern. (In Dr. Williams' Introduction to Sociolinguistics, a class taught in the spring of 2014, several of the male students said that they are content to just think in terms of the eight colors in the basic Crayon box. As one said, "My shirt is red. Not reddish-pink or reddish-orange, just red!")

Starting individually, brainstorm as many alternate words as you can for the following colors. After about 3-5 minutes, share your answers with a classmate, comparing and discussing any similarities or differences you might find. Next, see how your other classmates responded. Do you see any clear differences between the terms supplied by women and those supplied by men? Are there patterns that might be explained by other factors, such as area of study? (For example, an art major might be expected to know more color terms.)

Red: (crimson, scarlet, vermillion, etc.)

Green:

Black:

Yellow:

White:

Purple:

Blue:

Pink:

Gray:

Sociolinguistic Research

Sociolinguistics, when viewed as the scientific study of the relationships between language and society, aims to draw from observable data rather than opinion or emotion. However, since personal beliefs and attitudes influence human speech, and since sociolinguists are obviously humans as well as scientific researchers, it is virtually impossible to render a pure observation of data as one could do in the natural sciences. This has been called the **Observer's Paradox** by William Labov, among other linguists. Researchers want to observe language as it happens naturally within a given context, but once they become part of the context, it is no longer natural. There are ethical standards regarding covert research with human subjects, so secretly recording conversations is not an option. Hence, sociolinguists are like other social scientists in that they must be mindful of how objectively they attempt to collect, observe, interpret, and present data.

The field of sociolinguistics draws upon knowledge from other avenues of language study, as well as areas of research outside of linguistics, such as anthropology, psychology, physiology, and pedagogy. As stated in the first chapter of this book, the act of communication is perhaps the most complex feat of human behavior, requiring multiple points of view for the most complete explanations. While linguists are more driven by the "what" of language, sociolinguists, like pragmatists, are interested in the "how" and the "why." The entire context of a given act of communication is relevant. Who is speaking? To whom is the speaker speaking, and what is their prior relationship, if any? What is the setting of the exchange? What is the purpose of the exchange? Who leads the conversation? What voice inflections and aspects of body language are involved? How is the exchange concluded?

These questions, along with others, help to illustrate the main principle of sociolinguistics, which is that language does not exist in a vacuum, as in the discipline of linguistics, and that human communication can only be fully explored when social factors are taken into account.

Descriptivism vs. Prescriptivism

One of the major tenants of sociolinguistics (and indeed of nearly any branch of study that claims to be scientific) is that effective research is **descriptive** rather than **prescriptive**. This is what makes sociolinguists, as well as linguists and pragmatists, quite different from grammarians; a grammarian sees fit to prescribe correct ways of speaking, whereas a sociolinguist aims to describe language usage as it occurs naturally in a given context. In this latter view, there is no such thing as "bad grammar" in the inherent sense; a given way of communicating is only seen as bad if it fails to carry out its task of successfully conveying meaning between speakers. One simple way to remember this distinction is that a prescriptive approach to language focuses on what "should" be said (quotations here indicating that this value judgment is subjective), while a descriptive approach simply describes what is actually said in a given context.

To illustrate this point, think of the use of double negatives in a sentence. You can probably recall a parent's or teacher's voice in your head exclaiming *You can't use double negatives in a sentence!* Your reply might very well have been a defiant *Oh, yes, I can. Listen: I ain't gonna listen to you!* A prescriptivist would maintain that the usage of double negatives marks incorrect grammar, something to be avoided by educated speakers. A descriptivist would simply note that it is indeed possible to make such an utterance, and that many people do this every day, either naturally as part of their dialect or intentionally for some communicative purpose.

Sociolinguists are descriptive but they also take into account that language usage carries social consequences. Therefore, they might remind you that while you certainly can string together two negatives in a sentence if you want or feel the need to do so, your speech might be judged negatively in certain situations. This accounting for both realities can be liberating in helping you to understand that you have control over your own speech. With your consciousness having been raised regarding this dual reality, you can choose to avoid double negatives when writing a formal essay, but use them with abandon when talking to friends in a casual situation if you wish, or even purposely employ them for emphasis or humor.

It is this understanding of the balance of language usage and social consequence that makes many people who study sociolinguistics adopt a "time and place" attitude towards language, meaning that there is a time and a place for more formal versions of language and a time and place for less formal versions. While still considering concepts such as appropriateness in a given context, they abandon the idea that any particular aspect of language is inherently better or more correct than another.

Even after intellectually accepting that the concept of correct language usage is relative, many people still believe that their own way of speaking is the right way. It's human nature, but before you judge the speech of others, take this little quiz to see if you yourself are using language in ways that are considered to be incorrect by some. Which ones do not conform to your perception of "Standard English?" The difference may lie in spelling, word choice, syntax, or semantics. After considering these examples for about 5 minutes, compare your answers with a classmate or with the entire class.

Answers and explanations for each of these examples can be found at this link:
From Common Errors in English: http://wsu.edu/~brians/errors/errors.html

Phrase	What is "non-standard" about it?
Just between you and I, I don't like it.	
What's your PIN number?	
Do you want a complimentary drink?	

I wrote my boss, but he didn't reply back.	
I have a deep-seeded hatred for grammar.	
Why? For a myriad of reasons!	
Please RSVP if you're coming to the party.	
Do you like both of your sister-in-laws?	
Do you need to lay down?	
Supposably you think you speak better then me!	
I should really eat less cookies.	
I'll try and call you later.	
My parents called both my brother and I last night.	
That's a very unique purse.	
Many black slaves were hung in the south.	

Instead of using the terms "correct" and "incorrect," many sociolinguists advocate the use of the terms **marked** and **unmarked**. Using these terms, we can say that any given utterance that strikes the listener as strange or inappropriate for whatever reason is marked. Conversely, an utterance that draws no attention to itself can be called unmarked. Rather than calling any particular speech variant "correct" or "incorrect," it is the context that matters.

For example, Dr. Williams grew up in rural Iowa, where it is common to delete the verb *to be* in sentences like *This shirt needs ironed*. Since this was a practice she grew up with, the absence of the verb was not marked to her. When she moved to Athens, Georgia for graduate school, however, she was chided for doing this because speakers there do not generally drop that verb. This morpho-syntactic variant was marked to them. After a year or so of living in Athens, Dr. Williams abandoned this aspect of her home dialect so as to not be called out by her peers and professors. She has now lived in Erie, Pennsylvania for nearly two decades, where the majority of speakers do not delete the *to be* verb either, so she has maintained her learned use of it. Now when she visits her family in Iowa and her cousin says *The corn needs planted soon*, it is marked to her. Hence, for Dr. Williams, this isn't a matter of which version is correct; it's a conscious decision to use the linguistic practice of whichever speech community she finds herself in.

As another example of the importance of context, what would happen if you used the following greeting with a potential employer at a law firm: *Yo, what's up?* Conversely, how would you react if your best friend ended a conversation with you by announcing *Well, then, I shall take my leave. It has been a pleasure conversing with you. Farewell.*

What is problematic with these examples is that the tone of the utterances does not match the context. You would not be wise to use such an informal greeting as the first example with a potential employer that you do not know, and the formality of the second seems odd in a casual conversation with a close friend. Since such behavior would call attention to the speaker, these utterances are marked. If the speakers had used phrases more fitting to the situation, no one would have thought twice about the choice of words, so the utterances would have been unmarked.

Read the following statements, and discuss when each would be appropriate, socially acceptable, and linguistically advantageous to use (i.e., by whom, with whom, at what time, during what sort of social engagement/circumstance, etc.). What is the cultural significance of each? Why would society allow or disallow each under various conditions?

Comment	Discussion
Could you please provide me with the telephone number?	
May I have the phone number please?	
What's the number?	
Gimme the number.	

For the statements above, how would you react if the following people used such statements with you? (Note: You should address each statement for each of the people listed here.)

Person	Comment	Reaction
A client/customer	Could you please provide me with the telephone number?	
A client/customer	May I have the phone number please?	
A client/customer	What's the number?	
A client/customer	Gimme the number.	
A colleague	Could you please provide me with the telephone number?	
A colleague	May I have the phone number please?	
A colleague	What's the number?	
A colleague	Gimme the number.	
A son or daughter	Could you please provide me with the telephone number?	
A son or daughter	May I have the phone number please?	
A son or daughter	What's the number?	
A son or daughter	Gimme the number.	

The Internal Variation of Language

As we communicate in different social situations, we vary our language use in a number of ways. This variety can exist within the speech of one particular individual as he or she attempts to communicate within different contexts, such as a college student using different vocabulary to describe a person of romantic interest to a friend than he would to a parent. It can also occur between groups of individuals, such as people living in Boston as compared to people living in Atlanta. Some sociolinguists prefer to perform in-depth studies of individual people or communities, while others concentrate on a larger picture of more than one group of speakers coming into contact with one another, such as the language use exhibited among Spanish-English bilinguals in many parts of the United States.

Variations within Speakers

As mentioned before, we all vary our language usage depending upon context. We use different levels of formality in the classroom than we do at a party with friends. We use varying levels of slang when talking to employers, family, and friends. We may try to modify our language usage to match that of people around us, or to differentiate ourselves from those people. For the most part, these choices are made subconsciously, supporting the idea that language usage is, at least in part, an innate human behavior.

Variations between Speakers

Language usage also varies between different speakers. As one example, think about the terms you or your friends use for being intoxicated. Even limiting yourself to terms used by people of your same generation and at the same moment in time, you will likely be able to come up with a variety of answers. A quick survey of college students in Dr. Williams' 2014 sociolinguistics course offered the following terms for being intoxicated: *blotto, bombed, buzzed, crocked, fried, juiced, lit, loaded, pickled, plastered, polluted, sloppy, sloshed, smashed, tanked,* and *wasted,* among others. These variations might be due to differences in where these particular students were raised, or they might possibly break down into usage by women vs. men, or they may have other social and historical explanations. In any case they are colorful examples of the creativity of human language. One student even remarked that just about any combination of letters (forming a real word or not) combined with the suffix *-ed* could be taken in the proper context to mean intoxicated, as in *Jake got completely flooped last night!*

> Take a quick survey of your classmates, listing all the terms they currently use or hear for being intoxicated. How much variation do you see? Are there any terms that cause disagreement?

Language Change over Time

The study of language change over time seeks to trace the progression of language usage. Despite what some self-appointed language experts might lead you to believe, language has always evolved, and it always will. For instance, double negatives were considered to be correct grammar in Shakespeare's time, but are no longer acceptable in formal speech or writing. (As just one example, Maria's character in *Twelfth Night* uses the phrase, "nor this is not my nose neither.") As another illustration of language change, the vocabulary seen as appropriate during the Civil War would seem quaint if you used it in everyday speech today, such as Scarlett O'Hara's description of Melanie in *Gone with the Wind* as "a pale-faced mealy-mouthed ninny." The short life-span of many slang terms shows that language changes even within a generation. For example, using the term *boo* or *shorty* for a significant other was popular with young people just a few years ago. Now, in 2016, one popular term is *bae*.

Of course, just like with fashion, disfavored terms often reappear in subsequent generations. Dr. Williams recalls that in her middle school and high school years (the 1980s), girls referred to cute boys as *hunks*, while guys called cute girls *foxes*. When she first started teaching at the university level in the mid-1990s, her students snickered when she mentioned these terms. To her surprise, however, students in 2013 reported that they sometimes use these words now.

For a quick investigation of language change, complete the following survey individually first. Then work with a partner and write down his or her answers. Finally, make a few notes as to why you agree or disagree with each other.

Question	Personal Answer	Partner's Answer	Notes
Do you think young people today use more slang than their parents?			
Do you use slang? (If yes, what words or phrases do you use, and when do you use them?)			
Do you think people swear more than they used to?			
What can you say about your own use (or non-use) of "taboo" language?			

Language as an Identity Marker

Language usage as an identity marker is a broad area of study that encompasses any number of social factors, even overlapping with other topics of inquiry in the field. For example, there might have been terms in the above list of synonyms for *intoxicated* that you would not consider using, as they wouldn't seem to fit the language usage of your group of friends. Your choice of term might also be influenced by your opinions on drinking and being intoxicated, reflecting what you see as either a positive, negative, or neutral activity.

> Some examples of language usage as an identity marker can be seen in urban speech, such as the phenomenon dubbed as "hip-hop-slanguistics." MTV presented a show about this language in 2012, some of which can be viewed at: http://www.mtv.com/videos/misc/214963/yo-slangulistics-101.jhtml#id=1584322

Often misattributed to racial or ethnic differences, a closer look at urban speech and its speakers reveals that race or ethnicity is only a tangential factor, rather than a causal one. A comparison of the speech patterns of rap artist Eminem and golfer Tiger Woods works as a quick illustration of this misconception. Rather than citing race or ethnicity as the relevant factor in their speech patterns, we can assume that Eminem speaks the way he does to lay claim to the rap community, and Tiger Woods' speech reflects his membership in the traditionally white, middle-to-upper-class golf subculture. Those particularly familiar with the rap and hip-hop scene know that there are subdivisions within this culture itself, with East Coast differing from West Coast, and the South distinguishing itself from the North, both in music and in language usage, further disproving race or ethnicity as the sole predictor of speech patterns.

Another example of language usage as an identity marker can be seen in the technical terms and language (**jargon**) that is used by lawyers and doctors. Whether they are consciously attempting to sound more intelligent than their clients or patients, or perhaps even intimidating, or whether they are simply using the terminology that they feel most accurately and efficiently describes the matter at hand, it is clear that they use words that are not normally used by the general public. Therefore, this language usage marks their identity as lawyers or doctors.

> Provide at least two examples of situations where you have felt intimidated by the language of various professionals, such as doctors or teachers. How did you respond to them?

You yourself may use language to signal membership to any number of social groupings, from ethnicity to religion to a sports team affiliation. This usage marks you as a member of a group, and judgments about others' potential membership will be made according to their language usage, among other factors, whether these judgments are conscious or subconscious. Likewise, judgments will be made about you and your language usage as you go through college and enter the work world, and as you form all manners of relationships with others.

The topic of bilingualism will be discussed in detail in Chapter 13, but it is clearly related to the concept of language usage as identity marker. Those who speak two or more languages on a regular basis usually identify with two or more cultures as well. With language and culture boundaries rarely being rigidly drawn, many of these people consider themselves to be part of a unique subculture as well, one that bridges the separate languages and cultures sufficiently enough to create an entirely new combination of language and culture. One of the most fruitful areas of research stemming from this phenomenon is called code-switching, or the use of more than one language or "code" in one conversation. Given our understanding that language usage is a marker of cultural identity, it is easy to see how people who see themselves as belonging to more than one culture, perhaps even living in a blend of cultures, would choose to communicate in a form that blends languages as well.

Language Variation and Social Norms

As stated above, sociolinguistics is a descriptive field, rather than a prescriptive one. However, while there is no linguistic or sociolinguistic basis for classifying "correct" or "incorrect" ways of speaking, we must certainly admit that there are societal norms for what is considered to be acceptable language usage in a given situation. We could argue, for example, that all of the previously mentioned synonyms for *intoxicated* are valid choices. While this is true, one might consider using a term such as *intoxicated* rather than *wasted* when relating a story about a weekend's activities to a boss or a parent. Conversely, using the term *intoxicated* with your friends might strike them as unnecessarily formal as you tell them the same story.

There is no escaping the fact that we are judged every day based on our use of language. In other words, there is no linguistically superior variety of speech, but society may *believe* that there is, and that is an important realization. Sociolinguists do not seek to tell us how to speak, only to remind us that there are often consequences for our linguistic choices.

One of the advantages of studying sociolinguistics, then, is to raise our own consciousness about the variations in language, the contexts in which the variations occur, and society's reactions to a given variation. Whether or not it should be a stated goal of the scientific study of the relationships between language and society, we should also note that such consciousness-raising can often lead to increased tolerance of others and the way they communicate.

Conclusion

- The aim of this chapter has been to illustrate the inextricable relationship between language and culture.
- Any utterance that is made occurs in a particular context, and is unavoidably affected by this context.
- Sociolinguists believe that it is impossible, or at least irrelevant, to study language as a set of isolated parts separate from the social setting in which it occurs.
- In addition to this guiding principle, it is important to remember that sociolinguistics, like linguistics, is a *descriptive* field rather than a *prescriptive* one. Sociolinguists do not attempt to prescribe "correct" ways of speaking; they gather evidence, analyze and describe it, and perhaps make comments on how that particular sample fits into its social context and what consequences it might carry.

As you continue through this text, you will learn more about the various social factors that shape the way we communicate as human beings.

Additional Activities

1. While sociolinguists try to be as descriptivist as possible in observing language usage, they can harbor linguistic "pet peeves" just like anyone else. Admitting these irritations can be liberating sometimes, if you keep in mind that your particular "hang-ups" are based on prescriptivist notions.

    a. Skim through this website: http://thelanguageguy.blogspot.com/2005/02/linguistic-pet-peeves.html
    b. Create your own "pet peeves" list regarding language. (One example might be the use of *'s* as a plural marker instead of a possessive: *3 Taco's for $1.*)
    c. Are there some items on this list that are more geared towards formal usage than informal usage? Can you tolerate them more in certain situations than in others?
    d. Do you know where your distaste for each item came from? Did a parent or teacher drill it into your head that these were inappropriate? Do some just sound worse to you than others? Have you ever used some of these forms yourself?

2. Survey 10 people (friends, family members, teachers, etc.) and ask what their biggest pet peeves are regarding language usage. You might need to prompt them by giving an example or two, such as the overuse of *like* as a filler word.

3. Present 10 people with the list of phrases that are on the chart below. Have them mark which ones they deem incorrect, and if possible, explain why they think so. Do not offer any hints, or mention how many are supposedly incorrect.

    a. Analyze your results:
        1) When you review your results, which phrases received the most negative ratings? The most positive?
        2) What analysis can you make of the explanations given?
        3) What conclusions can be drawn from your results?
        4) What implications might your findings have for you as a student?
    b. (optional) If you are particularly interested in the concept of grammar and attitudes regarding the perception of correct language usage, you could follow up this activity by doing some web research on the history of the constructions shown below, such as double negatives, ending sentences with prepositions, and splitting infinitives.

Statement	#1	#2	#3	#4	#5	#6	#7	#8	#9	#10
Where is Shakira originally from?										
Who are you speaking to?										
I want you to carefully put that vase on the mantle.										
It is all over between you and I.										
I'm not going to take no stupid sewing class!										
I could care less about whether you come to the party or not.										
The tavern was serving ten wing's for a dollar last night.										
Grandma said that she was feeling good today.										
You run fast!										
I can't believe that you didn't get bit by mosquitoes last night.										
Were there less customers in the store today?										
So, anyways, I guess I'll see you later.										
Is he the one that called you after the party?										
This data is incorrect.										
Each of the puppies are equally cute.										
It's too bad I'm not as rich as him.										
Has the cat laid down yet?										
Where did you get that hat at?										
I need to go to the ATM machine.										

That's a woman that I could live with.										

4. Examine a variety of clothing catalogs and make a brief written analysis of their use of color terms. Along with your observations, make sure you record the name of the store and who the intended market might be (young women, businessmen, etc.). As you analyze, think about why the company might have chosen to use those particular terms. Do you see any patterns regarding the gender of the intended market? Age? Socioeconomic class?

5. In your own life, you likely speak differently from your parents or grandparents. To prove this, ask your parents and grandparents (or other adults of their age groups) what words were popular in their teen years for the following situations:

    a. two people showing physical affection for each other (*necking* and *making out* are two examples)
    b. being intoxicated (such as *bombed* or *schnockered*)
    c. the unfortunate regurgitation process that can occur as a result of being sick (*upchucking, driving the porcelain bus*, etc.)

Web Resources

General Sociolinguistics

- This section of the *Do You Speak American?* website is written by noted sociolinguist Walt Wolfram. Links on this page will guide you to other sections of the site dealing with sociolinguistics as well. http://www.pbs.org/speak/speech/sociolinguistics/socialbehavior/
- The University of Texas offers this collection of resources on sociolinguistics: http://www.utexas.edu/courses/linguistics/resources/socioling/

Language Change

- An online dictionary of unusual, weird, no longer used, etc. words can be found at: http://phrontistery.info/ihlstart.html
- Are you interested in the fate of dying languages? Visit The Endangered Language Initiative page here: http://www.yourdictionary.com/elr/whatis.html

- This is an extremely interesting site describing the project that two linguists undertook to document endangered languages around the world: http://www.pbs.org/thelinguists/

Slang and Taboo Language

- Each year, the American Dialect Society announces its "Words of the Year" awards. Interestingly, the winner for 2014 was actually a Twitter hashtag (#blacklivesmatter), and the 2015 winner was the "Face with Tears of Joy" emoji! http://blog.oxforddictionaries.com/2015/11/word-of-the-year-2015-emoji
- The Urban Dictionary is a large site focused on slang and taboo language: http://www.urbandictionary.com/
- This sound clip from National Public Radio features linguist Geoff Nunberg speaking on the topic of profanity and how views of profanity have changed over time: http://www.npr.org/templates/story/story.php?storyId=1966954
- Even beyond the concept of profanity, some words are considered too "taboo" to be uttered in any context. Why is this so? Listen to another sound clip by Geoff Nunberg, who explores this topic in detail: http://www.npr.org/templates/story/story.php?storyId=1539100

Further Reading

Bell, A. (2013). *The Guidebook to Sociolinguistics*. Malden, MA: Wiley-Blackwell.

Bonvillain, N. (2013) *Language, Culture & Communication*, 7th ed. Upper Saddle River, NJ: Pearson.

Bowe, H., and Martin, K. (2014). *Communication across Cultures: Mutual Understanding in a Global World*. Cambridge: Cambridge University Press.

Chaika, E. (2007). *Language: The Social Mirror*. Boston, MA: Heinle ELT.

Edwards, J. (2013). *Sociolinguistics: A Very Short Introduction*. Oxford: Oxford University Press.

Meyerhoff, M., and Schleef, E. (2010). *The Routledge Sociolinguistics Reader*. London: Routledge.

Chapter 10

Dialects

In this chapter, we will take a look at language dialects, as well as delve deeper into the concept of "standard" language.

I used to say that whenever people heard my Southern accent, they always wanted to deduct 100 IQ points (Jeff Foxworthy).

Introduction

This quote from comedian Jeff Foxworthy manifests what you learned in Chapter 9, which is that we are constantly making judgments about other people based on their speech (whether or not we are consciously aware of it), and they are doing the same to us. The way we talk is as much a part of our personal style as the way we dress or the music we listen to.

Sometimes we make assumptions about how a person will speak based on externally visible information, such as ethnicity or gender. These topics will be addressed in subsequent chapters. Other times, we listen to people speak and make guesses about their social status, such as socioeconomic class or level of education. In many instances, we may simply note that something is different about a person's speech, and we might wonder where the person is from. We may not always be correct in our assumptions, such as determining a person's ethnicity over the phone, or guessing their sexual orientation, but it is amazing how much information we can deduce just from what people say and how they say it.

You already considered some of these social factors when you read the questions that open Chapter 9. If your grandparents or parents use different terms to describe the state of being intoxicated than you do, it is likely a result of their belonging to another age group. If you are puzzled by many of the expressions used by the comics of the Blue Collar Comedy Tour, you may be from a different socioeconomic class than they are representing during their routines. And if you and your roommate don't agree on whether a carbonated beverage is called *pop* or *soda*, you are likely from different geographical regions.

As we have stated before, most people notice some variation in how others speak, but they may not be able to pinpoint exactly what the differences are. Even those with no training in linguistics can usually tell the difference between a speaker from Boston and one from Atlanta, and whether they realize it or not, what they are likely noticing is variation in pronunciation.

Not only are many people able to note these differences in pronunciation, they find it an interesting subject of conversation. Asking where someone is from after hearing them speak is common even among strangers in our society. Many comedians capitalize upon these differences when they do voice imitations in their routines, such as the Jeff Foxworthy in the Redneck Comedy Tour epitomizing a rural southern dialect, or Gabriel Iglesias mimicking his Chicano or Mexican friends.

Revisiting the Concept of "Standard"

The historical, social and political aspects of distinguishing language varieties are perhaps most powerful when we consider the concept of "standard" language. When most people use the term *standard*, they are referring to some version of a language that is seen as "proper" or "correct." In the United States, what we call **Standard American English** (SAE) is taught in schools, used in official documents, and preferred for national news media. Those who deviate from this standard are often said to be using bad grammar and may face negative academic, professional or social consequences.

Bolstered by prescriptivist traditions carried on through formal education and popular beliefs, many people assert that there is a standard version of language, and that we are best served by using it. Some go so far as to claim that there is only one correct way of speaking in all contexts, and anyone who does not speak this way is considered to be uneducated. This linguistic elitism is quite different than the viewpoint of someone who simply acknowledges that there is a way of speaking that is considered to be more appropriate in any given situation.

Not all prescriptivists are aggressive or hostile in arguing their case, of course, but their attempts at correcting others are not always welcomed. With language being such an intensely personal thing, it is not surprising that most people do not like to be singled out as being incorrect, or worse, uneducated, ignorant, or even inferior. Pointing out every deviation from one's own idea of standard grammar is not a good way to make friends, and often impedes true communication. If people are constantly worried about whether or not their speech will be picked apart, they are not likely to continue conversation. There are also particularly inopportune or unwise moments to concentrate on such details. For example, informing a burly motorcycle rider that the identification on his jacket should be *Hell's Angels* with an apostrophe instead of just *Hells Angels* might not be the best way to make friends!

But what exactly is this standard we speak of, and who speaks it? And who monitors its usage? Unlike French (Académie française) and Spanish (Real

Academia Española), English has no governing body to establish rules of usage. We certainly have grammar guides, but who wrote them, and under what authority?

Actually, this complex topic offers a perfect illustration of why sociolinguists must consider both linguistic and social factors in their research. In purely linguistic terms, there is no such thing as a standard variety of a language, especially if the connotation is that one version is more correct than another. As we discussed in Chapter 9, most sociolinguists avoid the terms *correct* and *incorrect*. Linguistically speaking, all language varieties are created equal; they are equally complex, and are equally capable of conveying meaning between speakers.

It is also important to remind ourselves that language usage changes over time; what is considered incorrect grammar today may have been perfectly acceptable in the past. In Chapter 9, you saw the use of double negatives in Shakespeare's *Twelfth Night*. You can find them in Chaucer's *Canterbury Tales* as well. You'd have a difficult time finding someone to brand the writing of these two literary giants as improper. Indeed, the use of double negatives was the literary standard at the time. Interestingly, the rule about not using double negatives in English is not one that evolved naturally within the language. In the eighteenth century, learned scholars who were fluent in Latin borrowed several rules from that language and applied them to English. This is just one exemplification of how many of our grammar rules have been rather arbitrarily chosen, applied and enforced.

Another point to keep in mind is that language often "fossilizes" in written form, with old forms remaining intact long after their use has ceased in spoken English. Think of the first word in a popular holiday story written in the nineteenth century, *'Twas the Night Before Christmas...* You can easily see that this is a contraction of *It was*. It would not be used in spoken language today, but the written form has been preserved in that classic text.

The constant evolution of language is a fact conveniently ignored by those who warn that the English language is decaying and that no one uses proper grammar anymore. The most drastic of these doomsayers would have us believe that if we continue to let language usage erode, we will eventually devolve back into cavemen who communicate with grunts. Obviously, this is not going to happen; in the general sense, language has always fulfilled whatever needs a given group of people have, and it always will.

Despite these linguistic realities, credence must still be given to the abstract notion of a standard or proper way of speaking. Again referring back to terms from Chapter 9, those who use this perceived standard are using essentially unmarked speech, gaining society's approval. Those who do not use it stand out by using marked pronunciation, vocabulary, or grammar, especially if their speech includes stigmatized features. People who don't use this so-called standard language often face difficulties in school and in the workplace, with the best education and jobs being more easily attained by those who do. You would probably agree that it is in your best interest to write a term paper in a style acceptable to your professor or to avoid slang when speaking to a prospective employer. This is as much a reality as the fact that all varieties are linguistically equal.

So, where does this leave us? In many ways, language usage can be considered a game of sorts. In this game, the rules are often arbitrarily set and are frequently changing. Additionally, there is disagreement on who gets to make and enforce the rules. At any given moment, we make choices about how we play this game. There are advantages to playing it by the rules, and consequences for not doing so. The bottom line is that there is no such thing as a "standard" variety of language, but society behaves as if there is. Such is the sociolinguists' conundrum. Henceforth, the term **Standard American English** (SAE) will be used, but with the understanding that it is more of a concept than a reality.

Standard or Dialect?

Dialect is a broad term used for describing a way of speaking unique to a particular group of people. It is often viewed in terms of pronunciation, but it also encompasses lexical, morpho-syntactic, semantic, and pragmatic variants. Linguists usually reserve the term **accent** to refer to someone's pronunciation, whereas a dialect encompasses all of the variants that comprise language usage. Whether we focus on pronunciation alone or the wider range of factors involved in distinguishing one group's speech from another (socio-economic, occupational, situational, etc.), it is important to understand that we all speak a dialect.

If we define dialect as a way of speaking unique to a particular group of people, this definition is all-encompassing; everybody speaks a dialect. It's as fundamental and general of a concept as noting that everyone has a skin color. One person's skin color might stand out in comparison to that of other people in the same geographical area, but that certainly does not mean that the others do not have any skin color! In the same way, if people are singled out as having a different accent or speaking in another dialect, it simply means that their speech stands out from that of others around them.

You may have heard someone disparaging another person's speech by saying that she speaks with a heavy accent or a strong dialect. Sometimes people even apologize for their own speech, self-disclosing their usage of a dialect as if it were shameful. What they usually mean in these cases is that they believe themselves to speak a variety that is not considered to be the standard. Again, it is all a matter of relativity. No accent can be classified as heavy or strong in and of itself. It is only when one accent contrasts noticeably with another one that the difference is evident. To use the skin color analogy again, it wouldn't make any sense for someone to say that they have a heavy or strong skin color; it would depend on what color it is being compared to. Dr. Williams notes that if she, a woman of Irish-Scottish-English-German heritage, were to visit Zimbabwe, her skin color would clearly stand out, but if someone from Zimbabwe came to visit her family in Iowa, it would be his or her skin color that would be seen as different. Neither color could be labeled in and of itself as heavy or strong.

Most people remain ignorant of this truth, however. You might have heard people claim that they don't have any accent. Many people believe that the best news anchors speak without an accent, and dialect coaches are hired to work with people whose speech is seen as being something other than standard. It is true that many forms of media and entertainment strive for speech that does not distract the listener from what is being said. More accurately, the aim is to avoid stigmatized linguistic features, especially in pronunciation. With radio or television news, for example, network executives want you to focus on the story instead of wondering whether the newscaster is from Texas or Minnesota. In this way, the media is appealing to our abstract concept of a standard.

Sometimes, however, the media chooses to use a specific dialect to its advantage. Advertisers are experts at this, using language to appeal to a particular market. The following activity will demonstrate this.

If you were an advertising executive, what type of speaker would you use to advertise the following products? Think in terms of portraying the appropriate gender, age, education level and socio-economic status as well as a regional accent. Discuss your ideas and your rationale with a partner to see if there are similarities between your choices.

1. a new videogame about extreme skateboarding
2. an all-natural cosmetic product for the reduction of facial wrinkles
3. a cell phone network service that limits the amount of texts that can be sent in a month
4. a new line of hip-hop inspired clothing
5. a new line of ice cream bars in flavors like *dulce de leche*, mango, and mojito
6. a traditional New York deli
7. a family-owned restaurant specializing in traditional comfort food
8. a new halal market
9. a light beer
10. a fine wine

What is important to remember is that each dialect has its own linguistic traits, and those traits are not marked to speakers of that dialect, unless they have been brought to their attention. If those people never come into contact with people who speak a different dialect, they might think that their own dialect is the one that everyone speaks. (Interestingly, exposure to mass media and movies portraying other dialects does not seem to alter this position as much as you might think.) Perhaps you as a college student have had the experience of interacting with speakers of another dialect, maybe people from a different geographical region, or of a different ethnicity. You likely thought that their dialect was odd compared to your own. It's a good bet, however, that they were thinking the same thing about yours!

Language or Dialect?

Contrary to what you might think, it can sometimes be tricky to decide whether two varieties of a language are mere dialects of the same language or whether they are separate languages. One criterion we use for labeling two language varieties as dialects of the same language is **mutual intelligibility**. In short, this means that speakers of each variety understand each other, despite the differences. They might also share the same writing system, the same literary history, and the same government. One example would be that most people from New Jersey could generally understand someone from New Orleans, in spite of differences in pronunciation, grammar, or word choice. The same would hold true for dialects of other languages as well, such as Syrian Arabic and Moroccan Arabic.

But what about China, where speakers of different regions use the same writing system, share the same literary history, and function under the same government, but speak varieties of language as linguistically different as Russian is from English, with no mutual intelligibility? And how about Spanish and Portuguese speakers, who live in separate countries with diverging literary histories but understand each other quite well? It might seem that the answer is geography, with languages separated by boundaries between countries, but this, too, can be misleading. Spanish is spoken in more than 20 countries, with relatively high mutual intelligibility between speakers. French is spoken on five continents, representing cultures as diverse as Haitian Creole and the French community of Belgium. The degree of intelligibility would be high between Parisian and Belgian French, but maybe somewhat less between Parisian and rural Canadian-French. Intelligibility would take a bigger drop between these groups and Haitian Creole French, but there would still be evident similarities. And then there is English, spoken in every continent on the planet, with most speakers understanding each other relatively well.

Furthermore, it is worth remembering in this respect that the boundaries between countries have not always been where they are now, and many will continue to shift in the future. One has only to recall the history of the United States border with Mexico, or the breakup of the former Soviet Republic, to see this.

These complications have made it difficult for linguists to form concrete criteria for differentiating a dialect from a language. Additionally, there is more than linguistic difference at stake; any variety called a separate language will likely be given greater historical, social, and political status than a dialect. These varieties are sometimes called **prestige dialects**, insinuating that those using it are more prestigious than those who don't. A prestige dialect is more likely to be raised to the title of language, and this dialect is usually what is spoken by those in power.

A phrase that linguist Max Weinreich is said to have heard from an audience member during one of his lectures captures this sentiment: "A language is a dialect with an army and a navy."

Linguistically speaking, all dialects are equal in that speakers of any given dialect successfully communicate with others with the same dialect. They can usually converse with those who speak other dialects of the same language, but speakers of different dialects often view each other's speech as marked in some way. Regardless, there are some dialects that are considered more socially acceptable than others, and this fact often leads people to believe that they are more linguistically acceptable. The truth is that almost every dialect has been made the butt of a joke at some time or another, and there are definite stereotypes in our society; i.e., people with a southern drawl are lazy or unintelligent, people from New Jersey are street-wise and working class, and people from Fargo, North Dakota, are uptight and behind the times, just to name a few. Indeed, it seems that language-bashing is one of the last forms of prejudice still acceptable (perhaps even encouraged) in "polite society."

English Dialect Divisions in the United States

In the case of American English, if you try to prod someone into marking on a map where they think there is no discernible accent, or at least where the "standard dialect" is spoken, they will probably point to some area in the Midwest. A sociolinguist might agree that much of the Midwest uses a dialect that is accepted as more neutral than those of New England or the South. However, a sociolinguist would also remind you that *neutral* here is not a scientific denomination, but rather a social perception. Additionally, there are many variations within this large region, in pronunciation and in grammar and vocabulary usage, making it difficult to definitively pinpoint the boundaries of where this fabled accent-free land lies. Again, a sociolinguist must remember both sides of the paradox; it is not linguistically possible to speak without an accent, but our society has deemed the speech of this particular region as the most neutral, and so we operate as if this were an absolute truth.

Regional dialects of American English are the result of numerous factors, including geographical factors, such as patterns of settlement, subsequent migration, and isolation. In very general terms, there are more distinct dialects in the east than the west, which reflects migration patterns that started with the arrival of the British. The website below this paragraph shows a map that delineates the main dialects, although different maps show different levels of division. For example, in this map, Texas and Georgia are lumped together in the Coastal Southern dialect, though there are many sub-dialects within that area. However, these dialects are more similar to each other than they are to either the Great Lakes or Upper Midwestern dialects. This website is also a great resource for studying American dialects in much greater detail than we will here.

The American Dialect Homepage: http://www.evolpub.com/
Americandialects/AmDialMap.html

Dialects in areas that remain particularly isolated, such as Martha's Vineyard, the
Appalachian region, and the Outer Banks of North Carolina, tend to see slower
change over time. In some areas, dialects are affected by other languages, such as
Chicano English (Spanish) and Cajun English (French).

The dialect of a particular group of speakers is influenced by other factors
besides geography as well, such as ethnicity, age, gender, occupation, socioeconomic class and level of education. This means that people living in one geographical area could actually be speakers of different dialects. Boston provides
one good example of this, as the speech of the upper class (called the Boston
Brahmin dialect) is quite different than that of the working class. There are also
individuals who speak more than one dialect, shifting from one to another based
on context. Many African Americans fall into this category, speaking their ethnic
dialect in some contexts and more standard English in others. (African American
English will be addressed more fully in the next chapter.)

Phonetic Variants

We mentioned before that each dialect has its own distinct linguistic traits. One
of these traits is variation in pronunciation. For example, in parts of the Midwest,
the common pronunciation of the word *roof* is [rʊf] (with the same vowel sound
as *book*), while it is [ruf] (rhyming with *spoof*) in many other parts of the country.
Likewise, the addition of the [r] sound at the end of a word like *idea*, resulting
in the pronunciation [ai-diər] (as if it were spelled *ay-deer*), would sound quite
appropriate to a speaker from parts of New England. President Kennedy's pronunciation of Cuba as *Cuber* [kyu-bər] is another good example.

(As a reminder, we are using the IPA symbols described in Chapter 2, but we
have also approximated the intended pronunciations here using the traditional
alphabet.)

There are other dialects that drop the [r] sound at the end of words. While
they differ in other phonetic aspects, this happens in many southern dialects and
in some urban East Coast regions such as the working class speech of Boston
or New York City. With her southern Georgia dialect in *Gone with the Wind*,
Scarlett O'Hara pronounces her name without an [r] sound in her first name
and a weakened one in her last name. In the working class speech of Boston, you
can expect to hear the phrase, *Park your car in Harvard Square* without any [r]
sounds at all. You can hear an excellent example of this dialect with Matt Damon
and Ben Affleck's characters in the 1997 film *Good Will Hunting*.

MOD 5

A series of studies conducted in 1966 by linguist William Labov investigated the use and omission of the [r] sound in the pronunciation of shoppers in three different department stores in New York City. The department stores chosen were Saks Fifth Avenue (to elicit speech samples from the upper class), Macy's (to elicit those from the middle class), and the now defunct S. Klein (to elicit those from the working class). In each department store, the interviewer asked sales assistants where a particular item could be found (such as shoes), knowing that the answer would be *the fourth floor*. The retention of the [r] sounds in these two words was assumed to be a marker of the prestige dialect we are referring to as Standard American English. As you might guess, the most retention was observed in the Saks shoppers, and the least in S. Klein. The Macy's shoppers exhibited somewhat less retention than the Saks shoppers, but significantly more than those from S. Klein.

The term **isophone** refers to an imaginary line on a map that separates the use of one pronunciation from another. For example, one could envision an unseen line running somewhere along I-90 (the transcontinental freeway running from east to west across the northern portion of the United States) that separates the pronunciation of the word *college* as [kalIʤ] (with the first vowel sounding like the "a" in *father*) in Erie, Pennsylvania, from a pronunciation more like [kælIʤ] (with the first vowel sounding more like the "a" in *cat*) in Buffalo, New York. Another example involves the pronunciation of words such as *which* and *witch*. In some parts of the country, these two words begin with different sounds; the first begins with a [wʰ] sound, with a puff of air escaping from the lips, and the second with just the [w] sound, producing no puff of air. In other parts of the country, speakers make no distinction between the two words.

> This link takes you to a map that illustrates the isophone boundaries regarding the pronunciation of /wh/ vs. /w/ across the United States: http://www.ling.upenn.edu/phono_atlas/maps/Map8.html

Lexical Variants

If you want to start a lively conversation among people who come from various parts of the United States, ask them what word they use for a carbonated beverage, like a Pepsi or a Mountain Dew.

> There is even a website dedicated to the pop vs. soda controversy: http://www.popvssoda.com/

As this site attests, there are more possible answers across the United States than just *pop* or *soda*. When Dr. Williams first started graduate school at the University of Georgia in Athens, she became confused while ordering a Coke at a restaurant.

The server asked, "What kind of a Coke would you like?" She answered that she wanted a regular Coke (as opposed to a diet Coke.) The server then asked, "But what kind? A Sprite? An Orange Crush?" and looked at Dr. Williams expectantly. It was only later that a friend explained to her that the word *coke* is often used in the south as a generic term for what she would call *pop*. In this dialect, then, one could indeed order a Sprite coke, which was very marked to her.

These kinds of vocabulary differences occur all over the country, and cause the same kind of confusion for outsiders as the Coke experience caused Dr. Williams. Do you know what a *cabinet* is in Rhode Island? How about a *bubbler* in Wisconsin? And a *skeeter hawk* in the South Atlantic States? Unless you are from these areas yourself, you might not recognize a *cabinet* as a milkshake, a *bubbler* as a water fountain, and a *skeeter hawk* as a dragonfly. MOD 5

> The Dictionary of American Regional English (DARE) provides an interesting list of words used in different parts of the country.

An **isogloss** functions like an isophone, except the imaginary line refers to different vocabulary choices rather than different pronunciations. For example, you can envision another imaginary division somewhere along I-79 (a freeway running from north to south in the eastern United States) that separates the use of *rubber band* in Erie, Pennsylvania, from the use of *gumband* around the Pittsburgh area, just over 120 miles away. The *Pop* vs. *Soda* map, however, illustrates that the separation is not always clearly delineated, and pockets using one variant may exist geographically within an area that generally uses another.

To explore other lexical variants in American English, think about which terms you generally use for the following things. Do you use more than one in some cases, and if so, does it depend on context? Compare your answers with the class.

a. sack/bag (for groceries)
b. grocery cart/buggy
c. pail/bucket
d. pop/soda/soda pop/coke
e. bubbler/water fountain
f. cabinet/milkshake
g. rubber band, elastic, gum band
h. face cloth, wash cloth, wash rag
i. fireflies/ lightning bugs
j. dragonflies/darning needles
k. sprinkles, ants, jimmies, shots
l. sub, hero, grinder, hoagie, poor boy
m. faucet, tap, spigot
n. skillet/frying pan
o. see-saw/teeter-totter
p. cut school, skip school, play hooky

Can you match the following regional terms to their more common "standard" version? You can find the answers at the end of this chapter.

	1	davenport	a	shallow swamp or pond
	2	eavestrough	b	liquor store
	3	sweeper	c	something that catches rain on your roof
	4	nebby	d	hopscotch
	5	packie	e	chewing tobacco
	6	logan	f	closet
	7	potsy	g	whoopee pie or moon pie
	8	banquette	h	vacuum
	9	locker	i	nosy
	10	snooze	j	couch
	11	gob	k	sidewalk, foot-path

Morpho-Syntactic Variants

Morphology and syntax also differ between dialects, although less so than pronunciation or vocabulary. For example, it is perfectly acceptable in many parts of the Midwest and in various parts of the Mid-Atlantic Appalachian region to omit the verb *to be* in a sentence like *The lawn needs mowed.* As another example, in many southern dialects, it is not only acceptable but common to use double negatives in a sentence. There is also the use in the south of what are called double modal auxiliary verbs, as in *Yes, we might could go* as opposed to using either *might* or *could* alone. And finally, in the Upper Midwest, especially Minnesota, the phrase *Do you want to come with?* has no need for an object at the end of the sentence.

MOD S

While various socio-historical and linguistic explanations account for dialect differences, we often tend to focus on geography. There are some linguistic variants that are more widely known, or at least more widely stereotyped than others. With what area of the country do you associate these phrases? What exactly is the linguistic alternate in question (phonetic, syntactic, or lexical)? After the entire class has a chance to guess on each, you can check the answers listed at the end of the chapter.

	Phrase	Geographical Location
1.	Hey, Y'all!	
2.	Dude, that's an awesome wave!	
3.	Yo, fugeddaboudit!	

4.	Yinz have a gumband I can borrow?	
5.	The eavestrough on the roof needs cleaned.	
6.	If it quits a-rainin', we might could go.	
7.	Let's go to the ice cream parlor and get a cabinet.	
8.	Are you in line for the bubbler?	
9.	Grandma got a new davenport last week.	.
10.	That grinder was wicked good!	

The web resources listed at the end of this chapter will help you if you'd like to further research specific dialects, like the Mid-Atlantic dialects, Appalachian English, southern Californian, or "Pittsburghese."

English as a World Language

We noted at the beginning of this section that sociolinguists and laypersons alike take interest in noting differences in the speech patterns of people from different geographical regions. With the concepts of *standard* and *dialect* firmly in mind, we can explore the basic dialect divisions of present-day English as an example familiar to most students reading this book. It is the mother tongue to some-where between 310 and 380 million people, ranking it as number three in the list of languages spoken as a first language. (Mandarin tops the list of number of native language speakers, followed by Spanish.)

Without a doubt, English is truly a world language, spoken to some extent by an estimated one billion people. One could also claim that it is the most influential language. It is the dominant language of business, and is the official language of international aviation, science, diplomacy and various other major fields such as music and literature. Thanks to mass media, it has spread to all but the most remote corners of the planet, for better or for worse.

> The website for Ethnologue provides an extensive list of languages where English is spoken, from American Samoa to Zimbabwe: http://www.ethnologue.com/

Perhaps the first major dialect division that comes to mind when you consider English would be between England and the United States. Great Britain has its own issues with the idea of standard, with the label Received Pronunciation being given to the socially-esteemed variety. Within the British Isles, however, there are many subdivisions, such as Welsh English or Scottish English. This is the same of all major dialect divisions of English, such as European, North American, Caribbean, Asian, African, and Oceanic, which includes Australia and New Zealand.

In North America, the two largest divisions are Canadian and American. Within American English, the major divisions are often labeled as Northeastern, Mid-Atlantic, Midwestern, Southern, and Western, sometimes with Native American (or Amerindian) English as its own category. While these broad categories might suffice for English speakers in other countries as they attempt to distinguish our various dialects, anyone living in New England can tell if someone is from Boston or Baltimore after hearing just a few words. The same goes for the Midwest; people in St. Louis wouldn't find the North Dakota dialect so humorous in the movie *Fargo* if it didn't sound so different to their ears. We can also predict that few people born and raised speaking English in the United States would confuse the Texan speech of former President George W. Bush with that of former President Jimmy Carter from rural Georgia, although they both speak Southern dialects.

Dialects in Other Languages

Like with English, all languages have multiple dialects. Linguistic equality aside, each language also faces the issue of which dialect(s) is/are socially preferred. The Spanish language provides one example of how a prestige dialect was established by those with political power; during the period of the Spanish Inquisition, the Catholic King Ferdinand and Queen Isabella enforced their Castilian dialect throughout all of Spain, along with their religion. Indeed, the word *Castilian* is used by some as a synonym of *Spanish*. Yet it was not this dialect that took root in Latin America, but rather Andalusian, the southern Spain dialect spoken by many of the Conquistadors.

Similar situations occurred in other languages. During the powerful Qing Dynasty, beginning in 1644, Mandarin Chinese was chosen over six other major dialects, although drawing the line between dialect and language is particularly problematic with Chinese. While the different language varieties are many times referred to as dialects, many do not share mutual intelligibility. For this reason, many linguists prefer to label them as distinct languages.

In the case of French, Parisian French may be what is generally taught in foreign language courses, but Canadian French speakers (including Dr. Remillard, a bi-dialectical speaker) will be quick to defend their dialect as equally capable of communicating meaning.

One example of dialect differences in French is that Canadian-French uses more single vowel sounds and diphthongs than French spoken in France. There are also variations in lexical items between the two dialects, especially in the Anglicisms (words borrowed from English) that are adopted into French. In France you see many anglicisms with the *-ing* suffix (standing, parking, etc.), while in Canada the Anglicisms are often due to cultural products in North America, such as *bécosse* coming from backhouse. Many French Canadian car mechanics have never known the French words for car products (tools, car parts, etc.) since these used to all come from the USA and English Canada.

Not all prestige dialects belong to one geographical region. When one speaks of Standard Arabic, for example, it is a matter of formality rather than geography; the formal written version is fairly uniform across the Arabic-speaking world, but spoken dialects vary significantly. With Standard Norwegian, the distinction is one of social class, with the prestige dialect being spoken mainly by the middle and upper classes.

Many times, specific dialects are only discernible to people who speak those languages well. You would likely have difficulty determining what part of Japan was home to a classmate who spoke Japanese unless you had personal experience with Japanese speakers from more than one area of Japan. Vice versa, your Japanese classmate might not easily distinguish pronunciation differences between a professor from Texas and one from New York City, even though this would likely be very obvious to you.

Below is a brief sampling of phonetic, lexical, and morpho-syntactic variants from dialects of various languages.

Phonetic Variants

Pronunciation differences between dialects occur in almost all languages. A notable one in Latin American Spanish is the use of the allophones [ʒ] (or sometimes [ʃ]) for the phoneme /y/ in Argentina and some other parts of southern South America. The [ʒ] allophone represents the sound you hear in the middle of words like *pleasure*, and the [ʃ] is the sound the letters "sh" make in the word *shoe*. Thus, *Yo me llamo Yolanda* is pronounced as [ʒo-me- ʒa-mo- ʒo-lan-da] in Argentina but as [yo-me-ya-mo-yo-lan-da] in most other Spanish-speaking countries. Since this distinction would not diminish mutual intelligibility, we would label [ʒ] and [y] as allophones, rather than phonemes, which you learned about in Chapter 2.

MOD 5   In French-Canadian dialects, you have a choice between pronouncing the word *oi* as [we] (almost like the English word *way*) and the more prestigious [wa]. For instance, you could say the word *moi* as either [mwe] or [mwa], but both still mean *me*. The [mwe] pronunciation was the standard in France until the French Revolution, but it continues to this day in many French Canadian dialects.

Lexical Variants

Vocabulary choices can distinguish dialects as well. In Spanish, one has to be very careful when talking about catching a bus. The appropriate verb in Castilian Spanish (Spain) is *coger*, but this same verb used in many parts of Latin America
MOD 5   translates to a more vulgar version of the phrase *to have sex*.

A similarly tricky situation could occur between a Japanese speaker from Tokyo and one from Osaka. In both locations, the word *aho* is used. While the word means *idiot* or *fool* in both dialects, it is sometimes used as a term of endearment in the Kansai dialect of Osaka, just as *silly* can be used affectionately in American English. In Tokyo, it would be an insult, as only the most negative connotation would be assumed.

Morpho-Syntactic Variants

In Caribbean Spanish, a pronoun often precedes a noun in a question, such as *¿Qué tú necesitas?* (*What do you need?*) instead of the standard *¿Qué necesitas tú?* MUD 5 Most Spanish speakers from outside the Caribbean see this as marked, or even stigmatized.

Canadian French uses the linguistic interrogative form meaning *what Que c'est qu'il* for *Qu'est-ce qu'il*. In France they use this latter interrogative form in exclamations such as *Qu'est-ce qu'il fait beau!* meaning *How beautiful it is!* for the more standard form *Comme il fait beau* or *Qu'il fait beau!*

The Persistence of Dialects

It is somewhat remarkable that regional dialects have survived even though our society is a highly mobile one. Mass media has reached all but the most remote corners of the United States, providing similar linguistic input to people across the country, and yet differences in pronunciation, vocabulary, and grammatical usage remain, and have even increased. Perhaps the strongest argument that could be made for the maintenance of regional speech is that, as you already know, dialect is intimately connected to identity. Human nature leads us to seek both similarities and differences between ourselves and those around us, but our social tendency is to identify with people who are like us. From ancient tribes to modern towns, people have banded together and congregated with others who share the same background.

Most of us have strong feelings about the people and places that have been important in our development, even if we eventually leave those people and places. People often retain at least some aspects of their home dialects, as language can be one of the ways we maintain ties to our identity in terms of heritage. You may have experienced this yourself, encountering people who can guess where you are from based on only a few minutes of conversation. This is yet another example of the intertwining paths of language and identity. People who are raised in a number of places may employ traits from more than one dialect, but often consciously or subconsciously adapt their speech to match the people around them. When they are successful in their modifications, their communication is interpreted as unmarked, and their interlocutors can say, "You're one of us."

Where we are born and/or raised can play a major role in forming our linguistic and social identity. However, we are not necessarily bound to our geography. Sometimes people have specific reasons for avoiding certain aspects of their natural dialect. One reason might be wanting to fit in with a group of people from another geographical origin, such as a college student who attends a school in another part of the country from where he was raised. Indeed, many people who are particularly attuned to pronunciation tend to imitate those around them; while this can be misinterpreted as mocking, the person usually doesn't even know it is happening. There are also cases where people might strive to speak in a way that does not immediately reveal their origin at all, such as a person applying for a news broadcasting job at a major network. (You will remember that there is no such thing as a truly neutral dialect, but an avoidance of particularly distinctive traits can create that illusion.) Conversely, there are times when people might want to enhance their dialectical traits to demonstrate pride in their origins, or even to deliberately separate their identity from others in the group.

Indeed, we can consciously choose to play up or play down our dialect depending on our surroundings and interlocutors. Let's say that the aforementioned college student was a young woman from Pittsburgh who was attending a college in Minneapolis. When at school, she could avoid certain linguistic traits that would make her speech stand out, or marked (such as using *yinz* for the second person plural pronoun or the word *gumband* instead of *rubber band*) and then return to using these variants during breaks back at home.

The same holds true for actors who are required to speak in dialects other than their own for a particular role. Take Nicole Kidman, whose Australian accent is not obvious in most films, unless she is portraying someone from that country, of course. When she is speaking naturally during interviews, however, it is quite noticeable. Some movies specifically focus on the idea of dialect shifting, both through characters who decide to assimilate to others around them, and those who choose not to. In the movie *Bringing down the House* (with Steve Martin and Queen Latifah), Queen Latifah's character says that she knows standard English but chooses not to use it, preferring to use African American English as a badge of her identity.

Conclusion

- Our language choices are influenced by many socio-historical factors.
- Our dialects are an integral part of our identity, and help shape our view of the world. They can give us a sense of belonging, connecting us to our families, and even linking us to our ancestors.

- We are not necessarily limited to speaking one dialect for our entire life. The most important factor in determining how closely we adhere to a specific dialect (geographical or otherwise) is our will. As with all aspects of our personalities, we are an amalgamation of both nature and nurture; our speech patterns are strongly influenced by the social factors of our youth, but we can also use language to demonstrate the alliances we wish to retain.

In the following chapter, we will examine how ethnicity shapes our language usage. Like geography and other socio-historical factors discussed in this chapter, ethnicity plays an important role in forming our dialect, and in turn, our identity.

Answers to In-Class Activity on Lexical Variants

j	Midwest	1	davenport	a	shallow swamp or pond
c	Midwest and various other regions	2	eavestrough	b	liquor store
h	Pittsburgh, PA, among other eastern regions	3	sweeper	c	something that catches rain on your roof
i	Pittsburgh, among other eastern regions	4	nebby	d	hopscotch
b	New England	5	packie	e	chewing tobacco
a	Northern New England	6	logan	f	closet
d	New York City Area, including adjacent New Jersey and Connecticut	7	potsy	g	whoopee pie or moon pie (a type of baked goods)
k	Louisiana	8	banquette	h	vacuum
f	Louisiana	9	locker	i	nosy
e	Pacific Northwest	10	snoose	j	couch
g	Western Pennsylvania	11	gob	k	sidewalk, foot-path

Answers to In-Class Activity on Dialects

1. Southern United States
2. Southern California
3. NYC (Italian-influence)
4. Pittsburgh, PA
5. Canada and the Upper Midwest
6. Southern United States
7. Rhode Island
8. Wisconsin
9. Midwest, Adirondack Mountains
10. Boston, MA

Additional Activities

1. Listen to at least 15 minutes of a national newscast (NBC, CNN, Fox News, etc.). Did you hear any linguistic features that would make you think the newscaster was from a particular part of the country? Do the same with a local newscast. Were your results similar or different? Explain your answer.

2. Over the period of a few days, try to observe situations where you modify your dialect to fit the occasion. For example, do you use different words with your family than you might while speaking to college classmates or roommates from different places? Are you ever "accused" of having an accent at school, but then chided by your family for speaking differently when you come home? Write as much as you can about the changes, analyzing when and why they happen, and what aspects of your speech you change. Are there ever instances where someone makes a comment about you changing your dialect?

3. Conduct additional online research on the major dialects of a language other than English. It could be a language you are studying, or one you know very little about.

Additional Web Resources

- The American Dialect Society is a great starting point for researching American dialects: http://www.americandialect.org/
- The "Do You Speak American?" website includes an entire section on dialects: http://www.pbs.org/speak/seatosea/
- This site also provides visitors the chance to take "quizzes" to test their ability to recognize speech from different parts of the United States. Try these for starters:
    - http://www.pbs.org/speak/seatosea/americanvarieties/map/map.html
    - http://www.pbs.org/speak/seatosea/americanvarieties/DARE/wordpower/dare.html
- To listen to speech samples of many dialects of U.S. English, visit this site: http://web.ku.edu/~idea/northamerica/usa/usa.htm
- Dr. Barbara Johnstone, Professor of Linguistics and Rhetoric at Carnegie Mellon University, and Dr. Scott F. Kiesling, Associate Professor of Linguistics at the University of Pittsburgh's study of the Western Pennsylvania Dialect can be found at this website: http://kearneyclan.org/html/western_pa_dialect.html
- Do accent reduction programs help in the workplace? http://www.tustinspeech.com/htdocs/accent/chicagotribune.htm

For Further Reading

Wolfram, W., and Schilling-Estes, N. (2005) *American English: Dialects and Variation*, 2nd edn. Malden, MA: Blackwell.
Wolfram, W., and Ward, B. (2005). *American Voices*. Malden, MA: Blackwell.

Chapter 11

Language and Ethnicity

> In this chapter, we will consider the relationship between language and ethnicity. We will focus in particular on African American English, from both a linguistic and a societal point of view.

It's hilarious a lot of times. You have a conversation with someone, and he's like, "You speak so well!" I'm like, "What do you mean? Do you understand that's an insult?" (Jay-Z, hip-hop musician/producer)

Introduction

In the previous chapters, we have addressed how certain social variables affect the way we speak. Another variable that can influence speech patterns is *ethnicity*. This term can be related to *race*, but the terms are not interchangeable, as ethnicity can be shaped by cultural, linguistic, religious, or territorial characteristics, as well as racial. The Hispanics or Latinos of the United States and the Spanish speaking world are a good example of this, as there are representatives of every race within this ethnic group. (Think about the differences in physical appearance between the singer Shakira of Colombia and actress Zoe Saldana with parents from both Puerto Rico and the Dominican Republic.) Perhaps more importantly, even the very concept of race has fallen into disfavor as scientists in a variety of fields continue to find evidence that racial boundaries do not fit biological reality.

Ethnicity is also separate from nationality, although the two may coincide. Two prominent examples today are Iraq, a country that houses warring groups of people who speak different languages and practice different religions, and the Darfur region of western Sudan, which is experiencing a conflict among multiple groups, tragically resulting in mass genocide.

The truth of the matter is that ethnicity, nationality, and language seldom line up neatly. A particularly good example of this can be seen with the ethnic Tajiks, who speak Tajiki, but can be found living in Tajikistan, Afghanistan and Uzbekistan, all countries in central Asia. Tajikistan is a multilingual nation, with Tajiki being only one of 11 languages spoken there. It is, however, the official or national language there. Afghanistan has two official national languages, neither of which is Tajiki, and houses speakers of about 46 other languages. Uzbekistan encompasses nine languages, with Uzbek being the national language. To further confuse things, there are subgroups of ethnic Tajiks living in each of those countries who speak languages other than Tajik. Some Afghani Tajiks are now refugees living in Iran and Pakistan, and there are some small groups in other countries as well.

African American English

Scientific controversies aside, the terms *ethnicity* and *race* have often been closely linked, such as in the case of **African American English** (AAE). Often referred to as *Ebonics* in the media, African American English has been a topic of intense controversy in recent years. The very fact that it has been referred to by so many labels (Black English, Black English Vernacular, African American English, African American English Vernacular, Ebonics, etc.) is testament to the discomfort we have discussing it as a society.

Linguists, however, have been studying AAE as a legitimate language variety for decades, with increased intensity in the years following the American civil rights movements of the 1960s. In early research, it was described in terms of distinct linguistic features, much like any other dialect, although the label often used at that time, *Negro Non-Standard English*, suggested something less than total objectivity.

In regard to the early usage of AAE, one obstacle for researchers is that there are very few written records. Masters were hardly interested in documenting the linguistic behavior of their slaves, and it was illegal for the slaves themselves to learn to read and write. In recent years, however, letters written by semi-literate ex-slaves in the mid-1800s have surfaced, as well as some audio recordings, providing first-hand accounts. Additional evidence has come from the oral tradition of spirituals and stories that have been passed down from one generation to the next. Unfortunately, other impediments to the objective collection of early linguistic data were ignorance and racism, aspects that continue to taint public opinion of the dialect to this day.

Linguists agree that the origins of AAE trace back to the slaves brought to the United States from disparate geographical areas of West Africa. The different geographical regions, of course, represented distinct cultures and languages, with many inhabitants speaking multiple languages and/or dialects. When the slaves arrived on U.S. shores, they were often grouped with speakers of other African languages, creating the need for a pidgin language to be used for basic verbal interaction between slaves, as well as between slaves and their masters. A **pidgin** is a simplified language meant to facilitate communication between people who do not share a common language. It is less complex phonetically, grammatically and lexically than an actual language, although it shares traits with the languages that have come into contact with each other. A pidgin is essentially a stop-gap solution. It is never learned as a first language; if a pidgin form is passed along to the next generation as a mother tongue, it is then considered a **creole**, and it will reflect more linguistic complexity than a pidgin. (More explanation and examples of specific pidgins and creoles will be discussed in Chapter 13.)

In the origins of AAE, the various West African languages mixed with each other, and with English. A matter of controversy among linguists is the exact pattern of mixing that occurred. Some believe that the slaves were exposed to two varieties of English: that of their southern masters, and that of the Scots-Irish indentured servants that often labored beside them. Others point out that many traits of AAE are shared by other creoles spoken by blacks around the world, and some contend that many traits of West African languages remain in AAE, such as the use of the copulative verb *to be*, such as in *I be here* (though there is also discord on that point), as well as the prevalence of double negation. Whatever the true origin of AAE may be, it is further complicated by the fact that it has changed over time just like any other language variety.

We shall now take a closer look at modern AAE, which is arguably one of the most researched dialects in the United States. Many linguists believe that the dialect has become more ethnically-based than regionally-based, meaning that in the twenty-first century, there are fewer variations between speakers living in different regions of the country than we see with other dialects. While geographical mobility has increased for African Americans over time, a degree of social segregation often remains, creating a need for establishing a stronger ethnic identity that reaches beyond geographical location. As with any other dialect, speakers can demonstrate solidarity through its maintenance. The continued vitality of AAE is testament to the desire to sustain a distinct African American culture.

This being said, it is important to remember that not all African Americans speak AAE, and not all AAE speakers are African American. As referenced in the previous chapter, Tiger Woods displays few, if any, traits of AAE when he speaks, while white rapper Eminem speaks an "urban" dialect, with many traits of AAE. In Eminem's case, he associates himself with black culture, and thus, essentially adopts this ethnicity. Within the entire population of AAE speakers, some use this dialect all the time, while others use it only in certain contexts. Many can easily "code-switch" between AAE and Standard English depending on the situation. (**Code-switching** will be discussed in detail in Chapter 13. For now, consider what you learned in the previous chapter on dialects: a parallel to this code-switching would be a person from the Deep South who uses a southern dialect with friends and family, but a less-marked variety while working as a television newscaster.) Sometimes this switch is intentional, but sometimes speakers alter their own speech without consciously thinking about it. Someone who has deliberately used this to his advantage is President Barack Obama. During both of his campaigns, he used more AAE traits when speaking to groups including more African Americans than when he spoke to groups including more white constituents.

> Read this brief article for more information concerning President Obama's use of code-switching in and out of AAE, and how it mirrors other people switching dialects in various contexts: http://gawker.com/5948541/the-art-of-the-code+switch-obama-morphs-for-his-audience-just-like-you-do

The following are a few general characteristics of AAE, but we would encourage you to visit the links listed at the end of the chapter for more detailed information.

Phonetic Characteristics

You will recall from Chapter 2 that phonetics deals with pronunciation differences. The first phonetic trait of AAE we will analyze is the reduction of consonant clusters at the end of words. While this phenomenon occurs in all dialects of English during relaxed speech, AAE uses it in contexts where other dialects do not, such as at the end of an utterance. (Remember that you can refer to the International Phonetic Alphabet chart in Chapter 2 if you wish, but if your instructor has chosen not to incorporate the IPA symbols into your course, the accompanying descriptions should help you "hear" the sound in your mind.)

Examples:
We got a <u>test</u>?   [tɛs] (like the name *Tess*)
It's really <u>cold</u>!   [kol] (like *coal*)
That's a bad <u>word</u>.   [wʌr] (like *were*)

The second phonetic trait deals with postvocalic /-r/ (an r that follows a vowel), which is deleted more frequently in AAE than in other dialects of English. One rather infamous example would be the pronunciation of the word *whore* as [ho], which has even changed its popular spelling to *ho*.

The third phonetic trait we will examine is the modification of the **interdental fricatives**, which are consonant sounds that are made with the tongue between the teeth. In English, we use the letters "th" to represent these sounds, but they actually represent two distinct phonemes: [ð] (as in *th̲y*) is a voiced sound, meaning your vocal cords vibrate, and [θ] (as in *th̲igh*) is the unvoiced version, where your vocal cords do not vibrate. You can easily feel this difference if you pronounce both of them with your hand placed lightly on your throat. They are both considered fricative sounds, because the air is not completely stopped when you pronounce the sound, but there is considerable friction as air leaves your mouth.

In AAE, the **voiced interdental fricative** [ð] (again as in *thy*) often becomes the **alveolar** [d], as in *Dad*. In the alveolar [d], your tongue touches the bony alveolar ridge behind your teeth. The voiced interdental fricative [ð], on the other hand, is made when you place your tongue between your teeth.

> That [dæt] ain't right ([dæt] rhymes with *cat*).

In the middle of a word, the **unvoiced interdental fricative** [θ] may be pronounced as the **unvoiced labiodental fricative** [f]. You already know that an unvoiced sound is one in which your vocal cords do not vibrate, and fricative means that the air is not completely stopped, but there is tension as the air leaves the mouth. The *labiodental* portion of the term means that you use your upper teeth and bottom lip to create the sound, as *father*.

> I got nothing [nʌfɪn] to say ([nʌfɪn] rhymes with *muffin*).

When there is a **voiced interdental fricative** [ð] in the middle of a word, it may be pronounced in AAE as the **voiced labiodental fricative** [v], the sound you hear in *very*.

> Don't bother [bavər] her now. (basically like *bother*, but with a "v" in the middle)

The final phonetic trait to be mentioned here is the tendency to reverse two sounds, like we see with the consonant cluster [sk] at the end of words, resulting in the pronunciation of *ask* as [æks], which would sound identical to the word *axe* to non AAE speakers. It is interesting to note that this example in particular seems to elicit very negative reactions, though we know this is a value judgement that is not linguistically justifiable. You may have also heard speakers of this dialect pronounce *officer* as if it were spelled "occifer." This process of inverting sounds within a word, known as **metathesis**, occurs in many languages and dialects.

As with the *ask/axe* example above, these changes are sometimes (but not always) stigmatized; you may have heard someone chastised for pronouncing *foliage* more like *foilage* or *nuclear* as [nu-kyɪ-lər], as if it were spelled something like *nu-kyi-lar*. The stigmatization of pronouncing *ask* as [æks] (*axe*) is particularly ironic, as this pronunciation was actually the one that developed first. Chaucer used it in his writing, as did others until after the fourteenth century. At that point, the process of metathesis eventually changed the accepted pronunciation to [æsk] (*ask*). In other words, it was not AAE speakers that changed the accepted standard; they simply continued to use the earlier pronunciation. This provides yet another example of how arbitrary the creation of our currently accepted "standard" has been.

Sadly, these pronunciations are still seen by some as lazy or uneducated speech. As mentioned above, however, metathesis is a natural part of the evolution of many languages and dialects. Sometimes, this change is adopted on a large scale. For example, the French word for cheese, *fromage*, began as the Medieval Latin *formaticum*. Other times, metathesis is something that distinguishes one dialect from another; some dialects of Turkish are known for having more metathesis than others. In some languages, the process of metathesis is not only accepted, but required; the Fur language, spoken by the Fur of Darfur in western Sudan, uses metathesis as an integral part of its morphological system.

Metathesis has also played a role in the development of the English language. Below are examples of currently used English words and pronunciations, preceded by their earlier representations. Can you identify the specific sound change that has occurred in each?

Old English	Modern English
bryd	bird
hros	horse
wæps	wasp
thridda	third

Morpho-Syntactic Characteristics

The word-final consonant cluster reduction described earlier can sometimes lead to variations in morphology, which, as you'll recall, deals with the formation words. An example would be the word *desk*, which as a singular noun would be pronounced in AAE as [dɛs], while the plural version, *desks*, would become [dɛsɪs] (*desses*). This is the pattern that occurs in SE (Standard English) when pluralizing a noun that ends in /s/; *dress* made plural becomes [drɛsɪz]. Hence, *desks* in AAE is pronounced with the same "-es" [ɪz] ending as *dresses*.

Perhaps the most notable syntactic trait of AAE is its use of the copulative verb *to be*. The unconjugated *be* is generally used to mark habitual actions, as in *He always be here*, and *We be sitting here every day*. You may have heard a song popularized by Club Nouveau in the mid 1980s called "Lean on Me" where the lyrics *We be jammin'* occur multiple times. The omission of the *to be* verb, on the other hand, usually occurs in statements referring to the present moment, such as *We talking right now*.

Another example of a syntactic variable occurs with the past tense form of the verb *to do*. In AAE, it is used to indicate that an action has been finished, as in *I done broke my finger*. Curiously, this past tense can also precede another past tense verb to refer to an event that is to be completed in the future, such as *You be done rested by the time vacation ends*.

The absence of the third person singular subject-verb agreement found in Standard English is another characteristic of AAE:

> SE: She writes good.
> AAE: She write good.

A fifth trait of AAE is the use of *I'ma* as a future marker. As you may guess, it is basically a contraction of the phrase *I am going to*.

> I'ma be somebody someday.

Our last feature is the use of double negatives. Double negatives are used in other dialects of English as well, as seen in *I ain't gonna go*, where *ain't* is a contraction of *I am not*. With AAE, *ain't* is also substituted for *didn't*, as in *I ain't do nothing to you*.

The following sentences are taken from *The Immortal Life of Henrietta Lacks*, an award-winning non-fiction book by Rebecca Skloot. Identify as many AAE grammatical traits as you can.

1. ...I never known nothin different.
2. I don't wanna know where he buried...
3. You got to remember, times was different.
4. I hope he burn in hell.
5. But I always have thought it was strange, if our mother cells done so much for medicine, how come her family can't afford to see no doctors? Don't make no sense.

Lexical Characteristics

When many people listen to rap music, their attention is likely drawn to the lyrics. They may focus on the use of unfamiliar words, rhyme schemes, or the use of slang or taboo language. Particular consideration has been given to what are perceived as misogynist and violent lyrics. This has led to many people mistakenly equating the term *slang* to AAE. You may have heard someone making disparaging remarks about the Ebonics used in rap and hip-hop music, citing the negative effects such language has on today's youth.

What they are referencing, however, is not African American English; they are simply stating their disapproval of words that are meant to denigrate women and promote violent behavior. To confuse these word choices with those of an entire language variety is inaccurate and can contribute to racial prejudice.

Words that do form a part of the AAE lexicon include terms associated with the jazz culture, such as *cat* (derived from a Wolof suffix *–kat*, meaning a person), *dig* (from the Wolof *dega*, meaning to understand or appreciate), and *hip* (from the Wolof *hepi*, meaning to understand what's going on). A phrase common among jazz musicians in the early twentieth century would be *That cat be hip,* *can you dig it?* Some food-related words that have been adopted from AAE into mainstream English (like *banana, yam, okra,* and *gumbo*) have roots in West African languages and culinary culture.

Public Opinion and Politics

As with any other dialect, all linguistic variants in AAE are systematic. While linguists and sociolinguists agree that it is at least a dialect of English, if not a separate language, much of the general public remains ignorant of its legitimacy. It is often considered to be at best poor grammar, and at worst, a deficiency requiring speech therapists or special education teachers to rectify. Politicians, celebrities, and other public figures have decried its existence in general and in particular its use in schools.

One of the greatest controversies regarding AAE in schools originated in the Oakland School District in California in 1996 and 1997 when the school board passed resolutions recognizing what they labeled *Ebonics* as the primary language of African American children, placing it on par with languages such as Spanish and Chinese as a separate language. In this view, Ebonics speakers would essentially be learning English as a Second Language. The fundamental goal of the school board was to improve the poor academic performance of their African American students. They believed that by legitimizing Ebonics as a language, students would feel less marginalized, and teachers would be more sensitive to the language the students were bringing to the classroom.

It was the school board's hope that this increased sensitivity would result from making non-Ebonics speaking teachers more familiar with it, and in turn encouraging them to use this familiarity to make bridges between Ebonics and Standard English. They likened it to what the English as a Second Language teachers were doing with Spanish-speaking students, or any other students having a home language other than English. Like with the existing English as a Second Language program already in place, the end goal would still be to transition students to speaking Standard English, at least in the school setting.

While this was an admirable goal, the labeling of Ebonics as a separate language from English (especially in the original resolution which labeled it a "genetically-based language") caused unexpected problems for the school board. A number of misconceptions arose from the public regarding the school board's true intentions, fueled in part by the media and non-linguist celebrities. Many parents believed that all teachers would be forced to learn Ebonics, and the teachers would then force all the students in the school district to learn it. There was also the false assumption that students who did speak Ebonics would never be encouraged to learn Standard English in the classroom, thus leaving them unprepared for their future academic and professional lives.

Despite clarification attempts by the school board, numerous testimonies given by linguists at board meetings and eventually even in front of the U.S. Senate, along with a resolution from the Linguistic Society of America approving Oakland's attempts to recognize Ebonics as legitimate, the controversy continued. An amended resolution removed the phrase "genetically-based," but maintained that Ebonics was a language separate from English. It upheld the intent of the board to implement an academic program aimed at teaching Standard English to African American students, while still respecting their home language as legitimate. It also removed or revised any wording that made it sound like they were intending to teach students Ebonics. Unfortunately, but perhaps not surprisingly, controversy over the matter exists to this day. If you would like to research this further, you will find relevant sources at the end of this chapter.

Pragmatic Choices

Completely separate from the issue of linguistic legitimacy is the issue of practicality. While there is no linguistic justification for labeling AAE as sub-standard, it is, regrettably, often viewed that way by the general public. Even people who recognize its validity as a dialect question its use in academic or professional situations. There is no denying that speakers of this dialect (or any non-prestige dialect) have been subjected to prejudice, leading to instances of denial of educational, occupational, socioeconomic, and social opportunities.

For this reason, many AAE speakers choose to shift between dialects depending on the context, using more traits of the AAE dialect in informal situations, and fewer traits in formal settings such as in school or at a job. It is true that some parents, teachers, and other caretakers fear that allowing children to speak AAE will harm their chances of success in life, and indeed, some encourage children to abandon their home dialect completely. A more balanced approach, however, would be to use context to determine the degree of adherence to a dialect considered to be less marked in some situations. What is important to remember is that this could be said of speakers of any other less socially-favored dialect, such as Appalachian English or Texas English. The fact that not many people draw this parallel is further proof that AAE speakers face more than just prejudice based on their speech.

Conclusion

- African American English is a legitimate language variety with its own history and evolution.
- It is not lazy, uneducated, or inferior English, and it does not directly correlate to slang, taboo language, rap or hip-hop.

- Most linguists agree it is a dialect rather than a language, but there is some debate as to whether it descended from a mix of African languages only, or from the mixing of these languages with certain dialects of English.
- AAE shows systematic phonetic, morpho-syntactic, and lexical variants, many of which are shared with West African languages.
- Not all people who speak AAE are African American, and not all African Americans speak AAE. Like speakers of any other dialect, many choose to "dialect-shift" depending on the context of the communication. The degree of these shifts can reflect social and ethnic allegiance, or simply be decisions made for practical purposes. Either way, it is a speech variety as worthy of pride as any.

Our next chapter investigates the role that another social factor, gender, plays in language usage. As with previous chapters, we will look at both American culture and cultures around the world.

Additional Activities

1. What specific linguistic traits of AAE do you see in this passage? You should find phonetic traits (some words are written in IPA to illustrate how the speaker pronounced them), and grammatical traits. List as many as you can find, including phonetic, morph-syntactic, and lexical variants. (Sound descriptions of the IPA symbols are included below the passage.)

    > Miss Roth [raf] always be yelling [yɛ-lIn] at me about how I act in class. Last [læs] week she asked [æks] me if I took her keys from her desk [dɛs], but I tell her I ain't done nothin' and she don't [don] know what she talkin' about. She try to break me. Ain't nobody can bring me down like that [dæt]. I'ma show her she wrong.

[raf] = rhymes with *cough*	[dɛs] = rhymes with *dress*
[yɛ-lIn] = rhymes with *melon*	[don] = rhymes with *drone*
[læs] = like *lass*	[dæt] = rhymes with *bat*
[æks] = like *axe*	

2. One particularly disturbing example of how we use speech to make judgments about people is described in the section on linguistic profiling in the *Do You Speak American?* public television program and website. Listen to this audio clip from National Public Radio about an African American man trying to rent an apartment: http://www.npr.org/templates/story/story. php?storyId=1128513. Then write a 1-2 paragraph reaction to it. If you are personally aware of any instances of linguistic profiling, make sure to mention that as well.

3. Select a rap song that includes traits of African American English and translate it to Standard English.

4. In the early twentieth century, black writers associated with the "Harlem Renaissance" broke tradition and started using ethnic language in their writing rather than Standard American English. You can find links to some of the greatest literary works of this period at: http://www.pbs.org/speak/seatosea/ powerprose/harlem/. Choose your favorite, and identify all the AAE linguistic traits you observe.

Web Resources

-   The *Do You Speak American?* website has an excellent section on AAE: http://www.pbs.org/speak/seatosea/americanvarieties/AAVE
-   Here is a very approachable non-academic commentary that covers

historical, linguistic, and political aspects of AAE: http://www.plaid-der.com/ebonics.htm

- This is an excellent essay by sociolinguist John Rickford on the Oak-land Resolution: http://www.stanford.edu/~rickford/papers/Ebonics InMyBackyard.html
- *Dialect Education: Not Only for Oakland* by Carolyn Adger is another good assessment of the situation and its applications to other situations: http://www.cal.org/resources/archive/news/199703/9703Dialect. html

Further Reading

Alim, S., and Smitherman, G. (2012). *Articulate While Black: Barack Obama, Language, and Race in the U.S.* Oxford: Oxford University Press.

Green, L. J. (2002). *African American English: A Linguistic Introduction.* Cambridge: Cambridge University Press.

Rickford, J.R. (2000). *Spoken Soul: The Story of Black English.* New York: Wiley.

Chapter 12

Gender

> This chapter will highlight the relationships between language and gender, including grammatical gender, gender-biased language, myths and truths about the language usage of men and women in American culture, and gender's effect on language usage in other cultures.

When a man gives his opinion, he's a man. When a woman gives her opinion, she's a bitch (Bette Davis).

Introduction

Do women talk more than men do? Can men put their feelings into words? Do women not listen to men, or do men not listen to women? American culture is full of myths surrounding the language usage of women and men, and while the details vary, the same is true of all cultures. What the general public believes about gender's effect on language is often very different from what sociolinguistic studies have found, but as Bette Davis implies in the quote above, the public's opinions are difficult to change.

To test your own preliminary notions, answer the following questions honestly by circling YES or NO. Then quickly compare your answers with those of a classmate. Each of these questions will be addressed in this chapter, so you'll have opportunities to discuss your thoughts further.

1. Women talk more than men do.	YES	NO
2. Women interrupt more than men do.	YES	NO
3. Women can't accept compliments.	YES	NO
4. Women can't "get to the point" or just say what they mean.	YES	NO
5. Women have better grammar than men.	YES	NO
6. Men don't listen to women.	YES	NO
7. Men can't express their feelings verbally.	YES	NO
8. Men swear more than women do.	YES	NO

Before continuing, we must distinguish between **grammatical gender, physical gender (sex)**, and **socialized gender roles**. Grammatical gender, as it does not apply to modern English, will be discussed in the sections on other languages and cultures. While a full discussion is outside the scope of this text, the concept of "gender" has been broadened in recent years, encouraging us to consider gender identification as a spectrum rather than a binary system. This is very important, and will be addressed to some extent in this chapter. For this introductory-level text, however, we will mostly work within the framework of what has been delineated as male and female language use. There are web resources listed at the end of this chapter that deal with the growing field of research on gender identification and language usage.

The true/false questions you just answered have to do with how different genders use language, as in men and women. As straightforward as that might seem at first glance, an important thing to keep in mind as you read this chapter is that gender is a social construct. It is not necessarily tied to physical gender, but rather to society's expectations of each gender. In American culture, boys are taught to be independent, and adult males are expected to be assertive and authoritative. Most girls are still encouraged to cooperate with others (following expected politeness strategies), and adult females are often compelled to work well with others and not act too aggressively.

In many cases, physical gender and society's expectations align themselves neatly, but not always. You likely know men who are more conciliatory than other men and use what you consider to be effeminate language, and women who are more domineering than other women and use more brazen language. You can probably also think of situations where a given person uses "feminine" language in some contexts but "masculine" language in others. One example might be a female business executive who uses more assertive language in the workplace than she does at home with her family. It goes without saying that there are exceptions to the following characterizations, as there are with any of the generalizations made in this text.

English and American Culture

Early Research on Gender and Language

One of the first researchers to specialize in gender and language was Robin Lakoff. In her influential early work, conducted mostly in the 1970s, she proposed various assumptions about women's language in American culture at that time. Below are some of the main conclusions that Robin Lakoff drew from that research.

Together with a partner, or in a small group, decide whether you think these conclusions are still true now. Have you witnessed any of these behaviors, either in your own speech or that of others?

1. Women use "empty" adjectives, like *sweet*, *charming*, and *divine*.
2. Women don't swear as often as men, or use non-forceful expletives like *shoot* and *darn*.
3. Women speak less frequently than men, but are seen as interrupting more than men.
4. Women use more intonation variations, much like children, raising their voices at the end of statements.
5. Women use better grammar and clearer pronunciation than men do.
6. Women use hedges in their speech, such as *I guess*, *maybe*, and *kind of*:
   Honey, I was thinking that maybe your shoes are kind of informal for a dinner party.
7. Women use qualifiers or apologies before statements:
   You're going to think this is silly, but I like to read romance novels sometimes.
   Maybe I'm completely wrong here, but I think the main character in that movie was sexist.
   I'm sorry, but I think you're wrong.
8. Women use indirect requests:
   Is it cold in here? instead of *Shut the window.*
   Do you think the neighbors are already in bed? (instead of *Turn down the music.*)
9. Women use tag questions at the end of statements:
   This cake is really good, isn't it?
   We're going to be there at 8:00, right?
10. Women use super-polite forms:
    I don't mean to be a bother, but if you wouldn't mind, I'd like some more tea.
11. Women don't accept compliments well:
    This old thing? I bought it at a thrift store for less than $10.
    Dinner? Well, I'm glad you liked it, but it was just some leftovers I threw together.

Truths or Myths?

While Lakoff's assumptions were considered to be generally accurate for that time, are they relevant today, four decades later? Recent research has upheld some of these notions, and disproved others. Let's return to the YES/NO questions posed at the beginning of this chapter, many of which overlap with Lakoff's list. The answers and explanations we provide here are purposely simplistic (perhaps even pithy), but they capture the essence of much of the recent research.

1. Women talk more than men do.
   <u>Answer</u>: No. Except sometimes.

   Grice's Maxim of Quantity (Chapter 6) refers to how much, or how little, someone speaks. The majority of studies conducted in the past 10 years have showed that women do not talk more than men, with some finding that men and women speak equal amounts (Mehl, Ramírez-Esparza, Slatcher and Pennebaker 2007), and others concluding that women talk less than men (Leaper and Ayres 2007). Perhaps most important in this research has been the qualification of the question. When do women speak more or less than men? What kinds of things do women speak about, with whom, and in what contexts?

Two main generalizations can be made from these recent studies, when viewed as a whole, at least:

1. Women tend to speak more in the private/home setting, and men tend to speak more in the public/business setting (Holmes 1991).
2. Women tend to speak more when the goal of conversation is to make a connection or bond, while men tend to speak more when the goal is to influence or exert authority. Deborah Tannen has referred to this difference as "rapport vs. report."

2. Women interrupt more than men do.
    Answer: It depends on what you mean by *interrupt*.

    Current research holds that if the term *interrupt* means simply to speak while someone else is speaking, then yes, women interrupt more. However, if the term is taken to mean not only to interject oneself verbally while someone else is speaking, but also to take over the conversation or change the subject, then it is men who interrupt more (Zimmerman and West 1975 and Okamoto, Rashotte and Smith-Lovin 2002). With this distinction, we are dealing more with turn-taking phenomena, as you saw in Chapter 8 on Conversational Organization. The former action is sometimes labeled *overlapping*, with the overlaps consisting of phrases that are intended to support the speaker rather than stop him or her from speaking, such as *I know, right?* and *No way! Really?* These are examples of the backchannel cues you read about in that chapter.

3. Women can't accept compliments.
    Answer: Generally true.

    Compliments fall into the category of conversational routines. Researchers such as Janet Holmes have affirmed that women give many more compliments than men. It is also thought, however, that women in American culture are more likely than men to deflect a compliment than directly accept it. Also, women in American culture are more likely to give compliments to begin with, and compliment each other more on physical appearance and possessions, while men tend to limit compliments to performance/skills/abilities.

4. Women can't "get to the point" or just say what they mean.
    Answer: Generally true.

    As suggested by Robin Lakoff in her early work, women do tend to use more indirect statements and veiled requests, leading men to view their speech as overly wordy and ambiguous, perhaps resulting in mixed messages. While they might not state it this way, what men are requesting are more transparent directives, as we discussed in our chapter on speech acts. Since women tend to be more concerned with "rapport" than "report," they may be trying to avoid sounding too blunt.

5. Women have better grammar than men.
    <u>Answer</u>: Women *use* "better grammar" than men.

    It can be generalized that, in American society, women care more than men do about what others think of them. While things are certainly changing, many girls are still socialized (at least implicitly) from an early age to "act like a lady," which includes the appearance of speaking properly. We have established that the idea of proper or better grammar is a subjective one; here we are referring to what people perceive as the standard. There are some phonetic differences between men's and women's speech in American English that demonstrate this. One example is that women are more likely to pronounce the final [g] on a verb that ends with *–ing*, such as *talking*. Another is that women are more likely to pronounce the post-vocalic –r that was discussed in the chapters on dialects. As adults, many women spend a lot of time talking to children, their own or others', compelling them to act as a good linguistic role model, at least at the subconscious level.

6. Men don't listen to women.
    <u>Answer</u>: Maybe.

    Some studies (Phillips et al. 2001) have claimed that biological differences in the brain cause men to process sound differently than women do, reducing some speech to the level of "white noise." Sociolinguists generally prefer to focus on behavior rather than biology, positing that boys, especially teenagers, begin to tune things out, such as parental reprimands, as a form of rebellion. In adult speech exchanges between men and women, it may be the case that men tend to focus more on one thing at a time, thus blocking out any irrelevant stimuli. This could mean that men listen better to the "report" portion of speech than to the "rapport." Whatever the case, it is likely that a man is as equally capable of concentrating on the words being said to him as a woman. Perhaps the question then becomes whether or not he considers the words to be relevant, or at least relevant at the moment (Grice's Maxim of Relevance), and determining that within any given speech exchange would involve many variables besides just gender. One bit of evidence supporting this determination is that women use more attention-getting phrases to begin conversations, such as *Do you know what?* and *Guess what happened today!* These types of phrases function as backchannel cuing, another structural feature of conversation you learned about in Chapter 8.

7. Men can't express their feelings verbally.
    Answer: Depends on the man.

    As alluded to in questions 1 and 6, American men are generally more likely to use language that is relevant, succinct, and to the point. Many are more comfortable with imparting knowledge and information than they are with sharing feelings or other things of an ambiguous nature. Using terminology from our chapters on pragmatics, men give more representative illocutions, whereas women are more focused on expressive illocutions. Men are often socialized from a young age to be independent and "act like a man," which does not usually include exposing their emotions. Adolescent and teen girls are more often the ones who write sappy love notes to boys, not the other way around. Of course, there are always exceptions, such as boys who wish to become writers, poets, actors, or just someone labeled as the artsy type.

8. Men swear more than women do.
    Answer: Too many factors to make a clear decision.

    For the most part, this statement held true when Lakoff did her studies in the 1970s. Even then, one had to consider other contextual factors, but these factors are even more influential now. For example, do you think female student athletes swear more when playing sports than when speaking to friends between classes? Is the same true of male student athletes? Do teenage boys swear when they're on a date with a girl? Do you swear around your parents? You can likely come up with a variety of answers to these questions, all based on factors such as who is speaking, to whom are they speaking, the setting, and the topic. This having been said, it is still generally true in modern American society that females are expected to act like ladies, at least in most public or professional settings. When their language usage says otherwise, it is more noticed, more marked, than it would be with males. In semi-public, private, and informal settings, however, the overall rate of swearing by women is nearing that of men, especially in younger generations.

Why do so many of these research findings differ from public opinion? One of the main reasons is that many studies that have been done on language and gender did not adequately take context into consideration. This is especially true of studies aiming to measure quantity of speech; if a study only involves male and female business people, the results are likely to be skewed towards men speaking more. Likewise, a study focusing on talk in a home setting will likely favor women in that regard. Topic is another variable that must be acknowledged in any study; it stands to reason that if either men or women are talking about a subject they know well and/or feel comfortable with, they are likely to speak more than they would on a topic unfamiliar or uninteresting to them. The interlocutor must also be considered, such as women speaking to each other without the presence of men, or women addressing children.

Gender-Biased Language

Now we will move away from the differences in how men and women generally use language in American culture, and focus on the concept of **gender-biased language**. As you might guess, gender-biased language is language that shows a bias towards men. You can also think of this as "sexist language," and it's likely been the topic of discussion among your friends or in some classes you've taken (especially those involving writing). It might have even been addressed in your workplace. This is a concept that may be better illustrated than defined. The following exercises will help you more fully understand what gender-biased language is and how it manifests itself within American culture.

Work with a partner to complete the chart below. Do you note any patterns?		
	Women	**Men**
What verbs can you think of for the act of someone talking too much?		
What do you call someone who is sexually active with many people?		
What do you call a physically attractive person?		

Are the following "paired terms," which were at one time seen as equivalents, still equal now? Does either word in the pair have other connotations you're aware of? Do any patterns emerge?

Terms	**Still equal now?** (yes or no)	**Any other connotations for the male version?**	**Any other connotations for the female version?**
Master/Mistress			
Sir/Madam			
King/Queen			
God/Goddess			
Wizard/Witch			
Professional			

It is likely that there is at least some discrepancy in the answers you and your classmates have given, but you can probably agree on some overall observations. For example, how does each of the above examples show the existence of gender-biased language? Is the bias more in favor of men or of women? Is this important?

A larger societal question is whether or not gender-biased language leads to gender bias in general. Imagine that you found the following sentences in some middle-school level textbooks, perhaps belonging to your own child or to a younger sibling. Do you think that they could influence the child in any way (either positively or negatively)? Are some sentences more problematic than others? Would you have a need to discuss any of them with the child? After you've considered all of the sentences, share your thoughts with a partner.

1.   A good nurse always listens to her patients.
2.   The most powerful businessmen are able to delegate responsibilities.
3.   John had to babysit the kids while his wife was working.
4.   Katie got up immediately, brushed the dirt off her knees and picked up her skateboard.
5.   If there are eleven students available to work at the bake sale, for how many minutes must each one man the table if they are to split a three-hour shift evenly?
6.   The invitation was addressed to *Mr. Matt Smith & Amy* [his wife].
7.   Since their parents allowed them each to have one pet, Tyler had a snake and Allison had a bunny.
8.   It can be very difficult when a woman doesn't want to have children, but her husband does.
9.   Sarah Williams was a female soldier who served in Iraq for two years.
10. It turned out that Christopher was really good at writing poetry.

There can be no answer key to this exercise. Beliefs about how much our language affects our actual behavior are generally a matter of personal opinion; a woman in the United States can make her own decision as to whether she feels included within the term *mankind*, or whether she would feel more comfortable with the term *humankind*. Likewise, a teenage girl working as a server in a restaurant can determine whether or not she is being belittled by an elderly customer who summons her with the term *waitress*. There is no right or wrong answer when it comes to how a given person interprets what could be considered as gender-biased language. While some might argue that we need to be more proactive when it comes to combating gender-biased language, we believe that a good rule of thumb is that you can't really tell other people what should or should not offend them.

It is often the case that a society's language changes more slowly than its beliefs. We can return to ethnicity, the topic of the previous chapter, for one quick example. What does the "C" stand for in NAACP? Is that word used by itself these days? Should the acronym be changed to reflect currently accepted terminology? Some scholars, whether they focus on ethnicity, gender, or another aspect of sociolinguistics, believe that language change is a necessary first step towards societal change. For the purposes of our text, we are simply saying that linguistic and societal changes don't always match perfectly in the chronological sense.

Gender Neutral Language

In the past few decades, there have been movements to neutralize gender when referring to people or certain things. Some people believe this is a sign of evolution in attaining gender-equality, but others label it as political correctness gone wild. Your own opinion might depend on the specific case.

Which of the following terms seem natural to you? Which seem unnecessary or overly "politically correct"? Use a check mark to indicate whether you would accept these terms, reject them, or not care one way or the other about their use. Compare your choices with a classmate.

Term	Accept	Reject	Don't Care
chairman			
chairperson			
chair			
salesman			
salesperson			
mailman			
mail carrier			
waiter			
waitress			
server			
steward			
stewardess			
flight attendant			
freshman			
fresher*			
manhole			
person hole			
mankind			
humankind			

* This term was used at Mercyhurst University for a period of time as a gender-neutral term for first-year students.

If you were to try to gender-neutralize the following phrases, what would you propose? Do you think your answer is more appropriate, or just silly? Indicate your choice with a check mark. Compare your answers with the class.

Term/Phrase	Gender-Neutral Form	More Appropriate	Silly
All men are created equal.			
No man is an island.			

We're going to need more man-power.			
Man the table (e.g.: standing behind a table representing your major at a college fair for prospective students, ready to offer information or answer questions)			
Too many men on the field (sports like soccer, lacrosse, etc.)			

We stated earlier that modern English doesn't use grammatical gender in its nouns. This is true, but it does affect some other parts of our grammar system. We do mark gender morphologically in our third-person singular pronouns: the subject pronouns *he* and *she*, the object pronouns *him* and *her*, and the possessive pronouns *his* and *hers*. In the past, the tendency was to defer to the masculine version. In recent years, a few alternatives have been offered, such as the consistent use of *he/she, him/her*, and *his/hers*, or blended forms such as *s/he*. (Of course, the blended form *s/he* would only work in the written form.) Some people choose to simply use the feminine version, as in *The average student does her homework in less than an hour*, although this doesn't achieve gender-neutrality any more than exclusively using the masculine version. Since at least the early nineteenth century, there have been several proposals for gender-neutral alternatives, including a recent one that Harvard University adopted (*ze*), but none have really become widely used thus far.

> For further discussion on the history of proposed gender-neutral pronouns, visit this page of the Oxford University Press official blog, entitled "The gender-neutral pronoun: 150 years later, still an epic fail": http://blog.oup.com/2010/08/gender-neutral-pronoun/

A clear example of our lack of consent with this appears in phrases that require the third person singular possessive pronoun. How would you complete the following sentence? *Would everyone who wants pizza please raise _____ hand?* You likely said *their*, which is certainly considered common usage now. Note, however, that prescriptively-speaking, you violated the rule of number; *everyone* is a singular noun, but *their* is the plural possessive pronoun. Prior to the eighteenth century, the pronouns *their* and *they* were considered the proper pronouns for indefinite or general single subject references like you see in the above example. Grammarians then imposed the rule of subject-verb agreement to these instances, and this rule is still upheld by many prescriptive grammarians. The use of *their* and *they*, however, is the norm in ordinary conversation (Bodine 1975), and it is increasingly being accepted in academic settings and publications.

This is actually a perfect example of how awkward (if not silly) it can be to strictly adhere to some of our prescriptive grammar rules. If the question was worded a different way, how would you complete the sentence: *Everyone ate the pizza, didn't _____?* If the prescriptive subject-verb rule described above were to be followed, the answer would be *he* or *she*, or some combination like *he or she*. That probably isn't the answer you provided, and it would be unlikely for most American English speakers to do so.

Language and Gender in Other Cultures

Gender differences occur to some extent in all languages, and, like in English, they may or may not reflect current societal norms for gender roles. Differences in language usage between men and women may include pronunciation, grammar, or word choice. These differences may be absolute, in that men and women use a particular speech characteristic all the time, or customary, where the division happens most of the time, but not always. We will begin this section by focusing on grammatical gender differences.

Grammatical Gender in Romance Languages

English may not use **grammatical gender** to mark nouns, but about 25% of the world's languages do. By this, we mean that nouns and their modifiers (like articles and adjectives) are assigned a gender. In Spanish, for example, speakers must know that a book is a masculine noun and a house is a feminine noun in order to learn their correct spelling. This grammatical gender marker has nothing to do with physical reality, in that a Spanish speaker does not view a book as being an inherently more manly entity than a house. It is simply an aspect of grammar, no different than verb conjugations or rules of pluralization. It is also unrelated to the speaker's gender; a book remains masculine whether it is referenced by a man or by a woman.

On a historical note, there are some researchers who have posited that grammatical gender was *originally* based on physical reality. It is not a commonly held belief, and even if it is true, speakers have long forgotten any possible connection. On the other hand, some recent research in the field of psychology suggests that grammatical gender might affect our understanding of reality more than we realize. To keep things simple, we'll just say that grammatical gender is not something most speakers consciously relate to physical gender.

Romance Languages mark all nouns, articles, and adjectives as either feminine or masculine (and in a few cases, neutral), but except for nouns that refer to living creatures, these designations do not reflect any physical reality. It's easy to see this when you examine the following nouns:

English	French	Spanish
dress	la robe (f)	el vestido (m)
necktie	la cravate (f)	la corbata (f)
truck	le camion (m)	la camioneta (f)
motorcycle	la motocyclette (f)	la motocicleta (f)
high-heeled shoes	les chaussures à hauts talons (f)	los tacones (m)
boots	les bottes (f)	las botas (f)

Things that are considered to be more "manly" items are not necessarily masculine grammatically, nor are the more "girly" things all feminine. There isn't even a direct correlation between Spanish and French for all of these examples, even though they belong to the same language family. This can be quite a challenge for English speakers learning to speak these languages, as they are not used to thinking of inanimate objects as either masculine or feminine. In his book *Me Talk Pretty One Day*, David Sedaris speaks about his struggles with learning gender in French, wittily stating, "What's the trick to remembering that a sandwich is masculine? What qualities does it share with anyone in possession of a penis? I'll tell myself that a sandwich is masculine because if left alone for a week or two, it will eventually grow a beard."

Grammatical Gender in Other Languages

Other languages have more complex grammatical gender rules, such as German, which includes a neutral (or neuter) category. Some languages group gender together with other kinds of classification factors beyond gender, such as inanimate vs. animate, or based on the shape of an object. For example, Sesotho, a member of the Bantu group of Niger-Congo languages in Africa, separates human nouns from non-human nouns. Ojibwe, a language in the Algonquin family of Native American languages, divides nouns into animate and inanimate objects. Tamil, a language spoken in India, labels nouns as either rational or non-rational things. Swahili uses no fewer than 11 different noun classes.

> For a more thorough exploration of how noun classification works in Swahili, go to: http://www.webkenya.com/eng/kiswahili/grammar.php

One of the most interesting noun division systems is that of Dyirbal, an Australian Aboriginal language. The classifications are:

1. animate objects, men
2. women, water, fire, violence
3. edible fruit and vegetables
4. miscellaneous/other

Gender Differences in Language Usage

In the fifth edition of her textbook, *Language, Culture and Communication* (2008), Nancy Bonvillain explores a variety of languages that exhibit exclusive differences in how men and women use language. She explains that European explorers who first encountered the Carib people of the Lesser Antilles believed that the men spoke a completely different language than the women. This was not true structurally, but systematic differences in vocabulary did exist.

Using data from anthropologist Edward Sapir's research (Sapir 1929), Bonvillain also illustrates Yana, a Native American language spoken in California (Bonvillain 2008: 223). This language utilizes gender-determined morphemes, namely additional syllables added to certain words when spoken by men. Her descriptions of a Siberian language called Chukchee (Bonvillain 2008: 221) and Koasati, a Native American language spoken in the southeastern United States (Bonvillain 2008: 224), show that the gender differences in these languages are reflected in pronunciation rather than grammar.

Japanese shows several gender-based differences in language usage, but since many of the differences represent both linguistic and pragmatic differences, it will be discussed separately later in this section.

Gender-Biased Language

As we saw with English, gender-bias of some sort can be found in many other languages as well. One example from Spanish might look like purely grammatical gender on the surface, but many argue that it actually reflects gender-biased language. When referring to a group of mixed gender, no matter what the ratio, masculine nouns and modifiers are used. For example, a group of 100 women in Mexico would refer to themselves with the feminine second-person plural Spanish pronoun *nosotras*, but if even one man joins them, this switches to *nosotros*. Does this mean that that one man is seen as greater than the sum of 100 women? Most Spanish speakers would deny any conscious connection, but it does give more power to the masculine form. French operates in this same way, as do many other Latin-based languages.

This imbalance of power can also be seen with Spanish adjectives. The masculine form of adjectives is the "default" form listed in the dictionary, despite the fact that the feminine version would come first alphabetically. To check this, look up the Spanish word for *pretty* in an English/Spanish dictionary. You will find *bonito* and/or *lindo*, which are the masculine forms of this adjective. Alphabetically, the feminine forms *bonita* and *linda* would precede the masculine forms, and the word is more often used to describe females than males, yet the masculine form is what is almost always listed. The same male default form occurs in French dictionaries, as well as those of most other Romance Languages. To some people, this reinforces the societal view that the concept of male is "the norm," delegating the concept of female to being outside of the norm.

Another example of gender-biased language can be seen in a number of marital naming practices around the world. Historically, Hispanic women have added their husbands' surname to their own after marriage. This tradition often includes the use of the preposition *de* before the husband's surname. For example, Juana Suarez would change her name to Juana Suarez de Leon, literally translated as Juana Suarez of Leon, or Leon's Juana Suarez. This practice has been fading over the last decades, with many Hispanic women opting to keep their own surnames.

In Japan, women are required by law to take their husband's name. In Greece, however, the converse is true. A law passed in 1983 explicitly required women to keep their own names after marriage. In Quebec, there are extenuating circumstances for which a woman may change her maiden name, but marriage is not one of those circumstances. It is not customary for Muslim women to take their husband's names, as the Quran states that no one should claim to belong to anyone besides his or her father. In the United States, it is still fairly common for a woman to take her husband's name, but many choose to keep their own names, or to hyphenate their name with their husband's.

> What are your thoughts on women taking their husband's name after marriage? Discuss them with a partner to see if you have similar ideas, or very different ones.

Many languages have gender-biased language referring to unmarried women, too. In English, the term *bachelor* hardly carries the same connotations as the words *spinster* or *old maid*. In Japanese, one term for an unmarried woman is *himono onna*, which translates to *dried fish woman*. Another term is the Japanese-phonetized version of *Christmas cake* (*kurisumasu keiki*), which is used to correlate unmarried women with leftover Christmas cake. While less offensive, the Spanish *señorita*, the French *Mademoiselle*, and the German *Fräulein,* are all diminutive forms of the versions for married woman; diminutive forms are usually associated with something smaller or lesser than the word from which they were derived.

Gender in Japanese: Blending Linguistic and Pragmatic Features

In the Japanese language, the role of gender is less straightforward than it is in languages such as Koasati and Chukchee. A complex system determines which grammar and vocabulary choices are appropriate for men, and which are appropriate for women, but the choices are not always exclusive. Better described as socially-motivated norms, these variations form a bridge between pure grammatical gender (built into the language itself) and the use of grammar as a means of conveying pragmatic meaning. Nuanced as it may be, however, the level of impact gender has on the Japanese language is profound. Not only are there "female" and "male" ways of speaking, there are even specific terms for the speech of women, translating as *women's words* (*onna kotoba*) and *women's language* (*joseigo*). In general, these differences only apply to the spoken form of the language.

Lexically, there are specific words in Japanese that are considered to be more feminine, and some that are considered to be more masculine. Part of that distinction also involves levels of politeness. In general, women use language that is considered to be more formal and polite, so a word that is considered more "feminine" can also be considered more "polite." The word men are expected to use for *meal*, for example, is *meshi*, but for women, it is either *shokuji* or *gohan*. This distinction is not obligatory, however. Men generally have more freedom to choose their words than women do. Since women's speech is seen as more formal and polite, for example, a man could use the term *shokuji* in a formal setting, or when he wishes to seem more refined. Men can also employ more polite forms in situations where they wish to be perceived as less forceful or blunt.

Many features of formality and politeness manifest themselves within Japanese grammar itself, including a very complex set of prefixes and suffixes. To illustrate, we offer one brief example with the prefix *–o*, which is a formality or politeness marker traditionally used more by women than men (Shibamoto 1987).

Men's Form	Women's Form	Meaning
bentoo	obento	box lunch
kane	okane	money
hasi	ohasi	chopsticks

Another example of gender-based morphology is the use of first person singular pronouns, where both men and women refer to themselves as *watashi* (meaning *private*) or *watakushi* in more formal contexts, but men are more likely to switch to *ore* (meaning *oneself* or *myself*) or *boku* (meaning *I*) in informal contexts.

Additionally, Japanese women use more honorifics, which in this language are suffixes added to the end of a person's name that indicate the degree of respect a speaker is giving to that person. These suffixes themselves are not limited to use by women, but women use them more often. The degree of respect assigned by the use of these honorifics can be based on social status, seniority, or the relationship between speakers. Examples are –*san*, which is used as a marker of respect between people of relatively equal status, and –*sama*, which refers to someone of higher status. While most honorifics can refer to people of both genders, there are some that are used more often to refer to men (such as –*kun*), and others more often to women (such as –*chan*).

> To read more about Japanese particles, visit this website: http://nihongoichiban.com/home/japanese-grammar-particles/
>
> To further explore Japanese honorifics, check out this website, which includes a chart and explanations of their usage: http://goinjapanesque.com/honorific/

In addition to these gender-based linguistic and pragmatic differences, there are also social expectations for how the language is used by men and by women. The traditional gender roles in Japanese society are relatively well-defined, and are intertwined with social status. Many aspects of women's language are also used by male and female children, alluding to a lower status being assigned to both women and youth. As you saw above, however, when adult men chose to use certain features of women's language, it is not to reflect a lower status, but rather to make their speech more polite or softer.

Within this intricate system, however, if men employ aspects of "women's language" in contexts that are considered inappropriate, they can run the risk of being seen as effeminate. Conversely, if a woman does not use the linguistic features expected of her, she will likely be perceived as rude or vulgar.

Some of this reversal of gendered language can be observed in the Japanese LGBTQ (Lesbian/Gay/Bisexual/Transgender/Queer) community, but non-heterosexuality is still a relatively taboo topic in Japan. In their book, *Japanese Language, Gender, and Ideology: Cultural Models and Real People*, Shigeko Okamoto and Janet S. Shibamoto Smith write:

> Since there are prevalent gendered and sexualized stereotypes of language use and other behavioral aspects that speakers must negotiate, lesbians and gay men may alternately choose to comply with the existing stereotypes of masculine lesbians and effeminate gay men or remain invisible as lesbian or gay to those who do not see past these stereotypes by adhering to more normative feminine or masculine speaking patterns (2004: 94).

Other variations in the traditional gendered speaking patterns can be seen outside of the LGBTQ community as well. Adolescent and teen girls may adopt more traditional male speech with each other as a subtle form of rebellion, and adult women may use the language to intentionally appear impolite or vulgar. In the workplace, women are increasingly assuming positions of authority, where they may attempt a balance between using women's speech to seem polite and men's speech to appear worthy of respect. It remains to be seen whether or not the lines between the traditional gendered speech patterns will continue to blur.

The Worldwide Myth of the Talkative Woman

It goes almost without saying that different cultures expect different sorts of linguistic behavior from men and women, and it is difficult to make any generalizations. However, we end this chapter by revisiting the myth that women talk more than men do. Despite a significant amount of research suggesting otherwise, this myth has been difficult to debunk in the public's eye. Furthermore, it's a myth that is not only stubborn, but also widespread. The perception that women are too talkative is not at all limited to American culture, as evidenced by the sayings below. As you read each, consider the pragmatic implications and how they reflect societal views on gender and language usage.

> *Women's tongues are like lambs' tails – they are never still.* (English)
> *The North Sea will sooner be found wanting in water than a woman at a loss for words.* (Jutlandic)
> *The woman with active hands and feet, marry her, but the woman with overactive mouth, leave well alone.* (Maori)
> *Nothing is so unnatural as a talkative man or a quiet woman.* (Scottish)
> *Where there are women and geese, there's noise.* (Japanese)
> *The tongue is the sword of a woman and she never lets it become rusty.* (Chinese)

Conclusion

- The relationship between gender and language usage is not always a direct one, and certainly not one that is consistent between cultures.
- Grammatical gender is not the same as physical gender or socialized gender roles.
- Beyond grammatical gender, we have the issue of gender-biased language, a phenomenon that occurs in nearly all languages in one form or another.
- In American culture, some of the myths regarding the differences between the speech of women and men are supported by research, such as the myth that women aren't very good at accepting compliments, or

that men have a harder time putting their feelings into words. Other myths do not hold up under closer investigation, such as women interrupting more than men, or speaking more than men in all situations. Pragmatic factors must always be taken into account.

- Any link we observe between gender and language usage in American culture might not apply to men's and women's speech in other cultures. Therefore, it is important not to impose our cultural norms and expectations on others. As with all cross-cultural communication, we all need to make an effort to understand each other before judging each other.

This concludes our discussion of how various social factors affect our language usage. In the previous four chapters, we have examined several of them, such as geography, social status, age, ethnicity, and gender. In the final chapter of the book, we turn to the subject of bilingualism. The factors we have studied thus far also apply to this topic; after all, a bilingual person is simply someone who is shaped by these same social factors in more than one language.

Additional Activities

1. Ask at least eight people these questions, encouraging them to respond without thinking too much. Aiming for a balance of males and females, try to find people of different age groups. You can either write the responses by hand, or record them if the participant has given you permission to do so.

   a. Name linguistic habits that women are often blamed for.
   b. Name linguistic habits that men are often blamed for.

   Did you find any recurring answers or themes? Were there any answers that were given for both men's *and* women's habits?

   Were there any patterns to how participants answered? (Did men or women answer more readily? Did men have more responses regarding women, or other men? etc.)

2. With a friend or a group of friends (preferably a mix of males and females), organize an informal debate to try to argue both sides of a woman changing her last name to her husband's when she gets married. Prepare a chart illustrating both the pros and cons.

3. Do you think children's books & movies, and/or young adult books and movies help to propagate gender stereotypes? Can you think of examples that aim to dissolve stereotypes? (Some ideas to consider: Disney books and movies, the Harry Potter books and movies, the Twilight Series books and movies, and *The Hunger Games* books and movies.) Write a 1-2 page position paper based on your findings.

Web Resources

- This website offers an in-depth description of language and gender studies, also covering major subtopics, leading researchers, and quizzes to test your knowledge of the subject. http://www.universalteacher.org.uk/lang/gender.htm
- This site, hosted by American University's College of Arts and Sciences, focuses on the study of "Lavender Languages", which explores language use in lesbian, gay, bisexual, and transgender life: http://www.american.edu/cas/anthropology/lavender-languages/index.cfm
- For people who still believe that women talk more in all situations, direct them to this article, "Psychology Today Study: Men and Women Equally Talkative": http://www.npr.org/templates/story/story.php?storyId=12633456

- This article addresses gender portrayal in the Bible: http://www.bible-researcher.com/inclusive.html
- For an alternate point of view, you can read this article by Dr. Kelley L. Ross, who argues that gender-biased language is not the problematic issue feminists claim it to be: http://www.friesian.com/language.htm

Further Reading

Coates, J. and Pichler, P. (2011). *Language and Gender: A Reader*. Malden, MA: Wiley-Blackwell.

Eckert, P. and McConnell-Ginet, S. (2013). *Language and Gender*. Cambridge: Cambridge University Press.

Shibamoto, J. (1987). The Womanly Woman: Manipulation of Stereotypical and Non-stereotypical Features of Japanese Women's Speech. In S. Philips, S. Steele, & C. Tanz (eds.), *Language, Gender and Sex in Comparative Perspective*. Cambridge: Cambridge University Press.

Tolmach Lakoff, R. and Bucholtz, M. (2004). *Language and Woman's Place: Text and Commentaries* (Studies in Language, Gender, and Sexuality). Oxford: Oxford University Press.

Chapter 13

Bilingualism

In this chapter, we will discuss bilingualism at the individual and social level. We will also take a brief look at bilingual education.

If you talk to a man in a language he understands, that goes to his head. If you talk to him in his language, that goes to his heart (Nelson Mandela).

Introduction

Before we begin this final chapter, we should clarify some terminology. Many teachers, researchers and authors use the term **bilingual**, and we will generally do the same here to maintain consistency. However, when we use this term, we are referring not only to people who speak two languages, but also to those who speak more than two. Some experts reserve the term *bilingual* to refer to people who speak two languages, using *trilingual* for those who speak three languages, and *multilingual* for anyone speaking more than three languages. You might have also heard the term *polyglot*, which can be applied to someone who has proficiency in many languages; a less frequently used term is *hyperpolyglot*, which defines someone proficient in more than six languages.

We will start with a discussion of just how multilingual our planet has been from the earliest times, and how the United States may be one of the most multilingual of all nations. Next, we will explore bilingualism at the individual level, including the phenomenon of code-switching, which is the use of more than one language in a given speech exchange. We will then turn to bilingualism at the societal level, and the linguistic and social results of more than one language coming into contact. After a brief look at bilingual education, we will end the chapter with some humor.

Our Multilingual Planet

One misconception held by more than a few Americans is that monolingualism is the norm around the world. They might know that more than one language is spoken in some countries, but for the most part, they believe that people

Based on your current knowledge, how would you answer these questions? Share your thoughts with a partner. The answers to each one will be revealed throughout the chapter.

1. How many languages are spoken on Earth? In how many countries?
2. In which country are the most languages spoken?
3. How many countries are monolingual?
4. How many languages are spoken in the United States?
5. Which world language has the most native speakers?
6. Which language has the most total speakers, either as a first language, or an additional one?
7. Can bilingual people speak each of their languages equally well?
8. Does speaking more than one language make you smarter?
9. To really speak another language well, do you have to start learning it as a child?
10. Do all countries have at least one language declared as "official"?

just speak the language of their country. So, Russians speak Russian, Chinese people speak Chinese, and Mexicans speak...well, Mexican! Even those who are more broadly informed might be surprised to know just how many languages are spoken in Russia (28), or in China (around 129, coming from 5 distinct language families). They would likely know that Mexicans speak Spanish, but they might not realize that Spanish is the official language of more than 20 countries.

So, globally speaking, just how many languages are spoken on Earth? One difficulty in providing a definitive answer is the fuzzy line between language and dialect. One of the most trusted print and internet resources for information on the languages of the world, Ethnologue.com, lists more than 6900 languages. More than 100 new languages have been added to the list since 2000, most of which were classified as dialects in earlier tallies. The fact that these 6900+ languages are housed in fewer than 200 countries is clear mathematical proof of how multilingual this planet is.

Which country claims the prize for most languages spoken within its borders? The answer is likely one you know little about: Papua New Guinea. Located in the southwestern Pacific Ocean, this country houses more than 800 distinct languages! As for the number of monolingual countries on Earth, the answer is that, practically speaking, there are none. A few countries are listed as having only one language, such as Japan and Rwanda, but even they house some speakers of languages other than Japanese and Kinyarwanda, respectively.

When you were asked about the number of languages spoken in the United States, what was your answer? If you said over 100, you'd be correct, but still on the low side; official data lists 162 different languages, and this does not include dialects. You're certainly not alone if this statistic surprises you, but the truth is that the United States is one of the most multilingual nations of all.

How about your answer for the language with the highest number of people who claim it as a first language? Mandarin tops the Ethnologue list, with over 847 million native speakers. Spanish is second, with just short of 400 million speakers. English takes third place with between 335 and 340 million native speakers, and Hindi comes in fourth, with 260 million native speakers. English and Spanish switch positions when we consider how many people speak English as either a first or a second language, with the total number of English speakers being around 850 million.

Individual Bilingualism

As stated in the introduction to this chapter, the use of more than one language in daily life is the norm for many people across the globe. Some are born into bilingual households, and begin from a very young age to function in both languages. Others start to learn a second language when they begin school. Depending upon their experiences, some can read and write their languages equally well, some can speak, read and write one but only speak another, and some speak them equally well, but cannot read or write either in a standard form. There are also **receptive bilinguals**, who can understand a language, but cannot use it to communicate themselves. An example of a receptive bilingual would be a woman living in the United States whose grandparents emigrated from Italy: the first-generation grandparents never learned English; the second-generation parents spoke Italian at home while they were growing up, but learned English at school; and now the third-generation granddaughter was raised speaking only English, but she can understand most of her grandparents' Italian.

How Do We Define *Bilingual*?

A major difficulty in classifying bilingual individuals is determining how well one has to speak a language for it to count. The most limited definition of bilingualism would be a person who speaks two or more languages equally well, although this only accounts for about 15% of people who consider themselves bilingual. The most inclusive definition, actually too inclusive, would be someone who can make "meaningful utterances" in more than one language. Since this would essentially include a tourist who can order a beer by consulting a phrase book, we might want to settle on a middle ground.

While it is still a vague description, we could consider someone bilingual if they can perform basic functions in more than one language. At minimum, this would include being able to communicate basic needs, such as asking for directions, requesting medical help, ordering food, and making basic purchases.

In summary, this leaves us with a fairly broad range of linguistic ability for people we can consider to be bilingual. On one end of spectrum we have people who speak their languages equally well (**balanced bilinguals**), and on the other end, those who can generally understand a second language, but not speak or write it well (receptive bilinguals.) The majority of bilinguals likely fall somewhere between these two extremes.

Bilingual Attitudes

Another aspect of individual bilingualism that differs from speaker to speaker is the way the speaker feels about his or her use of more than one language. For many, it is simply a way of life that has either been passed down through generations, or arisen from changing geographical or political realities. For these speakers, there are few strong feelings, either positive or negative, about being bilingual. For others, it is a source of pride, and it plays an important role in forming identity. And for some, it presents a certain degree of difficulty or disadvantage.

In his text *Life with Two Languages* (1984), Grosjean presents the results of a survey he conducted with bilinguals from a variety of geographical and social groups. The majority of respondents reported that they did not perceive any inconvenience from being bilingual. Some mentioned that they were sometimes frustrated with having to switch from one language to another when their competence in one language was stronger than in the other. Some expressed their dissatisfaction with having to serve as an interpreter in certain situations, and some explained that they felt like they were stuck between multiple languages and multiple cultures, rather than feeling like a legitimate part of either or both.

> In a letter written to Franco-American journalist Yvonne Le Maitre, author Jack Kerouac reflects similar feelings by saying:
>
> All my knowledge rests in my "French-Canadianess" and nowhere else. The English language is a tool lately found...so late (I never spoke English before I was six or seven). At 21 I was still somewhat awkward and illiterate sounding in my speech and writings. What a mixup. The reason I handle English words so easily is because it is not my own language. I refashion it to fit French images. Do you see that?

The prevailing attitude of respondents to Grosjean's survey mentioned above, however, was positive. They listed numerous advantages of being bilingual, such as increased educational and professional opportunities, the ability to communicate with many types of people, and a more open-minded attitude towards others. Some even mentioned the benefits of being able to communicate with friends and family without others knowing what is being said.

Unfortunately, some bilingual people face prejudice and intolerance from people around them, or even active discrimination in school, work, or social situations. As a result, some parents don't want their children to speak more than one language, as they might have to face negative attitudes from classmates or teachers. One example of this would be a Mexican immigrant father who has suffered prejudice based on his use of Spanish at work, so he discourages his children from speaking Spanish when they enter school. Even though their parents may still speak Spanish at home, without active use, the children's command of Spanish will diminish. At best, they will be reduced to being receptive bilinguals, and at worst, they will become monolingual in English.

American children in this particular scenario may encounter the same reality when they start looking for employment that those who were raised in monolingual families do; they realize that they must know Spanish in order to be marketable in many career fields. Thus, they end up in high school or college classrooms, learning Spanish as a near-beginner, when they could have maintained their Spanish-language skills from the beginning while still learning English well enough to succeed in school. Beyond educational and professional disadvantages, discouraging children from maintaining two languages can also prevent them from fully connecting with their heritage.

Benefits of Bilingualism

It is somewhat surprising that there are still several negative myths about bilingualism, including the idea that bilinguals can't speak either (or any) of their languages as well as monolinguals, or that being bilingual results in some kind of split identity. Indeed, at one time, it was believed that learning more than one language meant that none of the languages could be learned completely, resulting in less literate people. The idea was that there was limited room in the brain, and any space occupied by a second language was space that was being taken away from the first. This notion was based on flawed and biased research studies, and it has all but disappeared within the scientific community, if not from public opinion.

Now it is believed that speaking more than one language actually makes a person more intelligent in many ways. For one, it leads to an increased ability for divergent thinking, which means that one is able to think about something in more than one way, and to be capable of finding more than one solution to a problem. As Kerouac illustrated, bilingual people know that a thought can be expressed in more than one language; it stands to reason that they also understand that any given situation can be interpreted in more than one way. Additionally, there are several studies demonstrating that bilinguals are better at multitasking (Marian and Shook 2012; Poarch and Bialystok 2015) and they may score better on verbal and math-based standardized testing. A promising branch of research suggests that being bilingual can help adults prevent age-related cognitive decline (Fergus, Bialystok and Freedman 2010).

The benefits of bilingualism extend to social skills as well. Children raised with more than one language spoken in the home may be more tolerant and open to cultural diversity, and they are more likely to seek out friends from different backgrounds. This, in turn, allows them to interact with more people, and also grants them access to art and literature from other cultures. As a Czech proverb says, "Learn a new language and get a new soul."

Bilingualism and Age

Perhaps the most debated topic regarding individual bilingualism is the question of age, especially regarding learning a second language after learning a first language. Do you have to start learning an additional language as a child to really speak it as a native? Is there a critical period past which second language learning is more difficult? There are studies that support that notion, studies that refute it, and studies which offer qualified support. DeKeyser and Larson-Hall (2005) provide an approachable and balanced discussion of the role of age in learning a second language. While there isn't a complete consensus on the idea of a critical age period, many linguists believe that in order to learn a language well enough to be considered a native speaker of it, including having native pronunciation, you would need to begin learning it at a young age. Some think this age is around puberty, but others place it much younger, perhaps as young as five years-old.

Nonetheless, post-pubescent children and adults are cognitively capable of learning another language to a high degree of efficiency, if not native fluency. Older children and adults have the ability to abstract, classify, generalize, and infer, which are all useful skills in learning a second language. It is possible that they may always have a foreign accent or make minor mistakes in grammar, but there are other important factors that influence second language acquisition besides age, such as motivation and aptitude.

Interestingly, the two authors of this book fall on opposite sides of the age spectrum. Dr. Remillard spoke only French at home until he was about five years-old, and then learned English in a bilingual parochial school and with other speakers in the community. Dr. Williams, on the other hand, did not begin her study of Spanish until she was a 22-year-old college student majoring in music.

Code-switching

When two (or more) languages are deeply integrated within a bilingual person's life, we often see the phenomenon known as **code-switching**, or the use of more than one language (or dialect) in the same conversation, or even in the same sentence. This is especially common in societies where not only two languages co-exist, but also two cultures. As you saw earlier, for many bilingual people, the mixing of multiple languages and multiple cultures results in a unique blend that is its own distinctive reality.

The Spanish-English bilingual population of the American Southwest provides one example of this, as the two cultures and the two languages have intermingled there for generations. You may have heard of this combination of Spanish and English referred to as *Spanglish*. Linguists who study code-switching in depth point out that what we are observing in the case of Spanglish is somewhat different than true code-switching. In true code-switching, the two languages mix within one speech exchange, but not within one word. That is to say, an individual word does not include traits of more than one language. Contrary to what you might hear in a joke, a Spanish-English switch would not be *I want el book-o*. Spanglish does, nonetheless, demonstrate how languages are mixed within conversations. You can further explore examples of Spanglish in the activities at the end of this chapter.

One of the most fascinating aspects of code-switching is that the switches happen with little or no conscious thought on the part of the speakers. If you were to listen to a conversation with a high degree of code-switching, it would sound like the speakers flow seamlessly from one language to another, with no pauses or changes in tempo or rhythm. Both speakers understand each other perfectly well, seeming to not even notice the switches. It is important to note that these switches involve languages that the speakers understand well; they are not just examples of slipping a few foreign words into a sentence for effect.

Linguistic Factors

Even though the switches are for the most part done at the subconscious level, a careful examination shows them to be quite systematic. The factors involved are complex, but for our purposes, they can be grouped into two categories. The first covers switches made for semantic reasons, or reasons based on meaning. For example, some words or concepts only exist in one of the two languages, so they can best be discussed in that language. When that word or topic comes up in conversation, speakers will switch to the language that better captures what they are trying to say. The switch may last for only one word or a few phrases, or it may last for the rest of the conversation.

Other examples of semantically-based switches are topics that for some personal reason make the speaker prefer one language over the other (like speaking about a dear grandmother in the language that the grandmother spoke), or speaking about a topic in the language in which it was first introduced to the speaker (like speaking about physics class in English simply because the speaker learned about physics in English). Case in point, Dr. Williams first studied phonetics in Spanish as a graduate student, and even when she teaches the concepts in English now, she still sometimes accidently reverts to the Spanish terms. Dr. Remillard still says his prayers in French, as his early religious instruction was in that language. Yet another reason for switching based on meaning might be transitioning from one language to another to allow a monolingual third speaker to join the conversation, or conversely, to exclude them.

The second category of switches involves syntactic, or grammatical, factors. These are even more complicated to analyze than semantic ones, but a few examples will suffice. In many instances, switches occur between sentences. One of the most frequent types of code-switching involves a statement being made in one language, and then simply being restated in the other language, as in *Give me the keys. Dame las llaves.*

Another interesting phenomenon regarding the grammatical aspects of code-switching is that a speaker rarely switches languages between an article and a noun. For example, a Spanish-English bilingual might say, *I want to buy el libro,* or *Quiero comprar the book,* but not *I want to buy the libro,* or *Quiero comprar el book.* In other words, a switch can't occur just anywhere, and the grammatical patterns of each language are usually maintained, whether or not the speakers are aware of what they are doing.

Societal Bilingualism

Now that we've outlined the basic concepts of individual bilingualism, let's explore how it manifests within a given society. Bilingual societies can arise from a variety of circumstances. For example, the areas surrounding borders between countries often create both a social and an economic need for two or more languages to be used in daily life, such as the Spanish and English used around the U.S.-Mexico border. Other bilingual societies exist where there are large concentrations of a linguistic minority, such as in French-speaking Canada. In some instances, bilingualism is spread nearly equally throughout a country, such as in the tiny country of Luxembourg where most of the half million citizens speak at least Luxembourgish and French, and many among them also speak German.

Language and Geography

It is important to remember that language usage does not always break down neatly according to current geographical boundaries. Many countries have been bilingual for much of their history, such as Canada, India, and China. Even more importantly, the divisions between countries that we see on a map today have obviously not always been where they are now. Large countries have been divided into smaller ones (such as the former Soviet Union) and smaller ones have been combined into larger ones (as with East and West Germany.) Border lines have

Analyze the following bilingual speech exchanges, individually or with a partner. You do not need to speak the other languages to complete this exercise, as the non-English portions are italicized, with English translations in parentheses.

Address these questions as you analyze:

1. Where exactly did the switches occur?
2. Was the switch more grammatically-based, or semantically-based?
3. Do you think the context (situation, relationship between speakers, etc.) played a role in the switch?
4. Do you think the speakers are stronger in one language or another, or are they balanced bilinguals?

  a. A Spanish-English bilingual child to another:
      ...y el maestro me dijo (...and the teacher told me), If you don't stop bugging me, I'm going to kick your butt!
  b. A French-English bilingual grandmother speaking to her sister in the kitchen:
      I was thinking....um, thinking the other day, that it's been a long time since I've been to...*Aix-en-Provence...on y va*? (the name of a place in France...shall we go?)
  c. A Spanish-English bilingual businesswoman to another:
      Entonces, estaba trabajando en la computadora anoche cuando de repente, se me falló. (So, I was working on the computer last night when suddenly, it crashes on me.) Yeah, it freakin' crashes on me!
  d. A German-English bilingual child speaking to his English-speaking friend, and then to his grandmother:
      Mmmmm...these are so good! I love it when Gram makes these. You're gonna love 'em! *Danke, Oma!* (Thanks, Grandma!)
  e. One Spanish-English bilingual parent to another:
      I had to call Juanito's principal today, and I tell you, that man is practically impossible to deal with. I mean, really, *no entiende nada este gringo* (he doesn't understand anything, this gringo).

also been shifted for political reasons (like in Iraq, which has seen several border shifts since the fall of the Ottoman Empire) and religious circumstances (as we can see with the continuing border disputes between Palestine and Israel.)

This interactive website illustrates how the borders of what is now known as Iraq have changed from before 2000 BC up until the present: http://www.worldology.com/Iraq/iraq_history_lg.htm

The truth of the matter is that these divisions have been based on political and ethnic grounds far more often than on linguistic ones. In the United Kingdom, the division of England, Ireland, and Scotland has not been based on language for a very long time. That being said, in addition to English, there are versions of Gaelic spoken in both Ireland and Scotland, and Wales lists over 20% of its population as bilingual in English and Welsh. Another complicated example involves the country of Bosnia and Herzegovina; the country includes speakers of Bosnian, Croatian, Serbian and Romani, but Bosnian is spoken not only in Bosnia and Herzegovina, but also in Serbia and Montenegro.

Language and Politics

To further complicate matters, countries differ in how they describe their linguistic realities. Many countries claim only one official language, even when many of its citizens speak two or more. Some declare only one official language, but also list officially recognized minority languages, such as Guatemala, with Spanish as the official language, but 23 indigenous languages are recognized as well. The constitution of India, on the other hand, names 23 official languages, and estimates that about 20% of the population speaks two of them, if not three. As you learned earlier in this chapter, the island nation of Papua New Guinea tops the list of number of spoken languages at over 800, but only three of them are listed as official.

Some countries do not list any official language at all, including the United States. While there has been pressure (both historic and recent) to declare English as the official language of the U.S., thus far, this has not occurred. Nevertheless, according to the U.S. Census Bureau (2010), around 82% of the U.S. population speaks English as a mother tongue. While many people in favor of declaring English as the official language of the United States also recognize the importance of maintaining our bilingual heritage, there are radical factions that advocate the essential criminalization of speaking other languages. (For an in-depth look at this controversy, consult Jim Crawford's website regarding language policy listed at the end of the chapter.)

Not all occurrences of language contact are voluntary or welcome, and language mixing is sometimes actively resisted. One example of this is the conflict that has long simmered between French and English speakers in Canada. French explorers claimed lands along the St. Lawrence River in Canada and colonized it from about 1610–1759. Many French-speaking communities were established there, in the area known today as the province of Quebec. In 1763, France ceded this area to England, but England guaranteed the citizens of Quebec the freedom to continue to speak French.

Currently numbering about 7 million, the large majority of inhabitants of this area have for the most part maintained their usage of French, speaking several dialects of French labeled French Canadian. Since these areas eventually became home to English capitalists as well, French has co-existed alongside English. Some natives of Quebec consider themselves to be French Canadian, but do not speak French. There are also speakers of French in Canada that reside outside of Quebec.

Both languages were granted constitutional protection in 1867. In 1969, both French and English were declared official languages of Canada, even though less than 20% of Canadians speak both. Subsequent governmental policies outlined the specifics of how the two languages would be protected and utilized. In 1977, Quebec challenged the policies by passing legislation that would promote French over English in the province, including enforcing a law forbidding the use of any other language but French on public signs.

Currently, an English sign can be used as long as a larger French sign is visible. Alternately, a bilingual sign can be posted if the French portion is larger. The legal battle for the dominance of French over English continues in Quebec, and many even advocate Quebec's secession from the rest of Canada. Quebec's politics and social policies are beyond the scope of this text, but from a purely linguistic point of view, a region of French speakers surrounded on all sides by English speakers will not likely succeed in avoiding the effects of language contact altogether.

Bilingualism in the United States

Political controversy aside, the reality in the United States is that multiple languages are spoken here every day. This has been a fact of American life since the first settlers arrived from Europe, and it has been reinforced by continual waves of immigration. During each wave, ethnic groups have established themselves at various locations, and most have maintained at least some use of their first language.

Before continuing, see if you can match these geographical areas of the United States with the main languages besides English spoken there. (Some are obvious, but some are not!) Write the number of the corresponding language in the space to the left of the geographical area. Then compare your responses with a partner, then continue reading below to see how well you did.

	1. Little Italy, New York City	a. Finnish
	2. Little Canada, New England	b. A dialect of German
	3. Little Havana in Miami, Florida	c. Polish
	4. Chinatown in San Francisco, California	d. Arabic
	5. South Central and Southeastern Pennsylvania	e. Creole
	6. Hawaii	f. French
	7. Louisiana	g. Basque
	8. Idaho	h. various Asian languages
	9. Upper Midwest	i. Norwegian, Swedish
	10. Dearborn suburb of Detroit, Michigan	j. Spanish
	11. Upper Peninsula, Michigan	k. Italian
	12. Chicago, Illinois	l. Chinese

Besides the obvious matches of Italian in Little Italy, New York City; and Chinese in Chinatown, San Francisco; you likely identified Spanish as the prominent language of Little Havana in Miami, Florida. You might have also guessed Chicago as the home of many Polish speakers. Beyond that, knowledge of linguistic pockets in the United States is not as widespread. Louisiana is commonly associated with Creole, but it is actually French that forms the basis of the Creole. The Creole spoken in Hawaii, on the other hand, does not have any significant French influence. Hawaii is also home to speakers of many Asian languages. People living in the urban areas of New England referred to as Little Canada (or Little Canadas) have spoken French until quite recently.

It might have been more difficult for you to connect the German-dialect of Pennsylvania Dutch to Southeastern and South Central Pennsylvania, partly due to the misleading name. The *Dutch* in this case is an Anglicized name for *deutsch*, meaning German. The other matches include the Basque-speaking population in the northwestern United States (particularly Idaho); Norwegian and Swedish speakers in the Upper Midwest; Finnish speakers in Michigan's Upper Peninsula; and Arabic speakers in Dearborn, Michigan, a suburb of Detroit. Dearborn is actually home to the largest concentration of Arabic speakers outside of the Middle East. Of course, in addition to these examples, there are also numerous Native American languages from dozens of distinct language families spoken all across the country.

> If you are interested in learning more about the many Native American languages spoken in the United States, visit this website: http://www.cogsci.indiana.edu/farg/rehling/nativeAm/ling.html

One of the effects that this housing of multiple languages has had is one that isn't always easy to see. The English language is believed to have the largest vocabulary of all languages. The Oxford English Dictionary (OED) website explains how difficult it is to define what a *word* is, let alone make an accurate count of words within any given language, but it suggests that there are at least a quarter of a million distinct English words!

A large number of these words were borrowed from other languages. Some came from colonization while others came from language contact within the country. A curious phenomenon is that our language has historically borrowed the words in their original spelling, but then changed the pronunciation to suit the phonetic tendencies of English. If you had difficulty learning to spell as a child, it might comfort you to know that this phenomenon essentially means you've had to memorize and/or categorize spelling rules from dozens of languages!

Many times, we eventually forget which language a borrowed word came from, claiming it as one of our own. Can you (individually or with a partner) guess the original languages of these common words? Some are easier than others, but you can find the answers at the end of this chapter.

alcohol	apartheid	athlete	bagel	beauty
bizarre	calendar	cookie	Dracula	fjord
gauze	karate	molasses	orange	raccoon
robot	rodeo	sauna	shampoo	vampire

Diglossia

Bilingual societies exhibit a variety of patterns of language usage. In some of them, as you saw above, code-switching within one conversational exchange is common. In others, there is more of a tendency for speakers to use certain languages in certain situations or contexts. Linguist Charles Ferguson coined the term **diglossia** to describe a specific type of bilingualism that occurs in communities where nearly all members speak more than one language, but consistently use each of their languages in distinct situations. Many times, these situations are divided into two main categories; one category includes work, school, government, and business settings, and the other covers more personal settings, such as home or social life.

In some areas exhibiting diglossia, the two languages are closely related to one another, perhaps even a formal and a vernacular dialect of the same language. One example of this would be in Switzerland, where the Swiss use German in more official settings, and the dialect called Swiss German in more personal ones. Another would be areas where speakers use standard Arabic for more formal affairs and a vernacular or regional dialect of Arabic for everyday interactions.

In other situations, the languages used are not related at all, such as in Paraguay, where many people speak both Spanish and Guaraní, an indigenous language. Spanish is used for more formal settings such as business, government, law, and media; Guaraní is used for more informal settings such as communication between family members or in social situations. In the educational setting, both languages are used equally in the classroom and in textbooks. What is unusual about this particular case of diglossia is that these speakers include more people of European-descent than indigenous. In fact, it is estimated that more than 90% of the population of Paraguay speaks Guaraní (many of them being bilingual in both Spanish and Guaraní), but only 1-2% of the population is actually indigenous Guaraní by ethnicity.

Other examples of a colonizing group taking on the language of the native population are nearly nonexistent, and have not been observed elsewhere in the Americas. In Paraguay, however, there are a few historical factors that made this possible, the most important one being that the Jesuit priests acting as missionaries there chose to learn the native tongue and use it to teach the Guaraní about Christianity rather than forcing the Guaraní to learn Spanish. This adoption was later reinforced by the government when they declared both Spanish and Guaraní as official languages in 1992.

The Linguistic Effects of Language Contact

Whenever and wherever bilingualism occurs, we can observe the effects the languages have on each other. This includes border areas where there is only minimal contact, and areas where two or more languages are spoken by nearly everyone in the community. In cases of diglossia, the languages do not mix to any great extent. There may be some borrowing of words from one language to the other, but the structure of the languages themselves is not altered.

In other cases of language contact, the contact between the languages results in deeper changes at the grammatical level, even when the languages in question are not part of the same language family. In the most extreme instances of language contact, the languages intermingle so completely that a new language is born. You will read more about this in a moment.

There are many factors involved in determining what outcomes the contact will produce. To name just a few, we can consider the amount of time the languages have been in close proximity, the extent to which the speakers of both languages interact, the degree of linguistic similarity or difference the languages exhibit, and the socio-economic and political dynamics between the speakers of each one. The most visible mingling of languages occurs when the speakers interact on a daily basis. Languages can also be shaped through academic usage, such as the Latin we see in the United States through Catholic Church texts or the study of medicine and science. Some words taken from Latin church texts and adopted into English with very little modification include *gloria* (glory), *gratia* (grace), and *raptura* (rapture). Latin terms found in modern medicine abound, such as *dosis* (dose), *infectio* (infection), and *spasmus* (spasms or cramps).

Pidgins

In situations where the speakers of different languages perceive a need for communication and interaction, there is likely to be more evidence of integration between the languages. The example that linguists most often cite for this type of contact is the simplified hybrid type of language that arises where groups of people are introduced to each other through colonial or economic expansion. Seen frequently along trade routes such as rivers, this hybrid is known as a **pidgin** and it maintains distinct aspects of both languages.

A pidgin is not a fully developed language; it usually consists of juxtaposed content words and does not have the intact grammatical structure of either of the languages coming into contact with one another. It is simply a rudimentary form of communication meant to convey messages between speakers who do not understand each other's language. One example would be the communication system that developed on sugar and pineapple plantations in Hawaii between the English-speaking bosses and the workers imported from China, Japan, Korea, Portugal, the Philippines, and Puerto Rico. Pinker (1994) provides the following as an example of a pidgin phrase and its English translation:

> *Building-high place-wall pat-time-nowtime-and' den-anew tempecha eri time show you.*

> There was an electric sign high up on the wall of the building which displayed the time and temperature.

Creoles

The main difference between a pidgin and a true language is that it is not passed along from generation to generation in this relatively crude form. If a pidgin is expanded and adopted as a principle means of communication, and is passed along to the next generation as a mother tongue, it becomes a **creole.** A creole still has visible aspects of both languages, but also exhibits signs of each language affecting the other at a grammatical level, creating characteristics that are distinct from the parent languages.

For example, the children of the Hawaiian plantation workers mentioned above spoke a more evolved version of their parents' pidgin, developing a Creole English. This reinforces the fact that languages are not learned only through imitation; the children hear their parents' pidgin, but create unique grammatical structures, developing an independent language.

Bilingual Education

The topic of bilingual education is too vast to be covered extensively in this text, but a brief examination of the most crucial terms and concepts will serve to illustrate a very consequential manifestation of bilingualism within a society.

Types of Bilingual Education

While some children are raised speaking two languages from birth, a large number of them learn their second language at school. An example of this would be a child born to recent Bosnian immigrants to the U.S. who heard mostly Bosnian at home (English from the television being a notable exception), and was then exposed to English at school. Some immigrants settle in areas with a significant population of others from their homeland, and in these cases, the child may have the opportunity to be educated in both languages. This was true in Dr. Remillard's case; half of his school day was conducted in French, and the other half in English.

There are nearly as many different manifestations of bilingual education as there are institutions that offer it. Despite a multitude of differences, most programs can be broken down into two major categories. The first includes programs that aim to ease the student away from speaking the native language. These programs are called **transitional**, as the student makes a transition from the minority language to the majority language. The second group, labeled **maintenance**, encourages students to continue to speak the mother tongue even as they progress in learning the second language. The decision to employ one type of bilingual education over another can be as much social and political as it is pedagogical. When the goal of a society is assimilation, transitional programs are preferred. If the desired outcome is a bilingual and bicultural society, then the retention of the first language along with the second will likely be encouraged through maintenance programs.

The most extreme version of transitional bilingual education follows the "sink or swim" mentality. Students are placed in regular classrooms, and are expected to gradually learn the second language through constant exposure. Historically, these students were not only discouraged from using their mother tongue, but actively punished for doing so. While a small number of students have managed to acquire a second language under such circumstances, this approach is problematic in a number of ways, both pedagogically and psychologically. Until the second language is sufficiently mastered, the student will be behind the rest of the class in terms of mastering the material, and this may lead an inexperienced teacher to assume that the student is cognitively deficient. Such a stressful atmosphere also often leads to frustration on the part of the student, and some act out in ways that mirror behavioral problems. With this combination of confusion and resentment, it is not surprising that many minority speakers get inappropriately placed into programs for mentally or emotionally challenged students.

The recent trend has been to phase out programs like these and replace them with ESL (English as a Second Language) programs that allow for focused instruction in the second language rather than relying entirely on osmosis. Most ESL programs require the students to attend the majority of their classes with the rest of the school population, but separate them for periods of explicit formal language instruction. The end goal of ESL is still to move the student towards second language proficiency, but any given program may or may not seek to maintain the first language or culture.

Obviously, true bilingual education requires the use of both languages in instruction, but there is no consensus regarding the details of how such programs should be designed. Different countries view bilingual education in very different ways, and a great deal of variation occurs even within the United States. The aspect that varies the most between programs is the amount of instructional time spent in each language.

There is also the question of who is chosen to participate in these programs. The most obvious scenario would involve students who come into a majority language school speaking a minority language. There are also some programs that invite monolingual students from the majority culture to participate as well, resulting in them becoming proficient in the minority language as well the majority. These programs are often referred to as **dual-immersion** programs.

Effectiveness and Public Opinion

The lack of a universal agreement on the definitions and details of bilingual education has led to mixed results in research regarding its effectiveness. From the sociolinguist's perspective, if bilingualism itself provides the many benefits outlined earlier in the chapter, then any educational program that seeks to maintain and enhance a student's first language and culture while still striving for excellence in the second language should be seen as a positive thing. In the list of suggestions for further research at the end of this chapter, you will find a source that presents a meta-analysis of the studies to date on the effectiveness of bilingual education.

Public opinion on bilingual education in the United States has been swayed by bias from all sides, but especially from the media. Facts and statistics are often presented without context, and scare tactics are used to convince people that bilingual education poses a threat to English and the American way of life. Without proper information, taxpayers can believe that their hard earned money is being used to keep students from becoming productive citizens. Additionally, parents can believe that their children are being denied the best education. Even teachers can feed rumors about facing elimination if they do not become bilingual themselves.

Lost in Translation

We'll end this chapter, and indeed, this textbook, on a humorous note. As you've learned in this chapter, about 1 billion people speak English, in more than 100 countries, either as a native or as a second language. With so many countries and regions employing English as a second or additional language co-existing alongside one or more other languages, it is not surprising that this contact presents

interesting challenges. One of these challenges concerns difficulties in translation. Sometimes the difficulty occurs due to one single word being mistranslated;
other times, it involves errors at the morphological or syntactic level. Many times,
these linguistic conflicts are compounded by semantic and pragmatic mismatches
as well.

The following translations seen on signs from around the world were collected by Richard Lederer in his book *Anguished English*. You will find them funny, but can you identify *why* they are funny? Where did the translation issue occur; that is, what linguistic or pragmatic anomaly caused the problem? What would have been a more accurate way to phrase the English?	
In a hotel lobby in Bucharest, Romania:	*The lift is being fixed for the next day. During that time we regret that you will be unbearable.*
In a hotel elevator in Paris, France:	*Please leave your values at the front desk.*
In a hotel in Yugoslavia:	*The flattening of underwear with pleasure is the job of the chambermaid.*
In the lobby of a Moscow hotel across from a Russian Orthodox monastery:	*You are welcome to visit the cemetery where famous Russian and Soviet composers, artists, and writers are buried daily except Thursday.*
Outside a tailor shop in Hong Kong:	*Ladies may have a fit upstairs.*
In a dry cleaning shop in Bangkok:	*Drop your trousers here for best results.*
Outside a dress shop in Paris, France:	*Dresses for street walking*
In a hotel in Vienna, Austria:	*In case of fire, do your utmost to alarm a porter.*
In a dentist's office in Hong Kong:	*Teeth extracted by the latest Methodists*
An advertisement for donkey rides in Thailand:	*Would you like to ride on your own ass?*
In a bar in Tokyo, Japan:	*Special cocktails for ladies with nuts*
In a cocktail lounge in Norway:	*Ladies are requested not to have children in the bar.*

Conclusion

- Bilingualism (or multilingualism) is a way of life for the majority of people on Earth.
- Our planet has been multilingual since the earliest days of human existence.
- A bilingual person may know two languages equally well, or be superior in one.
- A bilingual's choice of language to use may be based on specific settings (diglossia), or the speaker may use more than one language in any given situation.

- The languages may be kept separate, or they may be mixed within one speech exchange, or even one utterance, and the change may or may not be conscious.
- Bilingual people may consider themselves as living in more than one *culture* as well as more than one *language*.
- Bilingualism occurs both within cultures and between cultures. Wherever languages come into contact, they affect each other in at least some way, with results ranging from some shared vocabulary to the creation of a new language.
- Different societies deal with bilingualism in different ways, including their approaches to bilingual education.
- Research supports the idea that speaking more than one language has many cognitive and social benefits.
- Bilingualism can be viewed as a sign of creativity in the human race, as it is perhaps our greatest demonstration of the balance we seek between the individual and the whole.

Answers to the In-Class Activity on Word Origins:

Apartheid	(Afrikaans)
Athlete	(Greek)
Bagel	(Yiddish)
Beauty	(French)
Bizarre	(Basque)
Calendar	(Latin)
Cookie	(Dutch)
Dracula	(Romanian)
Fjord	(Norwegian)
Gauze	(Hebrew)
Karate	(Japanese)
Molasses	(Portuguese)
Orange	(Sanskrit)
Raccoon	(Algonquin)
Robot	(Czech)
Rodeo	(Spanish)
Sauna	(Finnish)
Shampoo	(Hindi)
Yacht	(Dutch)
Vampire	(Serbian)

Additional Activities

1. Interview a number of bilingual speakers (you can include yourself if you are a bilingual), using the following questions as a starting point. You may record responses with an audio device (with speaker's permission), or record the responses by hand. When you are finished, take a look at the results as a whole. Did you find similarities between speakers? Differences? Can you identify any contextual factors that would lead to these similarities/differences, such as age or social class? Did any of the responses surprise you? What would you have liked to know more about?

   a. What languages do you speak?
   b. To what extent are you bilingual?
   c. What do you consider to be your stronger language(s)?
   d. In what context(s) do you speak each? With whom?
   e. Do you ever mix languages together? When? How do you feel about mixing them?
   f. What are some advantages of being bilingual? Disadvantages?
   g. What generation are you in this country?
   h. (Feel free to add other relevant questions.)

2. Choose a book that you can check out of the library or buy in English and another language with which you are generally familiar (two examples are books from the Harry Potter series or the Twilight saga). Depending on your level of familiarity with the other language, pick one page, one paragraph, one section, or one chapter and compare the two versions.

   Do you think the translations were generally accurate? Why or why not? What specific translation discrepancies do you note? Do you think it's a matter of poor translating skill, or a matter of things that do not translate well between the two languages? Is it possible that the problem was more due to pragmatic factors than linguistic ones?

3. Watch a movie, choosing one of the following strategies. You may choose to watch a portion of the movie several times and provide a detailed comparison, or make a more general comparison from the entire movie.

   a. Watch an American movie with the sound in English and the subtitles in another language with which you are generally familiar.
   b. Watch an American or foreign movie with the sound in the other language and the subtitles in English.
   c. Watch a foreign movie with both the sound and subtitles in the other language.

Do you think the translations were generally accurate? Why or why not? What specific translation discrepancies do you note? Do you think it's a matter of poor translating skill, or a matter of things that do not translate well between the two languages? Are pragmatic factors also at play? If you chose option C above, did the subtitles generally match the spoken words you heard?

4. If you speak Spanish, either as a native-speaker, or a learner at an intermediate or higher level, analyze the following examples of code-switching. Where exactly is the switch? Is the switch grammatical or semantic? Does the switch seem like true code-switching to you, or is it more characteristic of a creole? Can you guess if English or Spanish is the stronger language for the speaker? Explain your answers as thoroughly as possible.

   a. María tiene que ir al doctor, pues tiene un appointment a las 3:00.
   b. Tengo que dar para atrás el libro a la biblioteca.
   c. José tiene que arreglar las brekas de su carro.
   d. La marketa está como a unos cinco blokes de aquí.
   e. Maria me brifeo por nota el trabajo pendiente.
   f. Maria va a pagar todos los biles de la renta, etc.
   g. ¡Ten cuidado con ese bompe en la calle!
   h. Tengo que limpiar la carpeta con la aspiradora.
   i. Honey, apúrate a cuquear la comida que ya tengo hambre.
   j. Maria va a chequear al baby que va a babysit por la noche.
   k. ¡Quiero una cheeseburger, fries y una soda por favor!
   l. Haz clic aquí para visitar mi website.
   m. Maria se eskipea de la High School cada semana para irse con su novio.
   n. Tengo que ir a la marketa a comprar grocerías.
   o. Juan pertenece a la ganga de sur de L.A.
   p. Voy a la librería a estudiar un poco más.
   q. Mi vieja tiene que mopear toda la casa para que pueda watchar las novelas.
   r. ¡Mira! El gato está en el ruffo.
   s. José, pon los platos en el sink.
   t. Cada verano, trabajo sorteando cherries en una empacadora.
   u. Me acabo de comprar una troca nueva.
   v. Voy a la washatería a lavar la ropa.

Web Resources

- Linguistic Society of America's page on multilingualism: http://www.linguisticsociety.org/resource/multilingualism
- To research bilingualism in any country on the planet, start here first: http://www.ethnologue.com/web.asp
- Where did that word come from? Research the status of loanwords from 41 different languages via the World Loanword Database: http://wold.clld.org/
- What are the effects of immigration on bilingualism in the United States? http://www.migrationinformation.org/Feature/display.cfm?id=282
- Spanglish: Code-switching or Creole? To learn more about what's happening as Spanish and English mix in the United States, visit these sites:

    o NPR radio story on Spanglish: http://www.npr.org/templates/story/story.php?storyId=1438900
    o American Chronicle article on Spanglish and code-switching: http://www.americanchronicle.com/articles/view/7164
    o "Spanglish" in advertising: http://www.youtube.com/watch?v=-n0hr4ViFAA&NR=1

- Code-switching in American High Schools (a video to educate high school teachers): http://il.youtube.com/watch?v=SuDLCdwHrdg&feature=related
- Here is a meta-analysis of research on the effectiveness of bilingual education: http://www.languagepolicy.net/archives/greene.htm

Further Reading

Baker, C. (2006). *Foundations of Bilingual Education and Bilingualism*. Bristol: Multilingual Matters.

Grosjean, F. (2012). *Bilingual: Life and Reality*. Cambridge, MA: Harvard University Press.

Myers-Scotton, C. (2005). *Multiple Voices: An Introduction to Bilingualism*. Malden, MA: Wiley-Blackwell.

Glossary

Listed below are significant terms used within the text. Boldfaced terms within these definitions are found elsewhere in the glossary.

accent	One component of a dialect, specifically related to pronunciation.
active listenership	Related to the use of **backchannel cues** consisting of verbal and non-verbal forms to show attention to the other speaker(s).
African American English (AAE) *also known as **African American English Vernacular (AAVE)**, **Black English (BE)**, **Black English Vernacular (BEV)** and **Ebonics***	A dialect of English associated with African American culture rather than race/ethnicity. Not all African Americans speak it, and not all people who speak it are African American.
alliterations	**Stylistic device** wherein two or more words in a phrase or sentence have the same initial sound, like in the verses of the Mother Goose poem: *Betty Botter bought some butter, but, she said, the butter's bitter.* Such devices are used by speakers to focus on a topic, or for humor.
allophones	Non-distinctive sounds in a language, such as in the degree of plosiveness (air release) used in stop consonants like [p,t,k] in English. The degree of plosiveness in either [p] of the word *pop* does not change the meaning of the word.
articulation	The place in the mouth where a consonant sound is produced. An example is the bilabial sound [b], where both lips are used to produce it.
articulatory phonetics	The study of how speech sounds are physiologically produced.
backchannel cues	Verbal responses such as *yeah, sure, cool, uh uh*, etc. (or non-verbal cues such as nodding your head or a facial expressions) made during a conversation to let the addressee know that you are listening to (or boring) them.
balanced bilingual	A person who speaks two (or more) languages equally well.

bald politeness

Politeness strategy in which there is little to no effort to minimize the threat to the hearer's face. This strategy is usually used when there is a close relationship with the hearer(s), or in performing common tasks together, or to warn someone of danger.

bilabial

The use of both lips for producing a sound such as with the [b] in *baby*, the [m] in *money* and the [p] in *pepper*.

bilingual education

Any form of education that employs more than one language in its instruction.

bilingualism

The frequent use of two languages by a speaker or by a community. The term is sometimes used to mean the use of more than two languages as well (see **multilingualism**).

code-switching

The use of more than one language or dialect within a given exchange.

commissives

Speech act **illocutions** that commit the speaker in varying degrees to some future course of action as in promising, threatening and pledging.

communicative competence

The speaker's internalized knowledge of a language **(linguistic competence)** as well as its appropriate use in context and in the intended communicative purpose.

context

The conditions (setting, participants, topics, goal as well as everything involved in how something is said) that surround the use of utterances.

conversational organization

Refers to the structural interactions between speakers and hearers in a conversation such as **turn-taking** and use of cohesive devices between and within turns, such as repairs, repetitions, and backchannel cues that allow a conversation to proceed.

cooperative Principle

As defined by Paul Grice, this principle consists of an internalized operational understanding (postulate/assumption) that speakers will not normally lie, cheat, mislead, etc. Four **maxims** underlie the cooperative principle: **quantity**, **accuracy**, **relevance** and **manner/clarity**.

creole

A language developed for communication between people who speak mutually unintelligible languages. It is a combination of the original languages, but also has its own distinct grammar and lexicon. It can be considered a mother tongue.

| declaratives | Speech act **illocutions** consisting of a decree or declaration that results in a change in the world as when a duly certified cleric or justice of the peace pronounces two individuals as married. |

declaratives — Speech act **illocutions** consisting of a decree or declaration that results in a change in the world as when a duly certified cleric or justice of the peace pronounces two individuals as married.

descriptive grammar — A grammar that describes rather than prescribes language use.

descriptivism — A belief that language should be described as it occurs naturally in a given context, rather than prescribing what is correct and incorrect.

dialect — A way of speaking unique to a particular group of people. It is often determined by geography, but can also be affected by other factors such as age, ethnicity, or socio-economic group. It is often viewed in terms of pronunciation, but also encompasses **lexical**, **morpho-syntactic**, **semantic**, and **pragmatic** variants.

diglossia — The use of two languages within a society, but with one language being used in certain contexts (such as school and government) and the other used in other contexts (such as home and personal life).

direct speech act — **Speech acts** wherein the sounds, words, phrases and sentences directly perform the function. The sentence form (question, directive, etc.) and the speech act are in direct association with one another, as in the command *Clean up your room now*.

directive — **Speech act illocution** such as a command, warning, request, invitation etc. that consists of getting someone to perform a physical act.

dual immersion — This term refers to bilingual education programs that involve both minority language learners and majority language learners learning two languages side by side.

entailment — The logical connection between sentences so that if the first sentence is true the second sentence is also true. To say then, *My wife was murdered* logically means she is dead.

ethnicity — Factors shared by people who share the same cultural, national, religious, or linguistic traditions. It does not, however, always directly correspond to shared physical traits, national origin, religion, or language.

expressive — **Speech act illocution** that reflects the psychological state of the speaker as in an apology, a congratulatory statement, an expression of sympathy, or even a negative evaluation.

face	Term used in politeness theory referring to one's self-esteem (personal) or public self-image (social).
face saving act	A verbal act that lessens a potential threat to an addressee.
face threatening act (FTA)	A threatening or damaging verbal act that conveys a lack of sensitivity to the face wants of an addressee.
face wants	The expectation that individuals expect in regard to their self-esteem or public self-image (see **face**).
flouting	Occurs when a **maxim** is deliberately violated in order to convey a meaning that is the opposite of what is literally said, such as when one compliments another person's deliberate and ridiculous choice of dress by saying *It's a fashion statement.*
gender spectrum	A belief that gender assignment is not a simple binary system, but rather a more nuanced designation that is influenced not only by physical gender, but also gender expression and identity.
gender-biased language	Language that favors one gender over another, such as sexist language used in advertising.
gender-neutral language	Language that attempts to erase gender bias, such as using the term *chairperson* instead of *chairman*.
genre	The form of the speech event such as a speech, poem, joke, lecture, etc.
goal	Contextual component that refers to why something is said, that is, all the outcomes and personal goals or purposes of the speech event.
grammatical gender	Languages that involve grammatical gender have a noun class system in which a gender is assigned to all nouns and their corresponding parts of speech, such as adjectives and articles. The assignment is generally not associated with physical gender. Some languages have a binary system, while others include a neuter category as well as male and female.
high considerateness speakers	Verbal style defined by Deborah Tannen associated with speakers who tend not to interrupt or impose while another is speaking and who may even take more time than expected between speaker turns.
high involvement speakers	Verbal style defined by Deborah Tannen associated with speakers who tend to speak quickly and in an animated fashion, often with no gap between turns or with overlapping remarks.

honorifics	Linguistic markers (word, phrase, particle etc.) used for politeness or respect that reflect hierarchical social constructs. In Japanese, for example, an honored individual would be addressed with the particle suffix *–san* after his name.
hyperpolyglot	Someone who speaks many languages.
idiolect	A unique way of speaking that every individual has; it is based on various factors, but each person's idiolect differs slightly from others who speak the same dialect.
illocutions	**Speech acts** that refer to the force of the action, or what the speaker is trying to do (command, convince, promise, sympathize, etc.).
implicature	Occurs whenever speakers and hearers understand that one or more of the **maxims** are being flouted, that is, purposefully and deliberately violated. For example, implicature occurs in a letter of recommendation for a teaching position consisting only of a detailed description of how well that person dresses rather than a description of the person's competence in an academic field.
indirect speech acts	**Speech acts** wherein the performative verb does not describe the illocutionary type, as in rejecting an invitation to meet someone at a certain hour with a locution that does not directly imply rejection such as: *I have to be at work at that hour.*
instrumentalities	The means used to communicate both in terms of form (oral, written, code switching such as in the use of Twitter as opposed to e-mail) and style (dialectical features, slang, casual or more formal register used).
intercultural pragmatics	Use of **pragmatic** forms in social encounters in foreign as well as other English speaking cultures.
interlocutor	A person participating in a conversation.
interruption	An **overlap** in a speaker turn that is interpreted as overpowering the other speaker.
intonation	The pattern of **pitch** and **stress** that adds functions to a phrase or sentence such as expressives (emotions, attitudes, etc.) and grammatical meanings (declarative, interrogative).
isogloss	An imaginary line on a map that distinguishes one region's word choices from another, such as *rubber band* vs. *gum band*.

isophone   An imaginary line on a map that distinguishes one region's pronunciation from another.

jargon   Terminology used by a specific group of people, usually connected by a profession or interest, such as doctors or soccer players.

key   Contextual component that reflects the manner (rapid, imitative, etc.), tone (solemn, light hearted, etc.) or the attitude (satirical, ironic, sincere etc.) the speaker uses.

lexical variants   The aspect of communication associated with word choice, such as *soda* vs. *pop*.

linguistic competence   Native speaker knowledge of the sounds, grammar and semantic forms of a language.

linguistic variants   These variants include phonetic, morpho-syntactic or lexical usage.

linguistics   The scientific study of language forms (**phonology, morphology, syntax** and **semantics**) independent of context.

locutions   Sounds, words, phrases and sentences which when combined convey semantic (literal/direct) meaning.

maintenance bilingual education   A form of **bilingual education** that aims to have students learn a second language without losing their first language.

marked (speech)   Marked speech is language use that is subjectively deemed by the interlocutor to stand out as being unusual or even incorrect. This can refer to both linguistic and paralinguistic variants.

Maxim of Accuracy   Gricean principle of not saying what you believe to be false or for which you lack adequate evidence.

Maxim of Manner   Gricean principle of avoiding obscurity of expression and ambiguity and instead to be brief and orderly.

Maxim of Quantity   Gricean principle of making your contribution as informative as required and no more than is required.

Maxim of Relevance   Gricean principle of being relevant to the subject you are discussing.

minimal pairs   Two words that differ from each other by only one sound (regardless of spelling). An example is *bit* [bIt] and *fit* [fIt].

maxims	General principles underlying Grice's Cooperative Principle. The maxims impinge on four areas of communication: **quantity, accuracy, manner** and **relevance.**
morpheme	The minimal sequence of sounds that carries lexical meaning or grammatical function as in the word *boys*, which consist of two morphemes: the lexical unit, *boy*, and the grammatical plural marker -*s*.
morphology	The study of word parts, or **morphemes.**
morpho-syntactic variant	The aspect of language associated with differences in **morphology** or **syntax.**
multilingualism	Can be used as a synonym for **bilingualism**, or to refer to the use of more than two languages within a given exchange.
mutual intelligibility	The degree to which speakers of two or more varieties of a language understand each other. This is a somewhat subjective assessment, but it is often used to determine whether the varieties are **dialects** of the same language, or separate languages.
negative face wants	The desire to be independent of others in the sense of not being imposed upon or interfered with.
negative politeness strategy	Occurs when speakers take note of someone's **negative face want** to be independent and autonomous as verbally expressed, for example, in apologies and deferential utterances, such as *I hate to bother you but I could use some help with this assignment.*
norms of interaction	Contextual component that addresses the cultural speaking conventions of a group, such as when it is proper to be loud or silent, to speak or not speak.
norms of interpretation	Contextual component that reflects the cultural speaking practices and values of a group, as regards the set of norms and expectations in various contexts and in the use of communicative functions such as **speech acts** and politeness strategies, etc.
Observer's Paradox	This paradox occurs when researchers want to observe language as it happens naturally within a given context, but once they become part of the **context**, it is no longer natural.
off-record strategy	A verbal request that is not addressed to anyone in particular as when one remarks that *The meat is very rare* rather than stating directly that the meat needs to be cooked longer or that is the way meat should be prepared for eating.

on-record strategy   Politeness strategy (bald, positive, negative) wherein a request is directly addressed to someone.

overlapping   Circumstances where in simultaneous speaking, one or more speakers begins talking before another speaker has finished the turn, regardless of whether or not the speakers believe an interruption has taken place.

paralinguistic variants   These variants include factors such as voice pitch, volume, timbre, or speed.

participants   Contextual component consisting of all the individuals (*who*) involved in the speech event, which can include not only the interlocutors but the audience as well.

performatives   Verbs that semantically perform the **illocution** of a speech act as in *I sentence you to five years in prison.*

perlocutions   The intended or unintended effects that the illocutionary utterance had on the hearer. Following a **directive**, for example, several perlocutions are possible. An interlocutor may do the act willingly or realize it should be done or refuse to do the act and express anger and stubbornness.

Phatics   Verbal expressions, as in small talk utterances such as, *Hi, how are you, nice weather today,* wherein the communicative purpose is more social than informative.

phoneme   Sounds that a native speaker of a language recognizes as *distinctive*. The sounds [s] and [z] in *racer* vs. *razor*, for example, create different meanings in English. In Spanish, however, these are not distinctive sounds and thus are not phonemic. Consequently, the pronunciation of *rasa* as *raza* does not change the meaning of the word.

phonetic variants   The aspect of spoken language associated with pronunciation.

phonetics   The study of speech sounds, in particular how they are produced (**articulatory phonetics**) and perceived (acoustic phonetics) and heard (auditory phonetics).

phonology   The study of the sound system of a language.

physical gender/sex   Traditionally, the gender assigned to babies at birth, essentially determined by the physiological differences between males and females. Proponents of the idea of a **gender spectrum**, however, believe that physical gender is more than a simple binary designation.

pidgin	A rudimentary language created for communication between people who speak mutually unintelligible languages. It incorporates aspects of the original languages, but does not have any unique grammatical or lexical traits. It is used almost exclusively for context-specific communication (such as business/trade) and cannot be considered a mother tongue.
pitch	The frequency of vibrations of sounds as the voice rises and falls.
politeness strategies	Politeness strategies used to save the hearer's **face** especially when face-threatening acts are inevitable or desired. Brown and Levinson outline four main types of politeness strategies: **bald on-record**, **negative politeness**, **positive politeness**, and **off-record** (**indirect**).
polyglot	Someone who speaks multiple languages.
positive face wants	The desire to be connected with others.
positive politeness strategy	Occurs whenever the speaker seeks solidarity with another as in: *That looks difficult, can I help you with it?*
pragmatics	The study of how context and communicative functions express meaning, such as in the use of **speech acts**.
prescriptive grammar	A grammar that purports to show how a language should be used, as in the use of *I* rather than *me* after the verb *to be*, since this verb does not take a direct object pronoun. Prescriptivists would favor *It's I* rather than *It's me* in usage.
prescriptivism	The belief that there is only one correct way to speak (**prescriptive grammar**) and that this way should be prescribed to others. Deviations from this "correct" way of speaking are considered to be "incorrect."
prestige dialect	A **dialect** of a language that is considered to be more prestigious than another. These determinations are not based on linguistic superiority, but rather perceptions of social power.
presuppositions	An utterance in which the assumption is taken for granted, as in the utterance: *Did you see John at the park?* which assumes that there is a person that the addressee knows by the name of John and that he was at the park.

prosodic signals	Features such as **pitch**, **stress** and **intonation** that convey information and meaning beyond the phonetic segments of a locution in an utterance.
race	Traditionally described as shared similar and distinctive physical characteristics, this is a social construct rather than a scientific reality.
receptive bilingual	A person who can understand another language, but not speak it.
repairs	Structural devices used between and within turns to remedy errors in conversations, such as inadvertently providing inaccurate information, apologizing for interrupting or overlapping due to limitations in memory, distractions, swings in attention and interest.
repetition	Verbal device that renders conversations cohesive between and within turns.
representatives	**Speech act illocutions** varying in force, ranging from claims and conclusions to opinions and hedges, which are attempts to get someone to believe something.
rogatives	**Speech act illocutions** that occur when the hearer is asked to supply information, as opposed to a directive where the hearer is asked to perform a physical act.
routines	Verbal formulas used for purposes of social solidarity. They are found in ritual conversational openings, closings, thanks, apologies and compliments.
semantics	The study of meaning independent of **context**.
setting	Contextual component that refers to the time and place (where/when) of a speech event.
socialized gender roles	The roles, behavior, attitudes, and personality traits that a given society expects from boys and from girls. This socialization often begins shortly after birth.
sociolinguistics	The study of how social factors such as geographic origin, gender, age, ethnicity, socio-economic status and level of education affect language usage.
speaker meaning	Meaning is derived from the **context** and the communicative function, as opposed to literal meaning.
speech acts	Utterances that involve doing something with language such as in **illocutions** that are expressions dealing with promising, convincing, commanding, expressing emotion and making official declarations that change conditions in the world.

Standard American English (SAE)   What is considered by many to be the "proper" way to speak American English, also known as Academic English and Professional English. Sociolinguists assert that this is more of an abstract idea than a reality.

stress   The degree of emphasis given to a vowel in syllables or in certain words.

stylistic devices   Strategies that serve to render conversations cohesive. Among such devices are puns, **alliterations**, and other kinds of word play.

suprasegments   Prosodic features above the level of phonetic segments such as **stress, tone** and **intonation**.

syntax   The linguistic study of how words are combined in phrases and sentences.

tone   Quality of an individual's voice that can also reflect various attitudes toward the interlocutor, as in the degree of formality, intimacy, solemnity, seriousness, and condescension.

topics   Contextual component that refers to the subject matter (what) in a speech event, as well as its relationship to the language form used (dialectical/formal/casual speech).

transition relevance place (TRP)   The point in a conversation where turn taking occurs, such as after a question is asked, an offer is made, an apology is offered, etc.

transitional bilingual education   A form of **bilingual education** that has as its goal the transition from a first language to a second language, with no intent to maintain the first language.

turn taking   A basic structural requirement of conversation wherein speakers in a conversation determine who speaks next based on contextual and cultural factors.

unmarked speech   In contrast with marked speech, this is language usage that does not "stand out" to the interlocutor in any way. This can refer to both linguistic and paralinguistic variants.

utterance   A unit of speech of varied length depending on the speaker's breath groups.

utterance incompletor   A transitional entry device into a conversation wherein expressions such as *well, but,* and *so,* etc., are used to signal entry into the conversation.

voicing

A factor involved in pronouncing consonants. If the vocal cords vibrate, a consonant sound is considered to be voiced; if they do not, the sound is considered to be unvoiced (or voiceless).

Bibliography

Aijmer, K. (1996). *Conversational Routines in English: Convention and Creativity* (Studies in Language and Linguistics). New York: Routledge.

Akmajian, A. (2010). *Linguistics: An Introduction to Language and Communication*, 6th edn. Cambridge, MA: The MIT Press.

Alim, S., and Smitherman, G. (2012). *Articulate While Black: Barack Obama, Language, and Race in the U.S.* Oxford: Oxford University Press.

Apte, M. L. (1974). 'Thank you' and South Asian languages: A Comparative Sociolinguistic Study. *International Journal of the Sociology of Language*, 5: 67–89.

Austin, J., Urmson, J., & Sbisà, M. (1975). *How to Do Things with Words*. Cambridge, MA: Harvard University Press.

Baker, C. (2006). *Foundations of Bilingual Education and Bilingualism*. Bristol: Multilingual Matters.

Bell, A. (2013). *The Guidebook to Sociolinguistics*. Malden, MA: Wiley-Blackwell.

Birner, B. (2012). *Introduction to Pragmatics*, 1st ed. Malden, MA: Wiley-Blackwell.

Bloomfield, L. (1933). *Language*. Chicago, IL: University of Chicago Press.

Bodine, A. (1975). Androcentrism in Prescriptive Grammar. *Language in Society* 4: 120–46.

Bonvillain, N. (2014) *Language, Culture and Communication*, 7th edn. Upper Saddle River, NJ: Pearson.

Bowe, H., & Martin, K. (2014). *Communication across Cultures: Mutual Understanding in a Global World*. Cambridge: Cambridge University Press.

Brown, P., & Levinson, S. (1987). *Politeness: Some Universals in Language Usage*. Cambridge: Cambridge University Press.

Burgess, A. (1962). *A Clockwork Orange*. London: William Heinemann.

Chaika, E. (2008). *Language: The Social Mirror*, 4th edn. Boston, MA: Heinle Cengage Learning.

Chomsky, N. (1957). *Syntactic Structures*. The Hague: Mouton Publishers.

Coates, J. and Pichler, P. (2011). *Language and Gender: A Reader*. Malden, MA: Wiley-Blackwell.

Coulmas, F. (1981). Poison To Your Soul: Thanks and Apologies Contrastively Viewed. In F. Coulmas (ed.), *Conversational Routine* (pp. 61–72). The Hague: Mouton Publishers.

Darnell, R. (1985). The Language of Power in Cree Interethnic Communication. In N. Wolfson & J. Manes (eds.), *Language of Inequality* (pp. 61–72). The Hague: Mouton Publishers.

DeKeyser, R., & Larson-Hall, J. (2005). What Does the Critical Period Really Mean? In J. F. Kroll and A. M. B. DeGroot, *Handbook of Bilingualism: Psycholinguistics Approaches*. Oxford: Oxford University Press.

Eckert, P. and McConnell-Ginet, S. (2013). *Language and Gender*. Cambridge: Cambridge University Press.

Edwards, J. (2013). *Sociolinguistics: A Very Short Introduction*. Oxford: Oxford University Press.

Farb, P. (1977). Man the Talker, In V. P. Clark, P. Eschholz, & A. E. Rosa (eds.), *Language: Introductory Readings* (pp. 3–6). New York: St. Martin's Press.

Fergus, M., Bialystok, E., & Freedman, M. (2010). Delaying the Onset of Alzheimer's Disease: Bilingualism as a Form of Cognitive Reserve. *Neurology*, 75: 1726–729.

Ferguson, C. A. (1976). The Structure and Use of Politeness Formulas, *Language and Society*: 137–151.

Finegan, E., & Besnier, N. (1989). *Language: Its Structure and Use*. San Diego, CA: Harcourt Brace Jovanovich.

Fromkin, V., Rodman, R., & Hyams, N. (2013). *An Introduction to Language*. Boston, MA: Wadsworth Cengage Learning.

Frost, R. (1915). *"The Code." North of Boston*. New York: Henry Holt and Company.

Green, L. J. (2002). *African American English: A Linguistic Introduction*. Cambridge: Cambridge University Press.

Grice, H. P. (1975). Logic and Conversation. In D. Davidson & G. Harman (eds.), *The Logic of Grammar* (pp. 64–75). Encino and Belmont, CA: Dickenson Publishing Company.

Grosjean, F. (1984). *Life with Two Languages: An Introduction to Bilingualism*. Cambridge, MA: Harvard University Press.

Grosjean, F. (2012). *Bilingual: Life and Reality*. Cambridge: Harvard University Press.

Hollos, M., & Beeman, W. (1978). The Development of Directives among Norwegian and Hungarian Children: An Example of Communicative Style in Culture. *Language in Society* 7: 345–55.

Holmes, J. (1991). Women's Verbal Contributions in Public Settings. *Wellington Working Papers in Linguistics*, 3: 1–19.

Hong, B. (1973). The Chinese Language in its New Social Context. *Journal of Chinese Linguistics*, 1(1): 163–69.

Huang, Y. (2015). *Pragmatics*. Oxford: Oxford University Press.

Hymes, D. (1974). *Foundations to Sociolinguistics*. Philadelphia, PA: University of Pennsylvania Press.

Ide, S., Hori, M., Kawasaki, A., Ikuta, S., & Haga, H. (1986). Sex Difference and Politeness in Japanese. *International Journal of the Sociology of Language* 58: 25–36.

Irvine, J. (1974). Strategies of Status Manipulation in the Wolof Greeting. In R. Bauman & J. Sherzer (eds.), *Explorations in the Ethnography of Speaking* (pp. 167–91). New York: Cambridge University Press.

James, D., & Drakich, J. (1993). Understanding Gender Differences in Amount of Talk. In D. Tannen (ed.), *Gender and Conversational Interaction* (pp. 281–312). Oxford: Oxford University Press.

Keenan, E. O. (1976). The Universality of Conversational Postulates. *Language in Society* 5: 67–80.

Labov, W. (1966). *The Social Stratification of English in New York City* (2nd edn). Cambridge: Cambridge University Press.

Labro, P. (1988). *L'étudiant étranger*. Paris: Gallimard.

Lakoff, G. (1990). *Women, Fire, and Dangerous Things: What Categories Reveal about the Mind*. Chicago, IL: University of Chicago Press.

Lakoff, R. (1975). *Language and Woman's Place: Text and Commentaries*. New York: Oxford University Press.

Leaper, C., & Ayres, M. M. (2007). A Meta-analytic Review of Gender Variations in Adults' Language Use: Talkativeness, Affiliative Speech, and Assertive Speech. *Personality and Social Psychology Review*, 11(4): 328–63.

Lederer, R. (1987). *Anguished English*. New York: Dell Publishing.

Levinson, S. (1983). *Pragmatics*. Cambridge: Cambridge University Press.

Manes, J., & Wolfson, N. (1981). The Compliment Formula. In F. Coulmas (ed.), *Conversational Routine. Explorations in Standardized Communication Situations and Prepatterned Speech*. The Hague: Mouton Publishers.

Marian, V., & Shook, A. (2012). The Cognitive Benefits of Being Bilingual. *Cerebrum: The Dana Forum on Brain Science* (2012): 13.

Martínez-Flor, A. and Usó-Juan, E. (2010). *Speech Act Performance: Theoretical, Empirical and Methodological Issues*. Amsterdam: John Benjamins.

Mehl, M. R., Ramírez-Esparza, N., Slatcher, R. B., & Pennebaker, J. W. (2007). Are Women Really More Talkative Than Men? *Science*, 317: 82.

Meyerhoff, M., & Schleef, E. (2010). *The Routledge Sociolinguistics Reader*. New York: Routledge.

Mihaliček, V., & Wilson, C. (2011). *Language Files: Materials for an Introduction to Language and Linguistics*, 11th edn. Columbus, OH: Ohio State University Press.

Mitchell, M. (1936). *Gone With the Wind*. New York: Macmillan Company.

Mundy, L. (1996). Georgetown's Talking Heads: The Hidden Meaning of Conversation, *The Washington Post Magazine*, 4 February: 8–25.

Myers-Scotton, C. (2005). *Multiple Voices: An Introduction to Bilingualism*. Malden, MA: Wiley-Blackwell.

Okamoto, D. L., Rashotte, L., & Smith-Lovin, L. (2002). Measuring Interruption: Syntactic and Contextual Methods of Coding Conversation. *Social Psychology Quarterly*, 65: 38–55.

Okamoto, S. & Shibamato Smith, J. (2004). *Japanese Language, Gender, and Ideology: Cultural Models and Real People*. New York: Oxford University Press.

Ogiermann, E. (2009). *On Apologizing in Negative and Positive Politeness Cultures*. Amsterdam: John Benjamins.

Parker, D. (2011). *The Sexes*. New York: Penguin Classics.

Peccei, J. S. (1999). *Pragmatics*. London: Routledge.

Phillips, M. D., Lowe, M. J., Lurito, J. T., Dzemidzic, M., & Mathews, V. P. (2001). Temporal Lobe Activation Demonstrates Sex-based Differences during Passive Listening. *Radiology*, 220(1): 202–207.

Pinker, S. (1994). *The Language Instinct: How the Mind Creates Language*. New York: William Morrow & Co.

Platt, P. (1998). *French or Foe: Getting the Most Out of Visiting, Living and Working in France*, 2nd edn. Skokie, IL: Distribooks, Inc.

Poarch, G. J., & Bialystok, E. (2015). Bilingualism as a Model for Multitasking. *Developmental Review*, 35: 113–24.

Ravetto, M. (2012). Compliment Responses in Italian and German. *International Journal of Innovative Interdisciplinary Research*, 2: 77–100.

Rickford, J. R. (2000). *Spoken Soul: The Story of Black English*. Hoboken, NJ: Wiley.

Rosaldo, M. (1982). The Things We Do With Words: Ilongot Speech Acts and Speech Act Theory. *Language and Society* 11: 203–37.

Rousseau, J. J. (1968). *The Social Contract*. New York: Penguin Classics.

Sapir, E. (1929). Male and Female Forms of Speech in Yana. In St. W. J. Teeuwen (ed.), *Donum Natalicium Schrijnen* (pp. 79–85). Nijmegan-Utrecht: N. V. Dekker en Van de Vegt

Saussure, F. (1998). *Course in General Linguistics*. New York: Open Court Classics.

Searle, J. (1979). *Expression and Meaning*. Cambridge: Cambridge University Press.

Sedaris, D. (2001). *Me Talk Pretty One Day*. New York: Back Bay Books.

Shibamoto, J. (1987). The Womanly Woman: Manipulation of Stereotypical and Non-stereotypical Features of Japanese Women's Speech. In S. Philips, S. Steele, & C. Tanz (eds.), *Language, Gender and Sex in Comparative Perspective* (pp. 26–49). Cambridge: Cambridge University Press.

Skloot, R. (2011). *The Immortal Life of Henrietta Lacks*. New York: Broadway Books.

Stewart, Jr. T.W. & Vaillete, N. (2011). *Language Files: Materials for an Introduction to Language and Linguistics*. 11th edn. Columbus, OH: The Ohio State University Press.

Tannen, D. (1996). *Gender and Discourse*. New York: Oxford University Press.

Tannen, D. (2005). *Conversational Style: Analyzing Talk among Friends*. New York: Oxford University Press.

Tannen, D. (2011). *That's Not What I Meant!: How Conversational Style Makes or Breaks Relationships*. New York: William Morrow Paperbacks.

Tolmach Lakoff, R. and Bucholtz, M. (2004). *Language and Woman's Place: Text and Commentaries* (Studies in Language, Gender, and Sexuality). Oxford: Oxford University Press.

Trudgill, P. (1974). *Sociolinguistics: An Introduction*. Baltimore, MD: Penguin.

Wardhaugh, R. (1986). *An Introduction to Sociolinguistics*. New York: Blackwell.

Wolfram, W. (2006). *American English: Dialects and Variation*, 2nd edn. Oxford: Basil Blackwell.

Wolfram, W., and Ward, B. (2005). *American Voices*. Oxford: Blackwell.

Yule, G. (1996). *Pragmatics*. Oxford: Oxford University Press.

Zimmerman, D. H., & West, C. (1975). Sex Roles, Interruptions, and Silences in Conversation, In B. Thorne, and N. Hendley (eds.), *Language and Sex: Difference and Dominance* (pp. 105–129). Rowley, MA: Newbury House.

Index

CPSIA information can be obtained
at www.ICGtesting.com
Printed in the USA
BVHW040319120919
558234BV00002B/12/P

9 781781 793558